The Concept of Function in Twentieth-Century Architectural Criticism

Studies in the Fine Arts: Architecture, No. 2

Stephen C. Foster, Series Editor

Associate Professor of Art History
University of Iowa

Other Titles in This Series

The Concept of Function in Twentieth-Century Architectural Criticism

by
Larry L. Ligo

UMI RESEARCH PRESS
Ann Arbor, Michigan

Produced and distributed by
UMI Research Press
an imprint of
University Microfilms International
Ann Arbor, Michigan 48106

Library of Congress Cataloging in Publication Data

Ligo, Larry L. (Larry LeRoy)
The concept of function in twentieth-century
architectural criticism.

(Studies in the fine arts. Architecture ; no. 2)
"A revision of the author's thesis, University of
North Carolina, Chapel Hill, 1973"–Verso t.p.
Bibliography: p.
Includes index.
1. Architectural criticism–History–20th century.
2. Functionalism (Architecture) I. Title. II. Series.

NA2599.5.L53 1984   724.9'1   84-44
ISBN 0-8357-1542-6

To R. E. L.

Contents

List of Plates

In each case the source of the plate is included in parentheses following the description of the view. If the photographer's name is known, it is included in brackets. The plates are listed in chronological order according to the dates of the buildings' actual completion. Thus even though the Guggenheim Museum was commissioned before the Baker Dormitory, the dormitory appears first because it was completed eleven years before the museum.

1. Louis Sullivan. Carson Pirie Scott Store, Chicago, 1899–1904. *Exterior*. (Albert Bush-Brown, *Louis Sullivan*. New York, 1960, Plate 76). This reference will hereafter be listed as *Louis Sullivan*.
2. Louis Sullivan. Carson Pirie Scott Store. *Entrance pavilion*. (*Louis Sullivan*, Plate 76), [Henry Fuermann].
3. Louis Sullivan. Carson Pirie Scott Store. *Detail of ornament, entrance pavilion*. (*Louis Sullivan*, Plate 77), [John Szarkowski].
4. Frank Lloyd Wright. Robie House, Chicago, 1909–10. *Exterior*. (Vincent Scully, Jr., *Frank Lloyd Wright*. New York, 1960, Plate 39), [Hendrick-Blessing]. This reference will hereafter be listed as *Frank Lloyd Wright*.
5. Frank Lloyd Wright. Robie House. *View of exterior and plans of ground floor and first floor*. (*Frank Lloyd Wright*, Plates 40 and 41).
6. Frank Lloyd Wright. Robie House. *Living room showing environmental provisions*. (*The Robie House*. Historic American Building Survey, 1963, Sheet 10), [Drawn by Mary Reyner Banham].
7. Gerrit Rietveld. Schröder House, Utrecht (Holland), 1924. *Exterior from south*. (Theodore M. Brown, *The Work of G. Rietveld*. Utrecht, 1958, Plate 35), [Theodore M. Brown]. This reference will hereafter be listed as *Rietveld*.
8. Gerrit Rietveld. Schröder House. *Exterior view, and plans of three floors*. (Henry A. Millon, *Key Monuments of the History of Architecture*. Englewood Cliffs, New Jersey, p. 507), [Jan Versnel,

Amsterdam]. This reference will hereafter be listed as *Key Monuments.*

9. Gerrit Rietveld. Schröder House. *Exterior south-west side.* (*Rietveld,* Plate 36), [Jan Versnel, Amsterdam].

10. Gerrit Rietveld. Schröder House. *Detail, corner window, east.* (*Reitveld,* Plate 58), [Theodore M. Brown].

11. Gerrit Rietveld. Schröder House. *Exterior, south-west, showing its visual weightlessness.* (*Rietveld,* Plate 65).

12. Walter Gropius. Bauhaus Buildings, Dessau, 1926. *Ground floor and second floor plans.* (Sigfried Giedion, *Walter Gropius: Work and Teamwork.* New York, 1954, Plates 85 and 86). This reference will hereafter be listed as *Work and Teamwork.*

13. Walter Gropius. Bauhaus Buildings. *View on the left of heavy concrete construction upon which the glass wall (right) was to be hung.* (*Cahiers d'Art,* V (1930), p. 99), [Sigfried Giedion and Lucia Moholy].

14. Walter Gropius. Bauhaus Buildings. *View from the east with workshop building in the foreground.* (*Work and Teamwork,* Plate 90).

15. Mies van der Rohe. German Pavilion, International Exposition, Barcelona, Spain, 1929. *Exterior.* (Philip C. Johnson, *Mies van der Rohe.* New York, 1947, p. 67). This reference will hereafter be listed as *Mies van der Rohe.*

16. Mies van der Rohe. Barcelona Pavilion. *Plan and view from end of court.* (*Key Monuments.* p. 511), [Williams & Meyer].

17. Mies van der Rohe. Barcelona Pavilion. *View across one of the pools.* (Werner Blaser, *Mies van der Rohe: The Art of Structure.* New York, 1965, p. 33). This reference will hereafter be listed as *Art of Structure.*

18. Mies van der Rohe. Barcelona Pavilion. *Interior showing the independence of the walls from the load-bearing columns.* (*Art of Structure.* p. 29).

19. Mies van der Rohe. Barcelona Pavilion. *Interior with famous "Barcelona" chairs.* (*Mies van der Rohe.* p. 73).

20. Le Corbusier. Villa Savoye at Poissy (France), 1929–31. *North corner.* (Maurice Besset, *Who Was Le Corbusier?* Cleveland, 1968, p. 101). This reference will hereafter be listed as *Who Was.*

21. Le Corbusier. Villa Savoye. *Plan.* (Le Corbusier, *Complete Works, 1929–1934.* Zurich, 1935, p. 24). This reference will hereafter be listed as *Complete Works.*

22. Le Corbusier. Villa Savoye. *Entrance vestibule and curved wall with driveway returning toward Paris.* (*Complete Works.* p. 26).

Acknowledgments

If I were to list everyone who has contributed in some way to the completion of this manuscript, I would have a very long list indeed, and so I want to mention only those without whose help this project literally could not have been completed.

First, I wish to thank Dr. John W. Dixon, Jr. I am indebted to him for introducing me to many of the ideas which enticed me into the subject matter of this project.

Second, I am indebted to Dr. William J. Peck: the spirit of inquiry which he fosters provided the impetus for my initial work in this area, and his genuine humanity greatly influenced the direction which this project was to take.

I also wish to thank Dr. Joseph C. Sloane not only for his constant encouragement but also for his many penetrating comments and helpful suggestions.

I owe a special debt of gratitude to Dr. William A. Thompson for the meticulous care with which he proofread and edited the finished manuscript, and to Patricia T. Knox for the care and patience with which she undertook the typing of the final draft.

Finally, I owe an immeasurable debt to Christine G. Erskine. Without her competence to discuss the project with me every step of the way and her willingness to do so at the sacrifice of her own pursuits, it probably would have been abandoned.

1

Introduction

This book is the result of an examination of twentieth-century architectural criticism carried out in an effort to determine what developments have taken place in critics' concept of architectural function since the early part of this century. By way of introduction, it is necessary to explain how the terms "function" and "criticism" have been used in this statement and throughout the pages that follow.

"Function" is here understood in both a traditional sense and a new sense. The traditional understanding of "function," which is also the foundation of my use of the word, is "utility," "fitness for purpose;" it is the "task" a building is meant to fulfill, the effect it has on those who use or view it. It is thus the "commodity" of Vitruvius's "commodity, firmness, and delight," while "firmness" and "delight" are respectively technics and form. These three are the inseparable dimensions of a work of architecture, and we may speak of "function" by itself only for the purposes of analysis and only with the understanding that in reality it cannot exist without form and construction materials and techniques.

The less traditional sense in which the term "function" is understood here has to do with a recognition of the various ramifications of architectural "commodity." In addition to the more immediate "work" that a building must do, such as providing shelter or obvious traffic patterns or enough closet space, there are also the less tangible, farther-reaching, more profound underlying effects that architecture has on human beings. On this level architecture embodies and shapes our view of ourselves, our society, and our world. Although the recognition that architecture works to do this is actually not new, the systematic inquiry into how it does is quite recent.[1] Therefore the term "function" is commonly associated with practical utility and convenience.

The ramifications of architectural function need, of course, to be defined more precisely, and because my perception of those ramifications grew out of my research in criticism, I should like first to explain the procedure used in my research and, in the process of that explanation, to show the nature of the criticism referred to in the first sentence of this introduction.

The type of criticism which provides the data for this research is what has been termed "applied criticism,"[2] that is, the direct response to individual contemporary buildings, as opposed to the more theoretical or historical writings on architecture. The primary reason for basing my study on critical statements of this "applied" nature is that, collected into a body of material, they reflect the most widely held view of architectural function. Although critical theoretical writings often contain more complete definitions of terms and concepts, and are therefore in many cases easier to deal with, I am not concerned so much with the minority of relatively isolated advanced thinkers as with a consensus of the majority of practicing architectural critics of this century. I am interested primarily in the concepts set forth in applied criticism partly because I believe that this type of critical writing, because of its accessibility, is most likely to be influential in forming the opinions of architects, those who employ them, and those who view and use their buildings. This is not the place to debate what architectural criticism is or should be, but I would point out that my understanding of applied criticism does not restrict it to statements of judgment but may also include description, analysis, and interpretation; it does not therefore imply a narrow definition of the critics' task. I would also note that although statements of the "applied" type have provided the raw data of this study, more theoretical writings by critic-historians in this century, far from being ignored, have contributed greatly to the process of analyzing that data.

Because the purpose of this study is to discover the *profile* of the concept of function, to describe the consensus, it deals not with critics as individual thinkers but with their statements as typical of what was appearing in applied criticism at a given time or on a given subject. It is not within the scope of my project to search for the very first statement of a particular idea — I am more interested in when it became common enough to be influential; nor do I wish to become involved in arguments seeking to prove which critic was the first to state something — I am more concerned with the relative number of critics who held a common view. This attitude, I believe, is consistent with, even necessitated by, the focus on *applied* criticism. Search for "firsts" and treatment of individual critics' evolution in thought belong logically in a study of the more theoretical writings of architectural critic-historians. As a rule, therefore, this study will not deal with critics by name; when exceptions appear, they are usually in connection with the reference to the critics' more general remarks as aids in the analysis of observed trends in applied criticism.

Furthermore, this study will not deal with all of the architectural monuments of the twentieth century or all of the critical statements which they have elicited. A selection had to be made, but made in such a way as to be representative. I have chosen a method which permits me to approach the problem as directly and completely as possible. I have selected a series of key twentieth-century architectural monuments in order to examine in detail the critical statements which they have elicited. The choice of these monuments was guided by a number of essential conditions.

In the first place, since I have limited my inquiry to the architecture of the twentieth century, the selection of monuments had to span a period of nearly seventy years without leaving any wide gaps. Second, these monuments had to represent as many different types of building as possible. Third, my selection had to include monuments which were truly important: they would have to be representative of various phases in the growth and development of twentieth-century architecture, or, to use Professor George Kubler's terminology, they had to be "prime objects."[3] Fourth, and most important, the monuments had to have elicited a considerable amount of significant critical discussion.

Keeping these four considerations in mind, I arrived at the following list:

Louis Sullivan. Carson, Pirie and Scott Department Store, Chicago, Illinois, 1899–1904.

Frank Lloyd Wright. Robie House, Chicago, Illinois, 1908–9.

Gerrit Rietveld. Schröder House, Utrecht, 1924–25.

Walter Gropius. Bauhaus, Dessau, 1925–26.

Mies van der Rohe. German Pavilion, International Exposition, Barcelona, Spain, 1929.

Le Corbusier. Villa Savoye at Poissy (France), 1929–31.

Frank Lloyd Wright. Kaufmann House, "Falling Water," Connellsville, Pennsylvania, 1936–37.

Alvar Aalto. Baker House Dormitory, Cambridge, Massachusetts, 1947–48.

Frank Lloyd Wright. Solomon R. Guggenheim Museum, New York, 1946–59.

Mies van der Rohe. Farnsworth House, Plano, Illinois, 1945–50.

Le Corbusier. Chapel of Ronchamp, Notre Dame du Haut, near Belfort (France), 1950–53.

Louis Kahn. Richards Medical Research Building, Philadelphia, Pennsylvania, 1960.

Paul Rudolph. Yale School of Art and Architecture, New Haven, Connecticut, 1964.

Not all students of twentieth-century architecture would be in total agreement with this list. Some might point out what they considered to be glaring omissions, such as Peter Behren's A.E.G. Turbine Factory or Adolf Loos's Steiner house, while others would question the choice of Frank Lloyd Wright's Robie house instead of the Coonley house, Mies van der Rohe's Farnsworth house instead of the Seagram Building and Alvar Aalto's M.I.T. dormitory instead of his Civic Center in Säynätsalo. Still others would wonder why a building such as the Guggenheim Museum was included at all. There is no conclusive argument to support this particular listing over any other, but no such argument is really necessary for our present purposes. The important point is that although this list is not necessarily definitive, it does, nevertheless, include buildings that fulfill all of the above-listed conditions and as such is capable of providing the information necessary for the present inquiry.

There is another way in which the field of research has been limited naturally and conveniently: I have attempted to read only the statements concerning these thirteen buildings which I could find through the use of the Art Index. In addition to providing a workable quantity of material, this method, I believe, insures the material's consistently reputable quality. Thus, although this study often does not name or describe the critics, the reader may know that most of the observations made in this study are based on critical statements by reputable writers published in worthwhile books or sound periodicals. When a statement by a relatively unknown critic is quoted, it is because that statement is a clear expression of a typical view, and at that juncture I provide some information about the critic.[4]

Having read direct critical responses to the thirteen buildings, I had first of all to separate the responses on the basis of subject matter; those statements concerned with the function of buildings were separated from those concerned only with their forms as abstract, visual phenomena. Thus, that type of architectural criticism which may be called form analysis or style analysis was eliminated at the outset because it reveals nothing of the critic's concept of architectural function. If, however, a statement dealing with a building's function or effect was embedded in a context of form analysis, that statement was placed in the function category. The separation of the examples dealing with function from those dealing with form was not based solely on the presence of the word "function" or one of its variations in the critical statement. Although I examined all statements in which the word appears, many also were included in the study which only implied a concern with "building task" or with a building's effects on its users. This breadth of definition not only was recommended in theoretical discussions by such writers as Christian Norberg-Schulz,[5] but also was necessary to insure that no interpretation of architectural function held by critics of this century should be eliminated.

The first step in the actual analysis of the critical statements consisted of sorting out the various ramifications of the concept of function which they touched upon. These statements were then sorted according to subject matter, yielding categories based on the specific kind of function being examined by the critic in each statement. The types of function to which twentieth-century architectural critics refer fall into the following categories:

1. "Structural articulation" refers either to the revelation, in design, of a building's structural materials and methods (i.e., of the materials' and methods' "functions") or to the articulation on a building's exterior of the various areas of activity which are contained within it (i.e., of the building's uses or "functions"). Critics have referred to either or both of these ideas numerous times, almost always making use of the term "function" or "functional."

2. "Physical function" includes both the control of environmental factors and the building's accommodation of the physical aspects of its intended purpose, aspects such as traffic patterns and flexibility of space arrangement.

3. "Psychological function" refers to the "feelings" which buildings stir in their viewers, users, and critics, including vertigo, claustrophobia, directional confusion, psychic comfort, or less specific feelings and emotions.

4. "Social function" refers to the concretization of social institutions and values characteristic of particular cultures or eras.

5. "Cultural/existential function" refers to the concretization of universal values or subconscious structures of spatial and psychological orientation which are related to man's essential humanity rather than to his life in a specific time and place.

A discussion of each of these types of function and the salient characteristics of its treatment by critics will be found in Chapters 3 through 7. Chapter 2 provides some historical background of twentieth-century architectural thought as it relates to the concept of function. Chapter 2 differs from the following chapters in that its source material derives from the words of architects, architectural historians, architectural theorists, and architectural critics making statements of architectural theory, while source material for the following chapters, except where specifically stated otherwise, derives from what I call "applied criticism."

2

Historical Background

Because of the nature of architectural developments at the beginning of the twentieth century and the terms used to describe those developments, the word "function" can hardly be used in connection with architecture without our minds' leaping quite automatically to the word "functionalism." Functionalism, variously defined—and often not really defined at all—was the driving force in architecture at the beginning of the modern movement. In setting the scene for an examination of function in this century, therefore, a logical way to begin is to look more closely at the phenomenon of functionalism. This chapter will attempt to do just that and will concentrate on four main areas: the pre-1900 history of functionalism, the statements of the pioneer architects of the modern movement, the phenomenon of a narrow functionalist ideology which dominated the first four decades of this century, and the criticism during the early functionalist era.

The history of functionalist ideas has been comprehensively researched by Edward de Zurko, who demonstrates that functionalism is by no means a strictly modern phenomenon but actually originates in classical antiquity.[1] In a sense, my study is a continuation of his, since his ends in the mid-nineteenth century with Horatio Greenough and mine starts at the end of the nineteenth century with Louis Sullivan. But there are in our studies several important differences that arise because we are covering different time spans. De Zurko concludes that his research "has not revealed a clear semasiological development or orderly pattern of changes in the meaning of functionalism."[2] I believe that an orderly pattern of change has taken place in the twentieth century, and this study attempts to show that to be the case. Naturally, dealing with a shorter time span, as I am, makes such observations easier, but it is my belief that the twentieth century has been in the process of a change, unlike any before, in the general view of architectural function. Further discussion of this idea will appear in subsequent chapters.

De Zurko's study spans centuries and therefore touches upon many varying viewpoints on function; yet all those centuries have in common the fact that ideas of function have not been of central importance to aesthetics. In the twentieth century, on the other hand, such ideas have been central to such speculation—or rather to architectural theory and criticism. The term "aesthetics" is not appropriate in the twentieth century, and this points up another difference between functionalist writings before and after about 1900. The literature of functionalism before the twentieth century generally dealt with the relationship between function and *beauty* in form; beginning in the twentieth century, aesthetic criteria have been abandoned and functionalist writing tends to deal rather with value or worth of buildings than with beauty per se, or with function as an end in its own right rather than as a means to an end.[3] Crucial to the differences between pre-twentieth-century functionalism and that of this century is the fact that beginning about 1890, new structural systems made a true functionalism really possible for the first time.[4] Steel frame construction made possible the placement of walls according to convenience for the users of the building instead of according to the necessity of supporting the walls above. Thus some interpretations of the relation between form and function which previously had been only theory or metaphor now could become a reality.

In spite of the differences between earlier functionalism and that of our era, several important similarities exist. First is the variety of meanings attached to the concept of function. De Zurko states: "Functionalism implies a pluralistic, not a monistic, system of values;...a rich hierarchy of primary and ultimate values is intrinsically connected with the generic concept of function."[5] That I have found this to be true in the twentieth century is evident from the list of types of function given in the introduction. Close observation of the prevalence of these types yields a picture of a quite consistent trend from the early to the recent years of this century.

Second is the importance of rationalism in the development of functionalism. De Zurko concludes from his research that "the rational view of art is to a large extent responsible for functionalist theory."[6] Drawing closer to our own century, Peter Collins notes that "rationalism...was the most widespread and certainly the healthiest architectural movement of the nineteenth century."[7] The influence of this rationalist tradition on early twentieth-century functionalism becomes very clear in the closer examination of the types of function mentioned earlier. It is particularly interesting to observe the evolution of a less rationalistic "functionalism" in the latter part of this century, a development to be discussed in more detail in a later chapter.

A third similarity between earlier functionalist writing and that of the twentieth-century is the appearance of a number of analogies commonly used to help communicate some aspects of the way in which architecture functions. De Zurko discusses three analogies whose origins he finds as far back as classical antiquity: the organic, the mechanical, and the moral.

The organic analogy calls attention to qualities that architecture has or should have in common with nature as represented by either plant or animal life. The organic analogy began as a simple comparison of external forms and their relation to function; it developed, especially around 1750, toward a comparison of the *process* by which natural and created forms grow.[8]

The mechanical analogy, the history of which is not quite as long as that of the other two, draws a parallel between characteristics of buildings and characteristics of machines; although in our century the forms of machines have been seen to influence the forms of buildings, historically this analogy has had more to do with the principle of mechanical efficiency.[9]

Discussions of morality and art have taken so many forms and have been approached from such a wide variety of viewpoints that, in my opinion, the word "analogy" is sometimes not satisfactory to cover them all. When philosophers have declared that forms of buildings should reveal honestly their structural roles, they are comparing good buildings to honest men. When practicality is praised in architecture as it is in men, once again a *moral* analogy is being drawn. Related, but not exactly the same, is the idea that buildings should help to instill moral and ethical ideals in those who see and use them; this, it seems to me, is not so much a moral *analogy* as a moral *argument* for certain qualities in architecture. The use of these three "analogies," as de Zurko calls them, has continued into the period under study here, and indeed the relative strength of the three during the earlier and the later years of the twentieth century, as well as the changing meanings of terms related to them, provides insight into the modern concept of function to be discussed in detail in subsequent chapters.

Discussion of the three traditional functionalist "analogies" brings us to the writings of the pioneer architects of the modern movement, since allusions to the organic, mechanical, and moral analogies appear frequently in the verbal statements of Louis Sullivan, Frank Lloyd Wright, Le Corbusier, Mies van der Rohe, and Walter Gropius. The statements of these men are pertinent because of the major role they played in the establishment of that new architecture which came to be known as "Functionalism."

To determine what concept the pioneer architects had of the term "function," I looked first to see how they themselves use the word. Sullivan and Gropius, particularly, use it to refer to the structural techniques of a building and to the activity to be housed in it as the "functions" which should be clearly "expressed" in the design.[10] Thus the principle of structural articulation, as defined in the introduction, was an important aspect of the new style.

The architects also use the term in conjunction with what I have called "physical function," that is, the practical, utilitarian aspects of buildings. But often, when referring to the function of buildings on this physical level, the architect is making the point that this is not all there is to architecture. Mies van der Rohe, for example, writes: "In its simplest form architecture is rooted in entirely functional considerations, but it can reach up through all degrees of value to the highest sphere of spiritual existence, into the realm of pure art."[11] The architects generally do not use the word "function" to refer to those higher "degrees of value" even though they do make direct statements of the beneficial effects of those higher values on the viewers and users of buildings. Le Corbusier writes, for instance:

> The Architect, by his arrangement of forms, realizes an order which is a pure creation of his spirit; by forms and shapes he affects our senses to an acute degree and provokes plastic emotions; by the relationships which he creates he wakes profound echoes in us, he gives us the measure of an order which we feel to be in accordance with that of our world, he determines the various movements of our heart and of our understanding; it is then that we experience the sense of beauty.[12]

For Sullivan the word "function" meant the intellectual, emotional, and spiritual as well as physical aspects of the use of a building.[13] Generally, however, the architects reserved the word "function" for the practical dimension or for the principle of structural articulation. Thus, by their semantics they may have contributed to a narrow understanding of functionalism.

I cannot stress strongly enough, however, the clarity of the architects' statements about the higher value of architecture, even if these statements are less frequently quoted than the slogan-like ones such as "form follows function" or "less is more." Sullivan says, "I value spiritual results only."[14] Wright says that buildings "perform their highest function in relation to human life within and the natural efflorescence without";[15] he looked forward to a "new integrity of human life wherein art, religion and science are one."[16] Gropius writes:

> ...the New Architecture is a bridge uniting opposite poles of thought.... The liberation of architecture from a welter of ornament, the emphasis on its structural functions, and the concentration on concise and economical solutions, represent the purely material side of that formalizing process on which the *practical* value of the New Architecture depends. The other, the aesthetic satisfaction of the human soul, is just as important as the material.[17]

These statements point to what I call the cultural/existential function of architecture: the great architects, being artists, have always been aware of the far-reaching effects of their work.

After looking at the architects' use of the word "function," I investigated their use of the three traditional analogies. The analogies appear in their writings often without the actual use of the word function. The mechanical analogy became, for example, the foundation of the new "machine aesthetic," a concept associated primarily with Le Corbusier. He was outspoken in his admiration for the work of engineers and felt that architecture, on the other hand, was "in an unhappy state of retrogression."[18] His discussions of cars, ships, and airplanes as appropriate sources of inspiration for architects, his desire to "create the mass-production spirit," and his description of the house as "a machine for living in,"[19] all served to link the name of Le Corbusier with a machine-oriented architecture. But what seems to be a more important development in the first third of this century is not the continued comparison of machines and buildings, but rather the realization that mechanization presents profound problems that men must grapple with successfully or, probably, perish. Whereas for a while the machine had been allowed to become a god, it must be placed back in its rightful relationship to man — that is, in his hands, in his *control*, as a tool of civilization and humanization. Of the pioneer architects, perhaps Wright is the one who most frequently and forcefully made the "mastering of the machine" the subject of his exhortations.[20] Several of the pioneers expressed the hope that the machine would be the architect's means of liberation from the past, from the imitation of historic styles.

The "moral analogy" of de Zurko is difficult to trace, partly because its shape as an "analogy" was difficult to discern even in the periods covered by his book. Perhaps the most explicit appearance of it in the architects' statements has been the tenet that buildings should "honestly" display on their exteriors what their structure is and what their intended human users are, that is, through structural articulation. A more general but more fundamental echo of the pre-modern moral arguments for utility in buildings is the underlying belief that buildings which are designed with carefully analyzed functions in mind can serve men better and are therefore more "humanizing."

The organic analogy, after taking on a new meaning with the birth of the science of biology,[21] gained momentum in the early part of this century with the writings of Sullivan and Wright. With these men it ceased to be related to the prerequisites for beauty and became involved instead with the prerequisites for vitality in architecture. As a factor in "organic" — that is, living — architecture, the correspondence between form and function was seen by most of the "new architects" as the primary difference between their work and that of the copiers of old "styles." It is interesting to observe, in the writing of one associated almost exclusively with the mechanical analogy, how often Le Corbusier uses the word organic in a sense very similar to that of Sullivan and Wright: "I commence by drawing attention to this vital fact: a plan proceeds *from within to without*, for a house or a palace is an organism comparable to a living being." Le Corbusier calls the architect "a creator of organisms," and says that it was the engineers' "conception of *a living organism*" that contributed to their ability to achieve harmony.[22] Gropius states his convictions about the new architecture in terms of the organic:

> We want to create a clear, organic architecture, whose inner logic will be radiant and naked, unencumbered by lying facades and trickeries; we want...an architecture whose function is clearly recognizable in the relation of its forms.[23]

Even Mies van der Rohe, whose architecture is frequently thought of as the antithesis of Wright's, refers to the "organic," albeit in a sense which by contrast may be interpreted as rational/platonic:

> Let us recognize that the mechanistic principle of order overemphasizes the materialistic and functionalistic factors in life, since it fails to satisfy our feeling that means must be subsidiary to ends and our desire for dignity and value.... So we shall emphasize the organic principle of order as a means of achieving the successful relationship of the parts to each other and to the whole.[24]

In summary, all of the three traditional analogies appear in the verbal statements of the pioneer architects of the twentieth century. Of the three, however, only one continues to be of major concern after the establishment of the modern movement; that one, the organic, will be a topic of discussion again in this manuscript.

It is clear that none of these giants of the first generation of modern architects thought of purely practical, utilitarian considerations as the totality of architecture. None of them could have been called a "strict functionalist" according to J. M. Richards's definition:

> ...the idea of absolute functionalism...can be defined as the idea that good architecture is produced automatically by strict attention to utility, economy, and other purely practical considerations....[25]

But how, since their writings were so widely publicized and so influential, did the idea of absolute functionalism come to be so dominant, in fact to be thought of as a synonym for "modern architecture"? An investigation of the situation during the first four decades of this century reveals a number of factors which probably contributed to the dissemination of a narrow, utilitarian functionalism.

The first factor has to do with the effects of the architects' own polemic. I have already stated that the architects used the words "function" and "functionalist" in a narrow sense, that is, having to do with practical considerations or with the structural articulation of technics or utility. It is clear that some of those statements, if taken out of context and not balanced by their discussions of the higher value of architecture as art, could easily give the impression that practical considerations were all the architects cared about. An example of such a statement is found in Sullivan's autobiography in which he described his first year, 1881, with the firm of Adler and Sullivan in narrow functionalist terms:

> He could now, undisturbed, start on the course of practical experimentation he long had in mind, which was to make an architecture that fitted its functions—a realistic architecture based on well defined utilitarian needs—that all practical demands of utility should be paramount as a basis of planning and design; that no architectural dictum, or tradition, or superstition, or habit, should stand in his way.[26]

Unfortunately, even the slogans associated with the modern movement came to carry similar overtones of a "narrow" functionalism, such as "form follows function," or "a house is a machine for living in." And, of course, it was these slogans which received the most attention and were repeated even by those who never read any of the works from which the slogans came.

It must also be admitted that the number of narrow functionalist statements in any one architect's writing probably outnumbered the statements about the more profound aspects of architecture. The most blatant example of this imbalance occurs in Le Corbusier's *Towards a New Architecture*, in which there are many paragraphs praising the works of engineers. The overall effect of the book may be the result of the fact that it was made up of previously published articles which when strung together gave a picture of the modern movement which had strong rationalistic and mechanistic leanings.[27]

In contrast to these architects whose writings I have particularly examined, there were some who did sincerely espouse a narrow functionalist approach to architecture. Hannes Meyer, who in 1928 assumed the directorship of the Bauhaus for a brief period, was a "fanatical functionalist,"[28] who rejected all formalism and believed that beauty was not a proper aim of architecture.[29] In an official Bauhaus publication of 1928, Meyer made the following statement:

> All things of this world are products of the formula: function and economy. All works of art are compositions and therefore, not suitable. Life, however, is functional and, therefore, not artistic.... To build is not a process of esthetics but a biological process.[30]

And Meyer was not alone in this belief: in *The International Style,* Hitchcock and Johnson talk about "architects like Hannes Meyer...who claim that interest in proportions or in problems of design for their own sake is still an unfortunate remnant of nineteenth-century ideology." For the architects to whom Hitchcock and Johnson refer, as for Hannes Meyer, "it is an absurdity to talk about the modern style in terms of aesthetics.... If a building provides adequately, completely, and without compromise for its purpose, it is...a good building, regardless of its appearance."[31]

At the same time, narrow functionalist theory was coming from a new architectural organization in Russia called Sass (the section of the architects of socialists buildings). From 1928 to 1930 Sass published "a review called Sa (= contemporary architecture) which preached pure functionalism both in regard to the technical and the utilitarian aspects of building."[32] The Sass position declared that:

> All attempts to influence the spectator by means of composition of forms address themselves not towards the productivist psychology of the proletariat engaged in building up a life of its own, but to a class-enemy mentality, a consumer's psychology, based on ideological and religious premises.[33]

While it is true that Sass was a rather isolated and short-lived movement, and that Hannes Meyer's tenure as head of the Bauhaus was quite brief,[34] nevertheless, their position, coming as it did from "official" quarters, undoubtedly contributed to the growing belief that functionalism was a concept void of aesthetic and symbolic overtones.[35] Thus the statements of sincere "absolute functionalists" joined the somewhat ambiguous overall effect of the publications by the "giants" of the modern movement to give many lesser architects and thousands of "laymen" a concept of function in architecture which was not an accurate understanding of what the originators of the movement intended.

In addition to the effects of the architects' writings, part of the explanation for the spread of a narrow concept of function in architecture may lie in the words of some of the new movement's principal apologists. Reynor Banham makes a strong argument for the contention that some of the main apologists writing in the late 1920s, coming from countries outside the mainstream of the new architectural developments, came upon the movement too late to have an accurate understanding of its origins and "causes."[36] Even Sigfried Giedion, who was later to become such an important force in the widespread dissemination of the modern movement, at first interpreted the new architecture in narrow functionalist terms. His first exposure to the new architecture occured at the *Bauhauswoche* of 1923, an exposition of the new use of iron and reinforced concrete – and he apparently accepted the theme of the exposition as the primary concern of the entire movement. In 1928, Giedion published his *Bauen in Frankreich, Eisen, Eisenbeton*, in which, as the title suggests, he traced the origins of the new architecture to the "grands Constructeurs" of the nineteenth century.[37] Thus, readers of *Bauen in Frankreich* were led to believe that the modern movement was a purely rational and functional approach to architecture. Giedion's one-sided approach was subsequently corrected in his *Space, Time and Architecture* of 1941.

Similarly, Lewis Mumford, writing throughout the 1920s and into the 1930s on the new architecture in the United States, emphasized its limited concern with aesthetics. In 1921 he described the new architecture primarily in mechanistic terms—a monotonous "machine product" that for the most part ignored "the decent aesthetic requirements of humanity." He saw real potential in the "machine style" but felt that it had fallen short of its possiblities because of its one-sided emphasis upon the "logic of the machine" at the expense of a "regard for the vagaries of human psychology."[38] Writing in a similar vein three years later, Mumford warned against the inevitable results of permitting the engineer and not the architect to be in control of modern building. He felt that, by giving the engineer (and thus the machine) the controlling position in the new architecture,

> we have robbed the machine of the one promise it held out—that of enabling us to humanize more thoroughly the details of our existence.... With the features that govern the construction of modern building thus conditioned by external cannons of mechanism, it follows that...the esthetic element itself enters only by accident.[39]

In 1925, while discussing the architecture of Frank Lloyd Wright, Mumford suggested what he considered to be a continuing weakness of the "modernism of l'Esprit Nouveau" and singled out "architects like Le Corbusier" as prime offenders:

> [These architects] are not essentially concerned with humane building, and would be quite pleased to remodel our whole environment in accordance with the narrow physical processes that are served in the factory.... [They represent] but a continuation of an acerbic puritan philosophy that has degraded life and art throughout the whole period of the industrial transition.[40]

By 1933 Mumford saw Le Corbusier and the functionalist architects in a different light,[41] but that was after *The International Style* assumed the leading role of explaining the new architecture to America. Thus, during the crucial years of the 1920s some of the primary apologists of the new movement carried out a discussion of the new architecture in terms that ignored its aesthetic concern and symbolic meanings.[42]

Several other reasons for the confusion concerning the "functionalist movement" can be stated briefly. One of these, also suggested by Banham, is that some of the apologists for the new movement, including perhaps some architects, may actually have made a conscious decision to "fight on a narrow front" because of the economic and political situation in the Western world at the time. Banham explains:

> With the International Style outlawed politically in Germany and Russia, and crippled economically in France, the style and its friends were fighting for a toehold in politically-suspicious Fascist Italy, aesthetically-indifferent England, and depression-stunned America. Under these circumstances it was better to advocate or defend the new architecture on logical and economic grounds than on grounds of aesthetics or symbolisms that might stir nothing but hostility.[43]

Another contributing factor in the development of the "reputation" of the new movement is the picture painted of it by its attackers. In Germany and France particularly, there were those who for various reasons stood to lose if the new style were adopted and who worked to discredit it by accusing it of being a narrow utilitarian approach to building.[44] And finally, there were those numerous "rank-and-file" architects who were designing most of the buildings actually constructed at the time and who, through misunderstanding resulting from the situation I have described or through pure lack of creativity or artistic competence, produced an unfortunately large quantity of imitation functionalist, dehumanizing, and just plain bad architecture. Too often such architecture has been linked with the spoken and written ideas of the pioneers of the movement, and its ill effects have been blamed on *their* intentions, albeit wrongly understood.

Before beginning to discuss in detail the results of my research into the various layers of the concept of function as revealed in the applied criticism of twentieth-century architecture, I feel that it is necessary to make some statements about the general characteristics and overall shape of that body of critical material. The first, and most salient, characteristic of the criticism is that very little of it was written before 1930 and most of it appeared after 1940. Indeed there was a real dearth of architectural criticism during the first three or four decades of this century. Talbot Hamlin, in an article written in 1930, entitled "Criticism Might Help Architecture—Let's Try It,"[45] attributes the slump in criticism to "the confusion between architecture as a profession and architecture as a business": that is, architects who are inspired only by the profit motive respond to real criticism (and by this Hamlin seems to mean criticism which includes negative judgment on aesthetic grounds) with a libel suit. Consequently, critics become timid and meekly offer instead only praise or simple description.

Several reasons for the lack of criticism in the early twentieth century stem from developments in the field itself during the nineteenth century.[46] First among these is the rejection of aesthetic systems of criteria for judgment which accompanied the growing realization on the part of some critics that imitation of historical styles of building could not be a vital, viable approach to meaningful building. During the period of eclecticism, critics were reduced to the rather superficial task of determining whether or not such-and-such an architect's new building accurately duplicated the elements of Gothic, or Classical, or even Indian style.

Two elements which grew out of nineteenth-century Romanticism in literature contributed to the abandonment of aesthetic criteria in scholarly criticism. One of these was a new acceptance of the artistic virtues of ugliness which accompanied the birth in the 1830s of the school of literary Realism.[47] The other element growing out of Romanticism which helped to change the nature of criticism was the new emphasis placed on sincerity in the production of works of art. The idea that the design of a building should grow out of the architect's own convictions about how a building should be designed, rather than out of the preferences of his client or the public, places the emphasis on a very subjective aspect of architectural production — on the "private" relationship between the artist and his work.[48] Both of these elements, acceptance of ugliness and desire for sincerity, made it increasingly difficult for the scholarly critic to make aesthetic judgments.

Although scholarly criticism in the nineteenth century had been diminished, popular criticism, which was really a literary genre enjoyed by the general public, was definitely on the upswing during the same period. Yet even this popularity of criticism as literature had a detrimental effect on meaningful criticism, particularly of architecture. Because the important factor in this type of criticism was a verbal one — that is, the new work of art produced by the critic himself rather than the nonverbal phenomenon of the building which provided the excuse for the critique — the visual/spatial or structural aspects of architecture tended to be ignored while the surface decorations, being particularly conducive to literary interpretation, were given close attention.

This popular criticism was disseminated through the architectural journals. But these journals towards the end of the nineteenth century tended to become increasingly like fashion magazines, giving greatest coverage to the most photogenic buildings regardless of whether or not those buildings exemplified important or qualitative architectural development. And then even this medium of criticism declined early in the twentieth century, with the demise of the Art Nouveau it had espoused.[49] Partly because of the timidity of some editors about encouraging the new trends in architecture and partly because of the reluctance of some to damage the new movement's chances for growth by criticizing it too harshly before it had even gained a firm foot-hold, architectural periodicals carried out an undeclared moratorium on criticism for several decades.

It was not until the late 1930s and early 1940s that the critics gradually took a more active part in architectural debate and development.

Characteristic of the criticism that appeared in the forties, fifties, and sixties was a preoccupation with the formative years of the modern movement. Numerous articles were published whose purpose was to examine, reexamine, and reassess the products, the polemic, the style, and the significance of modern "functionalism" as it had grown since the turn of the century. It is convenient here to discuss the newly awakened criticism in terms of the two general types mentioned in the introduction — "applied" and "theoretical/historical." Certainly there was now an active production of applied criticism, which responded to specific new and recent buildings in various ways; it is that criticism which will be treated in detail beginning in Chapter 3. First, however, I should like to summarize briefly the kinds of statement made in the more theoretical type of criticism, and for two reasons: first, because such a summary can give a sense of the context or critical atmosphere in which the applied criticism was carried out, and, second, because it is in the rather theoretical writings by critic–historians that one can find more carefully stated definitions of terms and assessments of trends.

The reassessment of the early years was characterized by attempts to define what functionalism really had been. One result of this endeavor was the recognition that none of the "giants" of the early modern movement had ever been a "functionalist" in the narrow sense. Some critics argued that *no* architect could be a strict functionalist, that such an approach makes one no longer an architect but an engineer. Others pointed out that even engineers must make decisions on the basis of taste or preference. Thus there was an effort to counteract the impression of many people that "functionalism" was what rank-and-file architects had made it seem to be.

Central to the attempts to define functionalism was the tendency to differentiate between its aesthetic and its ethical aspects. Critics seemed to concur that although the period referred to as the "functionalist era" had produced primarily a new style, that is, an aesthetic development, the ideas implicit in functionalism constituted an ethic which could, and should, undergird a wealth of stylistic variables. The problem was that functionalism had been interpreted not too narrowly but rather too broadly — many architects lacking in creativity had attempted to use the values of functionalism as a substitute for artistic imagination.[50] In terms of the levels of function to be discussed in this manuscript, this would mean that the rank-and-file architects had concentrated on the areas of structural articulation and physical function to the neglect of the higher values or levels of function, since it is in terms of higher values that the essentially artistic factor comes into play.

Statements of applied criticism dealing with function were separated for this study from those dealing only with form as an abstract, visual phenomenon. The applied criticism which appeared after World War II, then, was of one or the other of these two basic types. The criticism of form has consistently outweighed that of function in this century, which may seem strange in relation to the earlier discussion of the factors working against aesthetic criticism. What must be realized is that the examples of form criticism in this century have been primarily simple description, something which is threatened by neither the emphasis on sincerity nor the likelihood of libel suits. Consistent with the emphasis on sincerity is the large proportion of what may be called a particular type of style criticism which places an individual work within the context of the architect's entire oeuvre and attempts to discern the influences, visual or otherwise, which may have helped to determine this design. The appearance of judgmental statements in any of the types of form criticism is very rare, while it is more frequent in criticism of function, a phenomenon to be discussed later. Thus the proportion of form and function criticism is consistent with explanations of the detriments to meaningful criticism that have been operating in this century.

3

Structural Articulation

"Structural articulation" is the term I have adopted to refer to a particular type of function in architecture. It covers a group of related concepts which have in common an emphasis upon the visual expression in form of some primarily non-visual aspect of a building—in one case the building materials and techniques, in another the nature or arrangement of human activities to be carried on within the building.

The category of structural articulation differs from the other types of function dealt with here in that its primary concern is with a visual phenomenon—the appearance of a building. Critics who discuss aspects of structural articulation concern themselves to a great extent with description of formal elements. Yet, more than any of the other types of function I have categorized, this one grows directly out of a frequent use of the word "function" by the critics. In one case it may be the "function" of the building that is seen as being expressed outwardly in a design; in another case it may be the "function" of a specific building material or technique which is revealed through the surface treatment.

This chapter contains a detailed summary of structural articulation as it is discussed by critics. The chapter deals first with articulation of structural materials and method, centering primarily around critiques of Sullivan's Carson, Pirie, Scott building, the one of the chosen thirteen which drew the most comment on the subject. The discussion of the articulation of plan centers around Gropius's Bauhaus. Then the critics' treatment of Kahn's Medical Research Laboratories illustrates a combination of the two divisions of structural articulation in a more recent building. After a description of the results of an investigation into chronological developments within the category of structural articulation, this chapter proceeds to an analysis of those results relating them to pertinent concepts and events (some of which were discussed in Chapter 2) that give insight into the significance of the results.

The way in which critics discuss the visible articulation of building materials and techniques can be seen clearly in an example from 1904 dealing with Sullivan's Carson, Pirie, Scott building:

> Its exterior frankly betokens its structural basis and rises in no uncertain fashion from sidewalk to cornice [Pl. 1]; . . . the design is thoroughly modern. It shows fully the structural function of the steel frame with the enclosing protection of terra cotta, treated with full knowledge of its plasticity in its natural state and hardness and durability after treatment in the kiln. The lower portion on the street is equally straightforward in its qualities of "plate glass" architecture.[1]

This example is typical in its use of the word "function" to refer to the use of structural materials and in its attribution of the quality of modernity to a design which makes such "structural functions" visible. The use of the terms "frank" and "straightforward" point to a value held in high regard during the early years of the modern movement.

The Carson, Pirie, Scott building was of particular interest because it used a relatively new structural system—the steel frame—the possibilities of which had only begun to be explored. It was one of the earliest successful "skyscrapers," and critics apparently were favorably impressed with Sullivan's treatment of it. This building was seen as the one in which "for the first time the steel frame produced its own expressive style of architecture."[2] The use of the word "expression," as in the phrase "the most magnificent expression of the steel structural system,"[3] is quite common, but it seems to me the word "statement" or even "treatment' would be more appropriate.

The "honest" revelation of structural methods on the surface design of a building is a characteristic which came to be associated with functionalism in the narrower sense. Some critical statements convey the implication that such a treatment is simply the logical outgrowth of the structure, as if in the formula "structural technique = form;" the role of aesthetic preference and of artistic choice is minimized.

One discussion of the Carson, Pirie, Scott building emphasizes that "the architectural lines follow exactly the form of the steel frame" and states that "the upper part of the building, almost bare of architectural detail, presents for the first time a strict and logical solution of the problem in question," the "problem" being the steel frame construction.[4] This statement is very revealing of the underlying assumptions of many critics and architects of the "functionalist era," and one can see how such critiques probably contributed to the conclusion that good architecture required only logic and restraint on the part of architects. This critic has by implication placed the concept of aesthetic choice in the area of architectural *detail*. In fact, his discussion of Sullivan's building proceeds to state that the artist's "urge and pleasure of self-expression. . . is worked off" in "a rich ornament of the most fanciful design"—that is, the ornament surrounding the windows of the first and second stories (Pls. 2 and 3). The critic points out the similarity between Sullivan's ornament and that of the Art Nouveau and says that "this ornament, springing from the unappeased desire for personal expression in architecture, remains a residue of the nineteenth century." Of course, the use of such surface ornament has turned out to be a thing of the past, of the nineteenth century. The point I wish to make is that the implied value judgments in this statement— implied in the choice of such words as "logical solution" (positive) and "worked off" (negative)—encourage the notion of rational, restrained, bare exposure of structure as an ideal and of artistic expression as a weakness.

A similar emphasis on rational functionalism is found in this statement:

> The logical directness with which the structure is expressed gives the building strength. This strength is softened, perhaps even weakened, by the rounded corner. A more logical solution would have been to have the fronts meet at a right angle.[5]

This example, written in 1964, shows that the narrow functionalist interpretation of structural articulation did not pass out of existence once the modern movement was firmly established.

By way of contrast to the conclusions of such rationalistic critiques, two points may be made which arise in other analyses of structural articulation in the Carson, Pirie, Scott building. First is the fact, pointed out in several different instances, that the articulation of the steel frame *does* involve artistic decisions. Hugh Morrison counters the rationalist view most directly:

> This dominant horizontality [of Carson, Pirie, Scott], so contrary to the dominant verticality of the Wainwright Building, although both are constructed on steel frames, should be conclusive proof that the horizontality of the one or the verticality of the other cannot consistently be interpreted as reflecting Sullivan's intention to reveal the steel frame; . . . the form in each case is an aesthetic choice, based to be sure on practical considerations, but far removed from literal structuralism.[6]

Similarly, another critic says that in his early skyscrapers, Sullivan "really achieved an abstract symbolic form far more than any direct expression of function."[7] The dates of these critical statements should be noticed and compared because they show that while the common language of strict functionalism was being used, along with its implications for artistic imagination, there were those whose vision was larger than the more limited rationalistic view and more in line with that of the great pioneer architects as expressed in their verbal and architectural works.

Again, by way of contrast with the rationalistic interpretation of Sullivan's design quoted earlier, there are those who see the ornament on the Carson, Pirie, Scott store not as an inconsistency or an archaism, but rather as an element which contributes to the principle of structural articulation in the building. One critic writes:

> The detail of the decorative treatment around these [window] openings enhances the outlook, and gives additional value to the exterior effect. The building terminates in a cornice based on the projecting roof beams and rationally functional.[8]

Thus the ornament, as seen by this critic, actually contributes to the modernity of the building by underscoring aspects of the structural system. Another critic shows how Sullivan's use of ornament in his Guaranty building — where the ornamental treatment is very similar to that in the Carson, Pirie, Scott design — declared honestly the function of the "curtain wall" material which was applied to the steel structure:

> In Sullivan's actual designs, wall surface was abandoned for a system of pier and spandrel. That the terra cotta which gave fire-protection was not self-supporting masonry, but merely a casing, was expressed with particular success in the Guaranty Building by a delicate surface ornament.[9]

This example, in addition to making a specific point in regard to Sullivan's use of ornament, also illustrates the application of the principle of structural articulation to the nature of individual building materials.[10]

Before leaving the subject of structural articulation as treated in critiques of Sullivan's building, it is worthwhile to discuss one last interpretation of Sullivan's use of ornament because, when seen in relation to those already quoted, it seems to illustrate beautifully how a critic's preconceptions can influence what he sees. Having seen how critics of the earlier part of the century view the ornament as enhancing the clarity of the structural articulation, now compare an example written in 1960 which, in talking about a technique used by Wright, mentions the same ornament of Sullivan:

> The band of ornament of the second floor [of Wright's Winslow house of 1893] also assists the cornice in denying the boundaries of the walls. That is, its broken surface texture splinters the light and sets up a play of shadows which denies any sense of structural solidity to the wall under the overhang. This then, itself assisting that effect by the shadow it casts over the visually non-structural zone, seems partly to float above the solid base of the ground floor. Sullivan was sometimes to use his ornament for similar effects, as in the Carson-Pirie-Scott Store of 1899–1904, where he visually separated the upper floors from the ground below by such ornamental masking of the structural solidity of that zone [Pl. 1].[11]

This time, the ornament is interpreted as a camouflage for the structural facts of the building, a camouflage which gives pleasure by fooling the eye, by presenting a contradiction to the fact and to what one's mind knows to be the case. Later I will discuss the 1960s taste for such contradiction, but for the present I wish only to make the point that the critical statements elicited by a building can depend as much upon the concepts a critic has in mind as upon the actual characteristics of the building he is describing. This observation is relevant to the method of the present study because it supports the assumption that conclusions about the development of a concept can be drawn with validity from the statements which critics have written in different decades about the same buildings.

This discussion of articulation of structural materials and techniques so far has been based completely on critiques of Sullivan's Carson, Pirie, Scott building because, more than any other early twentieth-century building of the group I chose, this one has evoked critical comment on this very facet of architecture. Many other buildings of the time were discussed similarly, particularly those which, like Carson, Pirie, Scott, made use of the new steel frame structure which made the "skyscraper" possible. Among the other buildings I deal with, the two by Mies van der Rohe have drawn comment on their articulation of structure. Only one of these, the Barcelona Pavilion of 1929, can be considered an early modern building, but because the Farnsworth house of 1945–1950 is so similar in structure and has drawn similar comment from critics, I shall deal with them both at this point before moving on to the second division of structural articulation.

Mies's Barcelona Pavilion caused quite a stir among architectural critics partly because of the architect's unique handling of its structure. It has been pointed out that "in this building Mies was able to dissolve the ordinary elements of enclosure—floors, walls, and ceilings—and magically to reconstitute them as abstract planes, divorced from structural function [Pl. 18]."[12] Discussions of the pavilion do not speak in quite the same way about *articulation* of structure as do those of Sullivan's work, since in this case the structural functions were so simple as to seem to be nonexistent. The Farnsworth house, if anything, exceeded the Barcelona Pavilion in structural simplicity. This example shows how a critic deals with that simplicity and links the house with the Pavilion:

> [T]he...relationship of by-passing horizontal and vertical lines is employed in the small Farnsworth House of 1950. Heavy steel columns are welded...to the edges of three horizontal planes: a floor, a detached terrace, and the roof [Pls. 38 and 42]. Exquisite details and flawless craftsmanship serve to make this building one of the most dramatic statements of the Miesian idea. It has the intensity of the Barcelona Pavilion. Nothing detracts from its perfect expression of structure: there is nothing left to detract.[13]

Critics have seen the Farnsworth house as the ultimate in articulation of structure precisely because the structure is completely bare and exposed. In the Carson, Pirie, Scott building, and others like it, critics were dealing with the "curtain wall," which somehow had to present an image, or an "expression" as they frequently termed it, of a structure which still remained an "internal" phenomenon and therefore to a great extent actually hidden.

The second division of structural articulation, as the critics approach it, has to do with a revelation on the exterior of a building of the nature or arrangement of the uses to which it is to be put by its occupants. Whereas the first had to do with an articulation *in* design *of* structure, the second has to do rather with the articulation *in* structure *of* design — design in the first case referring to external surface and in the second to floor plan. The concept can be better understood when one compares it with the older method of building in which rooms were partitioned off within a basic box structure which from the exterior gave practically no clue as to its inner divisions, and which gave rise to the practice of applying a facade as a painterly or sculptural beautification.

The early modern trend was a return to a more candid revelation of what went on inside of buildings; the idea of a decorative facade was anathema. But this principle of structural articulation can be fully understood only in relation to the principle of analysis and differentiation of functions. Consistent with the rationalist philosophy, architectural function was analyzed and differentiated according to the varying natures of the human activities to be housed. As a result, a building was expected to have an appearance which made evident the type of activity it contained. And in the case of more complex functional frames, the parts of buildings were expected to be differentiated visually to correspond with the actual differentiation of activity which was carried on inside. Domestic activities, for example, came to be separated into those demanding privacy and those of a communal nature, those demanding access to mechanical equipment and those free of such requirements, those demanding an enclosed space and those allowing communication with the out-of-doors, those calling for a formal arrangement of space and those calling for flexibility, freedom, and informality; and the exterior of a house was to reveal these variations rather than to present a uniform "false" front.

Along with the analysis and differentiation of human activities came a recognition of the particular requirements of certain twentieth-century building types. One of these new building types was the large department store, and Sullivan's Carson, Pirie, Scott building evoked comment which reflects the concern with the "commercial problem." For example:

> The Schlesinger & Mayer Building [later called Carson, Pirie, Scott] is a differentiation of the commercial problem and has been treated entirely on its own merits, both in the general design and the detail. This is frankly a department store — an establishment where goods of many kinds may be retailed to many people and so displayed over large

floor areas, that ease of examination and accessibility to products may be speedily achieved. Hence throughout its typical floors, the window openings are of maximum size and form a distinct basis of the exterior design.[14]

Again, the use of the word "frank" reveals the value placed on candidness in architecture.

Sullivan's building, however, stands at the very beginning of the twentieth-century development of such honest articulation. One authority writing in 1963 looks back on the early years and compares the work of Sullivan and that of his student Wright:

Sullivan's building was integrated facade design, at most a schematic description of the character of the spaces in contained, but Wright's was an integral embodiment of those spaces. Sullivan's building was conceived as a standing body, with a base, a middle, and an end, and can therefore be described, as Sullivan described it, in terms of the classic column [Pl. 1]. But Wright's solids, though supremely strong, expressed the volume of space they defined. Thus the exterior of his building was that of a container of spaces and is to be read not as a column but as a galleried cavern [Pl. 4].[15]

Once again the word "express" is used in reference to the articulation in structure. A typical example of an appraisal on the basis of this principle is the following one which includes the term "functional":

Of these [many houses of brick] the masterpiece was the Robie House in Chicago with its long horizontal bands of wall surmounted by long groups of small windows and capped finally with the widest eaves and the longest roofline he had ever achieved. The effect here is indeed exceedingly mannered but it expresses an admirably functional plan....[16]

Other typical examples use the phrase, "functional articulation of the plan," making the articulation itself a "functional" attribute.

If the Carson, Pirie, Scott building was the epitome of the functionalist concern with articulation of structure, then Gropius's Bauhaus has a parallel status in the concern for articulation of plan. Just as Sullivan's building dealt with a new structural system, so Gropius's building, completed in 1926, tackled a new problem of plan. Never before had such a large project been undertaken by a modern architect, and the complexity of its program, as handled by Gropius, made it a prime example of the differentiation of functions in one design (Pls. 12 and 14). In 1932 an assessor of the finished product stated that, among other aspects of its design, "the functional articulation of the plan... [has] hardly been surpassed." This discussion continues in a manner typical of critiques of the Bauhaus:

The different parts of the Bauhaus complex are clearly separated in plan and distinguished from one another in design.... the fashion in which the bridge joins the separate east wing containing the independent Dessau Trade School to the main building represents Gropius' talent for well-articulated functional expression at its best.[17]

Other statements about the Bauhaus point to the asymmetry of the plan resulting from its differentiation of functions.[18] Such asymmetry carried a great impact when the Bauhaus was new, and many critics deal with the surprising unity which they saw in the plan in spite of its asymmetry.[19] In attempting to pinpoint the source of that unity they speak of a visual rhythm or regularity of the composition, crediting Gropius, for example, with "a masterly adjustment of a variety of rhythms of monotonous regularity to produce a general composition at once rich and serene."[20] Since those rhythms were direct results of the structure, rather than some applied decoration, the use of structural means is of utmost importance; as a result the close connection between technics and aesthetics in the "functionalist" era figures in the critics' statements. For example, one critic, in 1929, calls the Bauhaus "assuredly the most successful demonstration in execution of the technical and aesthetic possibilities of the manner of the New Pioneers in dealing with a large and complicated functional problem."[21] An interesting assessment of the aesthetic value of the Bauhaus and the relation of that value to technics appeared in a critical statement of 1967:

> In this current condition of aesthetic disequilibrium, the rediscovery of the Bauhaus is a fortunate development, for its most impressive quality today is precisely its equilibrium, its effortless mastery of the means at its disposal. Nominally a mere technical fact, the rational balance of the Bauhaus is actually the secret of its aesthetic survival. An urbane justice marks every decision: the absolute clarity with which plan is expressed in volume; the simple assuredness of the concrete frame; the wide smooth flow of the stairs; the detailing of the light fixtures — even the considered placing of the exposed heating and plumbing pipes.[22]

Thus, for the critics of the new movement in architecture, the Bauhaus was heavily endowed with symbolic value because it exemplified so well the differentiation of functions which stems from the rationalist orientation, and the articulation of both structure and plan which grew out of that differentiation and out of the reaction against nineteenth-century facade architecture.

In the late 1940s, there appeared two buildings in which critics saw opposing trends in the handling of articulation of plan; one trend was toward an extreme simplification and re-synthesis of differentiated function, found in Mies's Farnsworth house, and the other was toward a renewed emphasis on articulation of individual functional elements, found in Aalto's Baker Dormitory at M.I.T.

A critic dealing in the sixties with the trend towards simplification and reunification that he sees in Mies's work compares the Farnsworth house with Philip Johnson's "Glass House" of 1949 in New Canaan, Connecticut:

> Several commentators immediately perceived a most important academic or stylistic difference between these two sister glass boxes. The Farnsworth house by the older man, Mies, was still a modern house in the early European twentieth-century tradition. It had the old revolutionary anti-gravity gestures of the raised floor and cantilever ends. It was still articulated to some extent, in that the outdoor living platform was separate and deliberately placed out of line from the box itself. The Johnson house on the contrary suggested a tentative move to a new solution to the ancient puzzle. This was the opposite from articulation. It was a move back to coherent form, to a more intense concentration on the old artistic principle of unity. The Farnsworth house carried the International Style's concept of simplicity practically to the end of the road. It concluded one investigation. The Johnson house opened another, extending the idea of simplicity into visual oneness. [23]

In the case of these houses, the idea of articulation of differentiated inner space has already evolved, via the Miesian urge to simplification, to the point of being no longer operative. Yet the critic's discussion reveals the centrality of the issue of articulation in the architectural developments preceding these.

Aalto's Baker Dormitory, on the other hand, represents the opposite trend. Critics writing in the sixties saw in this building a preview of a prominent movement which was to follow. One critic, for example, writes:

> In my opinion...a foretaste of Brutalism can also be found in Aalto; for example, in the M.I.T. students' dormitory, at Cambridge, Mass. (1947/48), one of the first buildings in which the access system is conceived as a sequence of interconnecting spaces; thus, the rear elevation, in which the staircases and passages, i.e., individual functional elements, are boldly emphasized as deliberate architectural features, becomes a characteristic device of later Brutalism [Pl. 29]. [24]

Aalto's dormitory has been seen as an "antidote" to the classicism which was a coexisting opposite trend of the fifties, partly because of its articulation of functioning elements:

> Here we had an architecture which was massive and solid, which most of all physically released functions to make forms, and went far beyond simple symmetry to a noble generosity in the fullness of its shapes.... [It was] a statement of the possible grandeur of architectural form [Pl. 30]. [25]

Yet another appraisal of Aalto's dormitory sees it as an antidote to a particular anti-urban trend in American architecture:

> American architecture, and especially Modern architecture with its antipathy to the "false front," has emphasized the free-standing, independent building even in the

city—the building which is an isolated pavilion rather than one which reinforces the street line has become the norm. Johnson has called this the American tradition of "plop architecture." Aalto's dormitory at M.I.T. is exceptional. The curving front along the river and its fenestration and materials contrast with the rectangularity and other characteristics of the rear; exterior as well as interior forces of use and space and structure vary back and front [Pls. 29 and 30].[26]

Once again, structural articulation is pointed to as the means to a particular visual and even symbolic end—symbolic, in this case, of a renewed faith in certain characteristics of urban architecture.

A building completed in 1960 stands as a kind of summary of what the principle of structural articulation had meant up to that point in this century. Louis Kahn's Richards Medical Research building at the University of Pennsylvania has been widely discussed as a building which demonstrates both types of structural articulation, making such articulation the prominent feature in its design. The differentiation of functional interior spaces in this case takes the summary form of a division between what Kahn has called "servant" and "served" spaces—that is, the laboratory spaces themselves and the spaces housing the mechanical services which make their operation possible.[27] One writer describes this differentiation thus: "Kahn separated the functions of the building into two categories... and made the latter, the laboratories, fragile glass boxes and the former, the mechanical service ducts, hefty workmanlike brick piers [Pl. 54]."[28] At the same time, the articulation of structural materials and methods figures large in the design:

> The early sketches for this laboratory complex show that Kahn had the tower cluster in mind from the start. Subsequently, he polished and made more explicit his first idea through a consideration of program and structure. In the end, it was the structural solution, with its interlocking web of precast ceiling and floor elements that determined much of the external and internal fabric [Pl. 57].[29]

Thus, the ideals of structural articulation, so central to early functionalism, have been seen to be embodied in Kahn's building. It has been called "a monument achieved within the rational code" and "a single unified thing, yet one which clearly followed some functional programme in its erratic external form, which was transparently honest and true to the spirit of the mechanized laboratories which it served."[30]

Yet, as one critic has pointed out, Kahn's building was "no mere essay in functional composition."[31] It has been seen as an important monument in relation to several twentieth-century trends.[32] It has been compared to the work of Mies in its "meticulous definition of architecture in structural terms, so that the building process clearly appears in what is built."[33] And yet, it has been seen also as part of the countertrend toward "the old regard

for functional flexibility" which "tempered. . .the new emphasis on wholeness, singleness or monolithic form,"[34] of which Mies was a prime mover.
Another statement puts it thus:

> Kahn. . .extends the ideal structure of Mies by giving it concreteness and tangibility in
> two respects. First, the structure embodies the spaces defined by the activities and ser-
> vices housed by the building. Second, it is more insistent on its own physical actuality.
> This extension makes Kahn less passive in his approach to design than Mies. After all,
> his architecture is not "almost nothing." It is "what it wants to be," while what "it"
> wants to be has been extensively preconditioned by Kahn's comprehensive philosophy
> of architecture.[35]

The first of these two points refers to the articulation of activity and plan
which had disappeared almost completely in Mies's Farnsworth house. The
second refers to a much less tangible quality, one which points to two
emphases prominent in the sixties: first, the celebration of the physicality
of materials, and second, the renewed appreciation of the creative role of
the artist in the making of architecture. Both of these will be discussed further in a later chapter, but for the present I should like to point out the
relation of the latter — the role of the artist — to the earlier, strict functionalist implications that design was simply a matter of technics and logic. In
this assessment of Kahn's work there appears the recognition of a truth
about architecture which in some of the criticism of this century had been
temporarily eclipsed — that is, the importance of the artist's creative imagination in determining the final design, no matter how derived from pure
logic it might appear to be.

In an effort to determine how structural articulation figured in criticism of
function as a whole, I obsesrved the relative importance of it in comparison with the other types of function.[36]

The profile of this type of function has very marked ups and downs.
Structural articulation was of major concern to critics writing before 1950,
much more so than any of the other types of function. A crude statistical
analysis confirmed my impression that roughly half of the functional criticism written between 1900 and 1950 elicited by the thirteen buildings I
chose was directly concerned with one or both of the divisions of structural
articulation I have defined here. Yet during the decade 1950–59, interest in
structural articulation declined quite sharply, so that considerably less criticism dealt with structural articulation than with each of the other types of
function. In the sixties, discussion of structural articulation increased
sharply once more, though now, unlike the period before 1950, the other
categories seemed more nearly equal in rank, both to structural articulation
and to each other. These characteristics of the "history" of the concept of
structural articulation may be seen in relation to several other ideas and

historical developments, yielding insight into various facets of the twentieth-century concept of architectural function.

First of all, the strong emphasis on structural articulation in the twentieth century can be seen in relation to two events of the nineteenth century already mentioned in the background material. One of these is the revolution which took place in structural materials and techniques. Concentration on both divisions of the category of structural articulation was brought about largely by this revolution. The excitement engendered by the new methods was bound to result in a great deal of attention paid, in critical writing, to their visual articulation in architects' designs. In the case of the actual leaving bare of the frame of a building, as in the Farnsworth house, one can sense the fascination which the pure structural skeleton holds for the architect. The steel frame and reinforced concrete certainly held the promise of an infinite number of formal potentialities just waiting to be explored. At the same time, the fact that the outer surface of a building no longer had weight-bearing responsibility meant that the new structural techniques could in fact be hidden completely behind a "curtain wall." Thus, if the advent of the steel frame was to be celebrated, it would have first to be made evident, or "articulated," on that curtain wall. In this sense, the insistence on articulation of structure just when, for the first time, obviousness of structural elements was no longer necessary might be interpreted as a conservative trend.

The other division of structural articulation—that is, the articulation in structure of plan—was likewise made possible by the revolution in engineering. Without the freedom of partition placement brought about by the liberation from the necessity of the load-bearing wall, the variety of human activities housed by buildings could not have been so successfully differentiated and accommodated, and the articulation of those functions would not have been a meaningful ideal. Furthermore, the new acceptance of asymmetry, which permitted the decentralization of buildings, was an outgrowth of new structural potentialities, the epitome of which is the cantilever.

The second event of the nineteenth century which has direct bearing on structural articulation is the concern for sincerity, or truthfulness, in art.[37] The articulation of the "facts" about a building, whether of its structure or its uses, was approved of as a "frank," a "straightforward" architectural statement. Indeed, the stress on articulation of structure on the potentially veiling curtain wall is certainly more the result of an aesthetic value than of necessity, and that aesthetic had roots in the nineteenth century.

Some insight into the rise and fall of critics' interest in structural articulation can be gained from viewing structural articulation in relation to some of the prominent trends in twentieth-century architecture. The first period, through the forties, was the time when one might have expected the more mechanical, efficiency-oriented category of physical function to be in the ascendancy. A great deal of the polemic accompanying the new movement, after all, stressed the economy and convenience of the new approach, and *beauty* was not often mentioned. And yet, in criticism, by far the strongest emphasis was placed on the appearance of the new buildings. And so one is left with the conclusion that the functionalist movement was primarily a stage in the evolution of style, so that by 1932 it was logical to entitle a book about modern architecture *The International Style.*

In that book, Henry-Russell Hitchcock and Philip Johnson outline three principles of the modern style,[38] all of which are directly related to what I have discussed here as structural articulation. The first principle, "volume rather than mass," has to do with the fact that the roles of surface and support now were played by different structural members and materials. Instead of a sculptured mass of masonry, there was now a cage or shell which surrounded a volume, and a surface which was stretched over that shell to protect the interior space from the weather. Characteristic of good modern architecture, according to Hitchcock and Johnson, is the consistent reinforcement of the visual effect of volume rather than mass. And this entailed an *articulation* of the facts about the structural system.

The second principle is "regularity rather than axial symmetry...as the chief means of ordering design." This principle, like the first, stems from the articulation of structural techniques but it touches also on the articulation of plan. Regularity is an intrinsic characteristic of the new structural methods: "The supports in skeleton construction are normally and typically spaced at equal distances in order that strains may be equalized."[39] But because of the differentiation of the purposes for which a building is intended, exact axial symmetry in the design is often a falsification of the facts. Thus articulation of both structure and plan demands regularity but not necessarily symmetry.

The third principle, proscription of "arbitrary applied decoration," also relates to structural articulation, particularly that of building methods and materials. Applied ornament is not honestly expressive of structural means and therefore has no *raison d'être* in a style consistently derived from the articulation of those means. Architectural detail, however, is a legitimate form of ornament, one that "is required as much by modern structure as by the structure of the past."[40] Thus, the main emphasis in Hitchcock and Johnson's comprehensive discussion of early modern architecture is on the stylistic aspects which result from the articulation of the new structural techniques. And one may conclude that the visual, stylistic results of structural articulation were what constituted the primary contribution of early functionalism to the development of architecture. Peter Blake has said that preoccupation with function is always characteristic of the beginning phase of a new style, while what is truly new is the visual "language" established in that style.[41]

The drop in critical interest in structural articulation during the fifties may be related to what has been called a "classicizing mode" in the architecture of that period,[42] inspired primarily by Mies. Although the tendency of the group of architects whose designs were in this "mode" was to articulate or even expose structure, they aimed at a unification and simplification in the expression of plan. The Farnsworth house, for example, is intended to house all the many varied functions of a domestic program in one glass box. Thus the decade of the fifties was a period when some architects counteracted one of the primary tenets of the modern style to explore other possibilities. Perhaps the decline of critical discussion of architecture in terms of structural articulation may have resulted from a "wait-and-see" attitude on the part of critics similar to that of the late nineteenth and very early twentieth centuries with regard to the new movement as a whole.

The sharp increase in critiques of structural articulation in the sixties may have been influenced by two factors. One is the Brutalist movement of the fifties and early sixties, which opposed the classicizing mode and stressed the growth of architectural forms from the needs of the activities they are intended to house. Reference to this movement appears in some of the critical discussions of Aalto's Baker Dormitory cited above. The second factor which may have contributed to my finding an increase of critical statements concerned with structural articulation in the sixties is the appearance of a number of books by critic-historians dealing with the early years of the modern movement as history. Many of these books discuss individual buildings in terms of their style and the manner in which function relates to that style. Naturally, articulation of structure and of plan is an important facet of that kind of discussion. Thus, some of the interest in structural articulation expressed in criticism of the sixties reflects a reporting of earlier concerns as much as it reveals an effort to deal with a present one.

In summary, structural articulation is a two-pronged principle of early functionalism which no study of the concept of function in twentieth-century architectural criticism could omit because of the critics' use of the very word "function." The critics refer to two kinds of "function" which should be articulated visually for the viewer of a building: one is the "function" of structural elements in combination; the other is the "function" of the spaces of the building, the activities they are intended to house. Both aspects of structural articulation were very important to the development of the modern style. Their importance is evidenced by the amount of attention given them in actual statements of applied criticism, and it is corroborated by Hitchcock and Johnson's definitive description of the modern style in terms of three principles, all of which stem directly from the tenet of structural articulation.

The emphasis in the kind of critical statements discussed in this chapter is upon the appearance of buildings: in their statements, critics deal with what is or should be the visible manifestation *of* function. Thus, critical discussion of structural articulation can be seen as a subsidiary of discussion of form; critics engaged in description of a building's form frequently refer to aspects of the principle of structural articulation as contributing to the final appearance of that form. In the following chapters, which deal with the other types of function mentioned in the introduction, the discussion revolves not around the visible form of a building but around the needs of the users of a building. It is characteristic of the critical statements to be examined in the next four chapters that they contain less reference to appearance and more reference to the actual "working" of the building as a whole, with the human occupant as the stated or implied center of concern. In a sense, structural articulation is a "sculptural" principle and critical statements based upon it deal with the more sculptural aspects of buildings—that is, the shape and appearance of their exteriors. Starting with the next chapter, the critic's concern moves inside the building to deal more directly with the peculiarly *architectural* responsibilities of buildings to their inhabitants.

4

Physical Function

The material dealt with in this chapter and in the next three chapters is qualitatively different from that in Chapter 3 in that it is concerned primarily with the well-being of the users of buildings. The four types of function which share this concern are related to each other in a particular pattern, a pattern which in a sense is hierarchical. Beginning in "physical function" with the most elemental, least complex of human needs, there will be a progression "upward" toward more "civilized," more complex, more highly differentiated and particularized human functions and needs. This is not to imply that a building must necessarily satisfy the "lower" requirements before it can answer the "higher" ones; in fact, critics frequently have accepted and praised a building for its "higher" significance while recognizing that in the more elementary aspects it decidedly failed. Nor should the reader infer that critics deal with these categories of function in a particular order; they are aspects of the same dimension of the architectural object—the dimension of function—and critics have dealt with them in a variety of ways, sometimes attending exclusively to one category, sometimes including discussion of more than one category in the same article or even the same paragraph. The upward progression does mean, however, that the types of function labelled physical, psychological, social, and cultural/existential can logically be referred to as *levels* of function. They are levels in the same sense that animals are on a lower evolutionary level than man.

This chapter deals with the criticism which has examined the effectiveness of a building in satisfying the purely physical requirements of its users. Physical function includes two basic areas of architectural function. On the very lowest level, that which I call "physical control,"[1] buildings must simply provide adequate shelter from the elements: thus temperature, ventilation, and sun-glare must be controlled. The second area of physical function, one which can be seen as "higher" than physical control, is what I call "functional frame"—the level on which buildings are space-frames through which men move and in which they carry out certain activities. Thus the problems of acoustics, artificial lighting, and traffic patterns are added to those of mere shelter. The term "functional frame" does not include the psychological ramifications of man as an actor in space. That is dealt with in the next chapter because it constitutes a discernible "level" of architectural function qualitatively different from the material of the present chapter.

Critical statements concerned with physical function have ranged in this century from a brief reference to an entire book.[2] Typical brief statements have referred to some feature of a building's design as being derived from the architect's desire to deal with environmental conditions. Le Corbusier's Villa Savoye, for example, is said to have been raised on "stilts" to get away from the dampness (Pl. 20),[3] and Wright's "heavy, low-slung roof planes" are seen as protection against the "threatening sky" of the American prairie (Pls. 4 and 5).[4] More recently, Kahn's Richards Medical Research Laboratories has been discussed as a building whose design was influenced greatly by the need to control certain physical elements, this time internally generated ones: the huge service towers function partly as exhaust funnels for the expelling of contaminated air from the laboratories (Pls. 53 and 57).[5]

Mies van der Rohe's Farnsworth house elicited lengthy critiques following the owner's conclusion that for her it was uninhabitable. One critic describes the problem this way:

> The Fox River house is located in one of the most difficult climates on earth, with an average annual range from subpolar winters to summers of Congo-like heat and humidity. Comfort, indeed survival, under such extremes as these would seem to indicate an architecture of flexible response and accommodation to environmental change. Mies's design makes no such concessions. All the exterior walls are identical; all are of glass; and none of the glass is shaded [Pl. 38]. Hence (so ran the owners' testimony at least) glare was often severe inside the house, especially in winter, when the ground was covered with snow. Drawing the curtains won summer relief, but also, of course, cut out the view, which was the reason for the glass in the first place [Pl. 42]. In fact, control of light and heat in a glass house posed all sorts of related problems of comfort for the tenant. Direct sunlight penetrated the unshaded glare, sharply raising the temperature inside the house, even in winter. All the glass in the house was fixed. There were no openable windows, and only a single pair of doors [Pl. 41]. Natural ventilation was therefore limited, and the house had no air conditioning. To escape this hot weather dilemma one could move out onto that beautiful porch and famous floating terrace, except that, without insect screens, they too were uninhabitable at this time of year [Pl. 40].[6]

Criticism was particularly strong when the Farnsworth house was compared with the house Philip Johnson designed for himself. It, too, was "an undifferentiated rectangular enclosure of glass," yet because of the architect's careful handling of environmental conditions, it was a very successful private dwelling.[7]

Critics writing in the sixties about some of the earlier architectural monuments of the century pointed out a rather common failing due to lack of care for environmental conditions. This time the initial result of the error was suffered not by the inhabitant of the building but rather by the external surfacing material. The material which suffered was the smooth white skin of stucco used to surface, among others, the Villa Savoye of Le Corbusier and the Bauhaus designed by Gropius. The stucco was a favorite surface, partly because it so enhanced the impression of a non-supporting, stretched curtain wall described later by Hitchcock and Johnson as so necessary to "good" modern architecture, and partly because "it looked wonderfully machine-made [Pl. 20]."[8] Unfortunately, before the finished building had stood for very long, streaks and cracks appeared, the inevitable effects of the weather on a not-so-durable material.[9]

A major piece of architectural criticism dealing with physical control appeared in 1969; it is Reynor Banham's *The Architecture of the Well-Tempered Environment,* a history of success and failure in solving problems of environmental control in twentieth-century architecture. Banham sees the years 1899–1910, culminating in the Robie house, not only as "Wright's greatest period of...environmental mastery," but also as a high-point in "the architecture of the well-tempered home" that was not to be equalled for another forty years—not until the appearance of Philip Johnson's house already mentioned as contrasting in this respect with Mies's Farnsworth house.[10]

Banham finds in the Robie house several ingenious techniques for environmental control which appear to be Wright's own innovations. Having paid careful attention to the environmental conditions of the site in various seasons, Wright devised some highly successful solutions for the difficult problems of lighting, temperature control and ventilation. For example, much has been made of the visual effect of the great overhanging roof of the Robie house, but Banham points out that its precisely designed contours solve a number of functional problems as well.

The great cantilevers of the roof, while they contain no hidden environmental secrets, are not quite so simple in their function as might appear. The western one certainly functions as a sunshade, particularly against the raking mid-afternoon sun which Latin cultures call "the light that kills," but the eastern one probably does more useful work as a permanent umbrella to keep the rain off the kitchen and service entrance area in the corner of the car-yard. Some have seemed surprised that the projections of the eaves on the south side of the house seem slight compared with those to east and west, and doubt that it is sufficient to shade the glass [Pls. 4 and 5]. In fact it is *exactly* sufficient—the sun stands tall in summer in Chicago's latitude, and at mid-day on Midsummer day, the shadow of the eaves just kisses the woodwork at the bottom of the glass in the doors to the terrace.[11]

Similar precision and care went into the solving of other problems in the Robie house such as ventilation, heating, lighting, and insect control (Pl. 6).

Wright's success in this area of environmental control reflects his attitude that the machine and its products are things to be mastered and used by man, not things to which man should be enslaved. Banham suggests that:

> With Wright's departure from Chicago, the subsequent splintering of the Prairie school, and the contemporaneous running down of the California school,...the architecture of the well-tempered home passed its first peak; the second was to be some way off, and the intervening period was to be largely occupied, and profoundly confused, by the European modernists' conviction that "the Machine" was a portentous cultural problem, rather than just something that the architect could use to make houses "perfectly sanitary, labor-saving...where the maximum of comfort may be had with the minimum of drudgery."[12]

Typical of the results of the European attitude is the Villa Savoye of Le Corbusier, in which the expanses of glass caused "tremendous solar heat gain due to greenhouse effects in summer, and...equally tremendous losses in winter due to the almost nonexistent insulating qualities of [the] window-glass."[13] The glass wall, like the stucco finish discussed above, was used because it reinforced the all-important intellectual and visual effect of a non-weight-bearing skin around a skeleton structure (Pl. 20).

The critic who is interested in discussing a particular building as a "functional frame" is typically interested in finding answers to such questions as the following: does the design facilitate the activities for which the building was intended? Are the spaces properly lighted? Is the permanent "furniture" conveniently arranged? If it is important to hear or be heard, are the acoustics adequate? In other words, does the building work?

Certain statements concerning Louis Sullivan's Carson, Pirie, Scott building illustrate the way in which a building may be discussed in terms of its success as a functional frame. One of Sullivan's major concerns was adequate lighting: the public must be able to see the merchandise on display. Sullivan's design, according to one critic, provides for this activity quite adequately.

> Since the fundamental interior arrangement was that of unbroken floor spaces for the display and sale of merchandise, it was important to have windows which would admit the maximum amount of daylight into these interior spaces.... The natural boundary of these windows would be the steel frame itself; the width determined by the distance

between columns, the height by the distance from floor to floor. These large window-openings of uniform size, established the basis of the exterior design...[and helped produce] one of the most intelligent solutions of the problem of the large department store that has ever been made.:.[Pl. 1].[14]

Sullivan's department store "works" in the opinion of this critic because the problems of functional frame were kept in mind throughout the design process.

Critics concerned with functional frame have not limited their attention to the interior of buildings. They also have been interested in such things as the proximity of parking areas to the building in question or the relative ease with which the individual is able to make the transition from such a parking area to the building's interior. In a discussion of the Robie house, for example, it has been noted that one of the "advanced concepts of function" in this building is the fact that "the garage is integral, perhaps for the first time in the history of American architecture."[15] And in discussions of the Villa Savoye, much has been made of the fact that "the ground-floor curve was calculated on the turning circle of...[the] automobile," and that the owners would "arrive by car, driving under the pilotis to their front door...[Pls. 21 and 22].[16]

In discussing buildings on the level of functional frame, critics have frequently referred to the virtue of flexibility resulting from movable or non-existent partitions, a flexibility made possible by the use of structural steel and reinforced concrete. All of Le Corbusier's family dwellings, for example, have been described thus:

[They all]...attack the same problem. He is always endeavoring to open up the house, to create new possibilities for connections between its interior and its exterior and within the house itself. We want rooms which can be thrown open or are enclosed at will, rooms whose outer partitions fall away when we wish. Briefly, it is a question of achieving dwellings of a sort which, up to the present, have been beyond the reach of conception and execution alike.[17]

Such flexibility is also a well-known concern of Mies van der Rohe. His Farnsworth house is, in the opinion of one critic, based upon the concept "of open, usable space, unhindered by columns, where function can be defined by flexible room dividers and furniture grouping [Pl. 39]."[18] Such flexibility, according to this same critic, makes this house "Mies's most important statement in residential architecture."[19]

Likewise, Gerrit Rietveld's Schröder house has been praised for the flexibility of its interior. The second floor of this house could be subdivided according to the whim of the owner by pulling collapsible partitions out into the center of the room along metal tracks recessed into the floor and ceiling (Pl. 8). One critic has said: "After forty years it is still the youngest house in Europe... [primarily because of its] provisions of flexibility for use...."[20]

One of the key buildings of this study has been found lacking in just this aspect — flexibility — for which all of these buildings just discussed have been so highly praised. Kahn's Medical Research Building elicited the following statement:

> The toughness and the clarity of the imagery suggest a functionalism made monumental and grand, though, in fact, the buildings, not mindful enough of the demands for flexibility on the part of the scientists, do not work very well.[21]

Thus for the critic interested in a building as a functional frame for human use, the handling of the problem of flexibility can determine whether or not the building is to be regarded as a successful solution.

Of the thirteen buildings chosen for examination in the present study, Wright's Guggenheim Museum is the one to have recieved the most critical attention in terms of its performance as a functional frame. Among those discussing the building in these terms there is almost universal agreement that although it is a remarkable architectural achievement, it presents serious problems related to the hanging and viewing of paintings.

One commentator jokingly compared the Guggenheim's failures in the realm of functional frame with those of Kahn's medical research laboratories.

> ...I'm still a functionalist enough to joke, maybe sourly, about moving the scientists from Kahn's masterpiece, the Richards building, into Wright's masterpiece, the Guggenheim Museum. The Guggenheim is a museum where you can't view pictures well; the Richards building is a laboratory where scientists can't work. Switching scientists with art objects might improve things.[22]

Another critic believes that Wright

> ...sacrificed the purposes of the Museum and created an empty monument as the sole prospective occupant of an untenanted world [Wright is reported to have said that if a nuclear bomb destroyed New York, his building, on its cushioned foundations, would merely bounce with the shock and survive.];...he turned an opportunity into an obstacle. Even as a fortress, even as a bomb shelter, it falls short of perfection.[23]

Some of the reasons for the building's failure on the level of functional frame are outlined in the following observations:

> The fact is that it is extremely difficult to display paintings on the Guggenheim's spiral ramps: to start with, the viewer stands on an incline; next, the wall slopes away from him at another angle; then the principle source of light (as conceived by Wright) would tend to light the viewer rather than the painting; and, finally, because of the absence of

all verticals and horizontals in the structure—and the prevalence of lines and planes slanting in all directions—no painting would ever look as if it had been hung straight [Pl. 36].[24]

It was because of just such problems as these that some rather drastic changes were later made in the picture-mounting arrangements and in the lighting of the museum. Many critics felt that Wright's excitingly effective structure was spoiled as a result, but apparently the changes did allow it, for the first time, to function well as a museum. The problems encountered here demonstrate clearly why critics necessarily have occupied themselves with what could have seemed to be an unimportant, uninteresting, and certainly unaesthetic aspect of architecture. Architecture is, after all, the creation of art objects which are intended to be *used*.

This difficult combination of practical utility with artistic value is one which architecture, more than any other of the arts, is required to achieve. Quite clearly the critics' statements which show a concern with practical utility refer primarily to the technical aspects of the building in question, aspects such as insulation, glare-control, durability of materials, accessibility by car, or flexibility of partitions. Or if the larger, overall "shapes" of the building are referred to, they are discussed rather as if they were primarily parts of a functioning machine. The visual or aesthetic aspects play a minor role when the critics' focus is on practical utility.

Characteristic of critical statements which appraise a building on the level of physical function is the frequency of value judgment. Many of the examples cited above include clearly negative assessments of the practical utility of the building in question. Often the negative response is not so much a matter of the critic's own personal opinion as it is a simple statement of the facts about the effects of a certain handling of the technical features. In fact, one could assume that in some cases, the negative response would not have come from the critic if he did not have access to information from those who have experienced the building more directly—the residents of a house, for example. Chapter 2 included a discussion of some of the elements operating in the early part of the century to make personal value judgment, aesthetic judgment particularly, difficult for critics to carry out. And as we progress upward through criticism of the higher levels of function, there is a noticeable decrease in value judgment. One can readily see, however, that making even negative judgments on the level of physical function is not likely to give the critic a heavy burden of personal liability: the facts, if ascertainable, are undeniable. It is somewhat surprising, therefore, that few of the examples containing negative judgments were written before 1950; and most appeared after 1960, even though some of them refer to buildings completed early in the century. This fact contributes to an analysis of the way in which critics viewed the concept of function on the physical, practical level—an analysis to be discussed further following a description of the "profile" of the material considered in this chapter.

During the entire period under investigation here, 1900–1969, critics' concern with the level of physical function was exceeded by their concern with structural articulation, a more visually-oriented facet of architecture. This lesser interest in physical function was the case particularly before 1950, when attention to structural articulation far outweighed that given to practical matters. After 1960, all the levels of function, including physical function, were in nearly equal proportion, though structural articulation still seems to have been of utmost concern. In view of the reputation of early functionalism for being preoccupied with mechanical efficiency and practicality, these observations of critics' general lack of concern with these matters are initially surprising. Similarly unexpected is the fact that of the two divisions of physical function—that is, environmental control and functional frame—the thirteen buildings on which I based my study received little critical comment of the former type before 1960. During the years leading up to 1960, critics were more interested in functional frame than physical control, even though the earlier years, if considered in terms of environmental control, saw the completion of both outstandingly successful and glaringly unsuccessful buildings.

These observations are surprising, however, only in relation to the reputation of early functionalism for making mechanical efficiency and practicality in architecture its ultimate goal, and, as is demonstrated by the writings of the pioneer architects and the critical reassessment of functionalism which took place around 1950,[25] that reputation was ill-founded. Once one recognizes that stylistic development and aesthetic value had never ceased to be the architects' and critics' main concern, the profile of the physical level of functional criticism is entirely logical. Appreciation of stylistic development, of course, places much emphasis on visual perception, while appreciation of mechanical efficiency depends much less upon the visual than upon the other senses. Thus the fact, reported above, that critics' concern with functional frame outweighed their concern with environmental control, can be seen as a natural result of visual bias. Glancing back over the kinds of building featured in the critical statements relating to functional frame, one can see that they depend more upon visual perception than do the majority of points covered under the heading of physical control. In addition, problems of environmental control in buildings completed early in the century often resulted directly from the use of materials such as glass and stucco which enhanced the desired visual effect; visually-oriented critics would tend to applaud the design for its appearance, perhaps letting that consideration eclipse the possibility of environmental drawbacks.

Similarly, the subordination of concern for physical function to that for structural articulation, particularly before 1950, is consistent with the primarily visual orientation of both architects and critics. As discussed in Chapter 3, the description of the new architecture by Hitchcock and Johnson in terms of three stylistic principles, all of which relate directly to structural articulation, supports the idea that aesthetic matters were of ultimate concern all along, while the intellectual concept of mechanical perfection was primarily a verbal accompaniment to the main event. The fact that after 1960 physical function was given critical attention more closely proportionate to that given structural articulation reflects a growing concern for the humanizing of architecture that was in evidence in more theoretical criticism in the decade and a half prior to 1960.[26]

Also consistent with the visual bias in criticism during the first half of the century is the late appearance of negative value judgments in criticism of physical function. Seemingly, problems of malfunction in the practical area tended to be overlooked in the search for exciting new visual forms in architecture.[27] This tendency to overlook practical faults is particularly characteristic of such buildings as the ones chosen for this study; these thirteen were all considered very important objects—that is, they generally received enthusiastic critical response on the basis of their plastic forms alone.

Indeed, during the sixties, when negative statements about the physical function of some of these buildings were being made, there was some critical debate concerning just which facet of architecture—the artistic or the practical—should be considered of greater importance. Some of this debate was prompted by and centered around Mies's Farnsworth house, in defense of which two important architectural critics, in particular, have spoken out. James Marston Fitch, writing in 1963, expressed his conviction that as a result of the changes made in the house to make it livable, "Mies's beautiful creation has been not merely maimed but destroyed."[28] A lengthy quote from Fitch's discussion of the problem is included here because it so clearly presents the "dilemma" presented by Mies as well as, to some degree, by other architects:

> The necessary modification of his design constitutes an exquisitely painful demonstration of the dilemma which he confronts us with: his architecture is literally utopian. It is a dilemma of which Mies is not altogether unaware, and there is something at once admirable and ornery in his Olympian refusal to lift a finger to help us. The size of his talent is so immense that, from an esthetic point of view, it confers an air of classic nobility upon everything he does. But the shape of his talent is so platonically restricted that it exposes many of the same buildings to serious challenge from an operational point of view. To acclaim Mies for the monumental purity of his forms, and yet to deplore their malfunction in some pragmatic details, is rather like praising the sea for being blue, while chiding it for being salty, or admiring the tiger for the beauty of his coat while urging him to become a vegetarian.

The fact is that Mies accomplished his ambition of an absolute purity of form only by doing what Plato did — that is, by resolutely suppressing many of the mundane details of everyday reality. The arbitrary limitations of material and palette in his buildings are self-imposed. He has found them essential to his integrity as an artist, to his peace of mind as a man.[29]

The critic who perhaps most consistently and forthrightly has taken up the defense of some of the great malfunctioning buildings of our century is Peter Blake. He admits that Mies is at his best when he has no practical problems of function to contend with, as for example, in the Barcelona Pavilion.[30] He states Mies's argument that "the only permanent ingredient a building can be expected to possess is beauty," and then continues:

History, of course, is on Mies's side; nobody remembers whether the Parthenon ever worked really well, but everyone remembers what Phidias did there for the eternal splendour and glory of architecture. By the same token no one will long remember that the German Pavilion at Barcelona contained no exhibits — and could not have contained many exhibits — in the conventional sense; but history will record that in 1929, on a hill above Barcelona, Mies van der Rohe built the most beautiful structure of an era.[31]

The Guggenheim Museum is another work in which serious practical problems, such as the difficulty of displaying paintings on its curved walls, have been cited. Wright's well-known egotism, perhaps like Mies's "Olympian refusal to lift a finger to help us," has been blamed for his failures to accommodate the programme of the museum. This building, too, has found a strong champion in Peter Blake. He admits that "the Guggenheim Museum is almost impossible as a museum in the normal sense,"[32] but he defends it much as he defends the work of Mies — from the standpoint of its long-term implications in history.[33] In addition, Blake sees Wright's building as a highly significant one for its possible influence on the immediate future of art:

[The Guggenheim] is an extraordinarily personal statement in the midst of a conformist city. It contains at least one of the most beautiful spaces created in this century [Pls. 33 and 37]. It is a dramatic glorification of the paintings and sculpture housed within it. It is not the most practical building in the world — but neither, one suspects, is the Pantheon. It will be remembered and debated long after its more efficient contemporaries have been forgotten. It is, undoubtedly, the most valuable piece in the Guggenheim collection. And it will be a constant admonition to all those who see it — and especially to architects, painters and sculptors — that creation is, among other things, a constant process of challenging and questioning accepted notions, everywhere.[34]

Thus, the artistic facet of architecture, having such a potential power to influence future building, and life in general, is seen to outweigh the practical component in importance.

A factor in the sixties which probably encouraged the acceptance of such buildings, in spite of their practical failings and in spite of the growing awareness of environmental control as an area of architectural concern, was the general consensus among critics that during the middle years of our century the *art* of architecture had been neglected — that following the initial upsurge of innovation and creativity marking the beginnings of the modern movement, we had suffered a slump. Thus when the Yale Art and Architecture building by Paul Rudolph, completed in 1964, was recognized as a "functional failure" because of the mishandling of such aspects as light and glare control, circulation, and acoustics and privacy,[35] it was nevertheless lauded for its artistic value. One defense of it declares:

> There is a vast difference between a leaky roof in a great building by a great master and a leaky roof in a building by a lesser architect. *Noblesse oblige*, they say. One could also say that, at times, *noblesse excuse*. But *noblesse* has to exist before any *excuse* can take place. There lies the glory and also the danger.

> I believe this is the present status of the functionalist controversy, and think that most architects today will agree that when a building is born which is a great work of art it is time for rejoicing. There are so few of them.[36]

Robin Boyd, a critic who in 1956 had deplored the lack of creative ideas in architecture,[37] in 1965 wrote that the practical oversights of Rudolph's building "should distract no one from understanding that this was a building which tried to claw its way back into the very heart of architecture."[38]

Thus, the question of whether the "heart of architecture" resides in its practical or artistic components is one which the critics of this century have answered in favor of the artistic, while, in comparison, concern for the physical aspects of the inhabitants' comfort, in terms of both environmental control and functional frame, has been somewhat neglected.

5

Psychological Function

Whereas the preceding chapter dealt with the pragmatic level of architectural function as shelter for the human body and as a frame for physical action, this chapter focuses on the psychological dimension: it deals with architecture in terms of its effects on the immediate orientation of the human psyche. This category has arisen from those instances in which critics describe what some people today refer to as a "gut reaction." Unscholarly as that expression sounds, it is quite a useful one; it is understood that it implies a reaction of the "feelings," but it keeps the focus on feelings closely allied to the sense organs and their neurological connections. Thus it helps to differentiate the "psychological" from the "social" or "cultural-existential" feelings. A crucial difference between critics' discussions of the psychological level of function and their discussions of the "higher" levels is that on the psychological level they do not refer to architecture as symbolizing some nonarchitectural concept. Rather their references are to immediate events—the architectural form and the psycho-physiological "feelings" of the occupant or viewer.

Critical statements about architectural function on the psychological level have tended to reveal one of two points of view. Either the critic responds to the building from the standpoint of the users of it—describing how the building affects or is likely to affect its users, sometimes actually reporting the responses of those who have occupied the building—or he quite honestly responds to it himself, describing his own feelings as he experienced the building. In the first case, the discussion often deals with what may be seen as the psychological aspects of the functional frame; that is, the critic appraises the building's establishment of an "atmosphere" appropriate to the activity it houses. In the other case, he usually expresses a less differentiated emotional response.

The perception of architecture as either contributing to or hampering the emotional experience that accompanies specific activities has sometimes received lengthy and detailed discussion, and has sometimes been alluded to only casually. An example of a brief allusion to this level of function is the critical statement which points to a "monastic" quality in Aalto's M.I.T. dormitory, which may help students resist worldly temptations in order to concentrate on their studies.[1]

More lengthy discussion has in numerous cases been elicited by the Guggenheim Museum. One critic, having seen the plans, predicted that:

> ...when the building is built, and people drive in off the street to the front door and see the great ramps swirling round and round to the dome of stainless steel and glass tubing, eight stories above them—when they ascend in the elevators to the top level through circular shafts of glass—when they stroll down an easy grade for an unbroken three-quarters of a mile without any feeling of fatigue—then they will have had their first real experience of what architecture can be like [Pls. 31 and 37]. Many will be uneasy and make jokes about it, because we are not accustomed to thinking of buildings in terms of an emotional experience.[2]

Another critic, apparently refuting predictions that the slanting ramp and walls will be disturbing to museum-goers, suggests that visitors would not even be conscious of those factors except in a positive way:

> As a matter of fact, the entire interior is so gently proportioned that the impression made upon one is of complete repose similar to that made by a still wave, never breaking, never offering resistance or finality to vision [Pls. 33 and 36]. It is this extraordinary quality of the complete repose known only in movement that characterizes this building, making it a more sentient and spiritual expression of human feeling by way of building materials and process than has yet been achieved.[3]

Yet, after the building was completed, some critics found that the design did contain psychological hazards for the visitors. One critic stated the problems in terms of "human traffic," on a psychological level:

> ...it appears that Wright himself slighted one important factor—human traffic—with unfortunate results. First seen from a standstill on the ground floor, the Guggenheim gives one a tremendous lift; it is indescribably beautiful at first glance [Pls. 34 and 35]. But soon the busy, dark figures ascending and descending the spiral ramps begin to blur the effect, and when oneself joins in the winding, pausing, spinning procession, incipient vertigo half spoils things; one cannot contemplate the pictures quietly [Pl. 37].[4]

This example is one of those which finds the Guggenheim an inadequate solution of the problem of functional frame, not because of physical difficulties, such as those mentioned in the previous chapter, but because of the manner in which the design hinders the perception and psychological well-being of the users of the building.

Critics in this century have frequently been drawn to the complex problems which arise from the differentiation of functions in domestic

architecture. The appreciation of contrasting needs for formal and informal settings for certain activities in the home has given rise to discussions
such as the following:

> Wright does not hesitate to say that the dining room is "always a great artistic oppor-
> tunity," but it is plain that he feels a certain uneasiness about the order of disarray
> which the living room seems to require; for such an order is intrinsically non-architec-
> tonic, if not antiarchitectural. Nevertheless, the problem one knows to be genuinely
> compelling for him is not the easy task of creating formal and symmetrical patterns but
> the difficult one of reconciling order with freedom. In such works as the Baker,
> Roberts, and Robie houses he goes as far as he can, within the limits of the prairie-
> house formula, toward infusing a "living-room" looseness into the shape and design of
> the house as a whole [Pl.5].[5]

Wright's willingness to deal with the informal spaces has been contrasted
with Le Corbusier's emphasis on rational planning in domestic architecture, an approach which replaces furniture with built-in "equipment" and
clears out the "vague and meaningless" clutter.[6]

The decade of the sixties has seen a renewed acceptance of the
informal and the complicated in domestic architecture. The major spokes-
man for "complexity and contradiction," Robert Venturi, has responded to
the "oversimplification" of Mies's domestic architecture with these words:

> Mies' exquisite pavilions have had valuable implications for architecture, but their
> selectiveness of content and language is their limitation as well as their strength.

> I question the relevance of analogies between pavilions and houses, especially analogies
> between Japanese pavilions and recent domestic architecture [Pls. 38 and 40]. They
> ignore the real complexity and contradiction inherent in the domestic program—the
> spatial and technological possibilities as well as the need for variety in visual experi-
> ence.... Where simplicity cannot work, simpleness results. Blatant simplification
> means bland architecture. Less is a bore.[7]

Privacy has been an important issue in the criticism of domestic architecture in this century of glass and the "open plan." It has been pointed out
that the Farnsworth house, for example, could so expose its interior space
only because it is located on a "considerable tract of land [Pl. 38]."[8] In
contrast, the interior of the Villa Savoye is very protected, a characteristic
which has been attributed to the influence of Mediterranean building, in
which "men have been forced for centuries to build vertically, and to
enclose what they built with walls that could guarantee privacy from close-
by neighbors."[9] The problem of interior privacy in a house naturally influences the plan. It has been pointed out that to create "a miracle of fluid
spaces" in the Robie house, Wright relegated to a parallel block at the rear
of the house all those rooms whose function demands privacy.[10] The

feeling of leading "an aquarium-like-existence" in one of Mies's houses has been expressed,[11] as well as the idea that man needs, for his psychological well-being, caves as well as goldfish bowls.[12]

A particularly good example of architectural criticism dealing with the psychological element of a building as a frame for a specific use is this statement about Kahn's Medical Research Building:

> So complex is the compartmentalization, what with the corridors angled in three directions from the elevators, that the initial effect is loss of direction. It is not, however, the total directional and psychic disorientation which occurs on stepping into the cramped angles of Wright's Price tower, since the rectangular logic and breadth of Kahn's structure keeps us psychically at ease while we locate our destination. What might be a serious defect in a building designed for visitors can, in any event, be a positive virtue in a research centre. And even on first stepping from the elevators, the short corridors are a welcome change from the remorseless bureaucratic alley. Welcome, too, is the lively play of natural light and shadow permeating that part of the building which is customarily relegated to the discomfort of semi-gloom or artificial illumination, at best intermittently punctuated by glare from the fenestration of an end wall or a distant stair tower.[13]

This statement spells out very clearly the opinion of the critic that the value of a psychological "atmosphere" created by an architect depends heavily on its "fitness for purpose," since even a factor that could have been seen as a flaw in the design has been interpreted as a virtue in terms of the specific function of the building.

The evolution of the skyscraper has included the use of some design techniques that have caused negative psychological reactions among its users. The following discussion of some of these reactions is concerned with Mies van der Rohe's Seagram building, one which is not included on the basic list of buildings studied here; yet the problems are so typical of those raised by the new building types of the modern era that the example is included:

> Users of this outside space [in upper floors of Mies's Seagram building] seem to be divided in their reactions as to whether the unusually deep glass area is pleasant, unpleasant, or an unimportant factor to be blocked out by floor-to-ceiling draperies or venetian blinds, so that one can get on with the day's work. Many do, quite seriously, experience a sense of vertigo. The sheer tower forms a sheer precipice, which to some tenants is rather terrifying.

> As for users of the interior space, they seem to be in unanimous agreement (off the record): being relegated, in a square-plan office building to space between the core (elevators, toilets, lobbies, etc.) and the outer offices, is most unpleasant. Seagram is basically a squarish building in contrast to the "...now standard thin, slab-shaped building..." which Mumford deplores. Thus it has a large proportion of this interior space which, no matter how well ventilated, is still interior, claustrophobic space. And the fact that many of the floors...use the Mies-Johnson floor-to-ceiling doors and other

trademarks of the building, does not make the space, as space, any more pleasant or any less confined.[14]

Critics' statements such as this one have undoubtedly had the effect of helping later, and perhaps lesser, architects to avoid the same pitfalls of skyscraper design.

Similar to the vertigo problem experienced in the Seagram building is the reaction of some visitors to another of Mies's buildings, the Farnsworth house. Because the walls are completely glass and the interior and exterior spaces are thus visually in total communication, some people "feel a sense of risk from stepping off the edge of the floor slab [Pls. 40 and 41]"[15]

Aalto's dormitory at M.I.T. may be cited here as an example of the care taken by an architect to avoid perceptual disturbances similar in nature to the vertigo experienced in the Seagam building.

> The site is located on a heavily-trafficed street along the Charles River. In order to avoid as much as possible the disturbing view out onto this street, a curving plan was chosen. By this means, no room was oriented at right angles to the street and its traffic. It is well known how much more tranquil it is to look, for example, from a diagonal line of sight out of the windows of a moving train at the passing landscape. An attempt to make use of this phenomenon was made with the form of the building: the windows face diagonally to the passing automobiles and thus afford a quieter environment for the person within the room [Pls. 29 and 30].[16]

The view from the windows in the curving plan also includes the river, as one critic has related: " 'How do you place your feet when you look at a river?' asked [Alvar Aalto] the admirer of Mark Twain. And forthwith he drew his plan...so most rooms could face...not straight across but either upstream or down."[17] In this case, the critic has credited the architect for his concern for the psychological well-being of the occupants of his buildings. It happens that Aalto himself had written at least one article urging architects to give more weight to this aspect of architecture, so critics could easily be aware of his concern. In many instances, as the previous examples show, the critic clearly had no such assurance of concern on the part of the architect and could only assume (particularly in view of the overall competence of the architects whose works are discussed here) that he had neglected this very important facet of design.

The second general type of response to buildings on the psychological level involves the critic's expression of his own emotional reaction. Quite often a critic describing a particular building is struck by his own feelings at the encounter and describes them or mentions them, sometimes in conjunction with a description of the actual forms which evoke those feelings and sometimes not.[18] For example, one statement about the Farnsworth house of Mies draws an interesting contrast between the Classicism of the design and the undeniable emotion inspired in the critic:

> The illusion of effortless organization is reinforced by the superb craftsmanship with which the building has been executed. . . . Each detail and each material, including the champagne-colored raw silk curtains, is used to clarify an absolute—one could say a platonic—architectural space, serenely independent of the transient emotional values of light, location, and atmosphere. But, in its cumulative effect, the Farnsworth house generates emotional overtones as insistent as the hum of a dynamo.[19]

In this example, various details of the building are mentioned but the critic's emotional response is to the building as a whole. Clearly his response in this case is on an aesthetic level: he makes no mention of the details of practical function.

Frequently, architectural critics in this century have responded to the buildings they appraise in terms of an emotional tension or disequilibrium generated by the particular way in which design elements have been placed in combination. An example of such statements is this one about Aalto's dormitory at M.I.T.: "The startling way in which Aalto's building plays sharp wall angles against curved walls has had the same disturbing and upsetting effect on critics as the dissonant passages in modern music. The force of the impact cannot be denied [Pls. 29 and 30]."[20] A similar statement concerning Le Corbusier's Villa Savoye reads: "The entire construction and its setting evoke a variety of stimuli, both architectural and non-architectural, providing a receptive viewer with almost bewildering allusions."[21] Even the Robie house of Wright, a building completed in 1910, was described in 1958 in a similar way: "[W]e are almost confused by the relationship of level to level and house to site. It is as if everything were held in place by levitation."[22]

Often a specific aspect of structure has been pointed out as causing the "disturbing" effect. This has been the case with at least two aspects of Rudolph's Yale Art and Architecture building. One statement dwells on the surface material, dealing with what is a typical "Brutalist" characteristic:

> The building thus repels touch; it hurts you if you try. The sense is of bitter pride, acrid acerbity rising perhaps to a kind of tragic gloom, since the light falls across the gashed ridges in long dusky veils, all brightness eaten by broken surfaces, no reflections possible, instead sombre absorption everywhere [Pl. 60]. Artificial lighting itself presents a special problem under these conditions. This is best seen in the exhibition area; spots of brilliance must hit the eye. . .since nothing can suffuse or glow across a plane.[23]

Actual structural technique is the topic of discussion in a statement by a critic who expresses "an irresistible urge to push a column into the center of gravity before the ceiling comes sliding by."[24]

Critical statements which speak of the confusing or disturbing effect of some buildings tend to be more common in the more recent part of the century, particularly during the sixties. Even in appraisals of buildings completed earlier in the century, critics seem recently to be particularly sensitive to the complex and contradictory nature of architectural design. I believe that this tendency is characteristic of the decade of the sixties. Robert Venturi's book *Complexity and Contradiction in Architecture* appeared in 1966 and was a statement of personal preference. I believe, however, that Venturi was not alone in that preference. The examples quoted above in which critics express bewilderment or confusion are not really negative assessments; the tone seems rather to be one of interest, even excitement.[25]

The effect particularly of the exterior form of buildings on those who view them has from time to time been expressed in terms of the correspondence of the forms and their visual "action" or "movement" with the movements of the human body, a concept which the nineteenth century termed "empathy," and on which Geoffrey Scott based his theory of architecture in 1914.[26] An example of the use of this concept in modern criticism can be seen in this statement:

> More forcefully, the late buildings of Le Corbusier culminate this modern expression of the human presence and its act. They stand as muscular forces, and mask, where necessary, both their interior spaces and their actual structure in order to appear to be the sculptural embodiments of powers with which men can identify their own.[27]

A similar approach is used here in respect to the visual relationship between two urban buildings:

> ...across York Street [from Rudolph's Art and Architecture building] stands Kahn's Art Gallery. Rudolph's structure now looms above it. Seen together, the former has a taciturn air, the latter a somewhat gesticulatory one. This occurs, I think, because the closed box of the one is visually contained within the open gesture of the other. They compliment each other exactly....[28]

A "history" of the critics' interest in psychological function during the course of this century can be very briefly stated: examples from before 1940 are quite rare, but beginning in the 1940s there is a steady increase in the appearance of statements dealing with this level of function. Assuming that the frequency of examples roughly corresponds to the amount of interest in or sensitivity to this level of function in architecture, one can conclude that before 1940, psychological effects of architecture did not play a major role in the critics' concept of function.

This finding is consistent with conclusions reached in the two preceding chapters, particularly the conclusion that the prevailing concept of function during the early period, as revealed by the criticism, had more to do with the visual awareness of structural function than with the actual functioning of a building *vis-à-vis* its human occupants. Just as purely pragmatic physical function has failed to spark the interest of the critics to any extent comparable to their fascination with structural articulation, so had psychological effects of architecture not been of major concern. According to one architectural writer, at least, such lack of interest on the part of critics had a parallel in the attitude of the majority of architects in the thirties. Catherine Bauer Wurster, writing in 1965, in looking back at the rational approach to human needs and uses in programming, planning, and design that one usually associates with the tenets of early functionalism, finds that:

> The rational approach was abandoned, because it would have required open minds and a real kind of collaboration and teamwork: architects working with engineers and social scientists, continuously trying to find better solutions, making experiments and testing them, working with business and government to encourage more research, experiment, and improvement.

What happened instead is that the innovators "reverted to the old prima donna role."[29]

How, then, can the marked increase in interest in psychological function during the forties be interpreted? It appears that this change is directly related to the call for a "humanization" of architecture which was voiced by many architectural writers beginning in the early forties.

The midcentury "call for a new humanism" was a many-faceted phenomenon taking almost as many forms as there were architectural writers participating in it. Its ramifications in terms of this study spread through all the "levels of function" and are by no means restricted to psychological function alone. But most of the important early statements of dissatisfaction with the status quo pertained to the psychological effects of modern architecture, and the profile of the criticism discussed in this chapter must be seen against the background of this more general development in architectural writing.

Long before the call for humanization in architecture became a common critical stance, one voice could be heard crying in the wilderness of urban American architecture. As early as 1921, Lewis Mumford urged the creation of building designs "which will respect the logic of the machine and at the same time have regard for the vagaries of human psychology."[30] Mumford believed that by making an idol of mechanization, our society and its builders were actually preventing the increased humanization which its proper use could bring about.[31] He described what he called the early machine style in this country—an architecture which sought to make plain its source of inspiration. He saw buildings whose smooth, hard, clean lines and surfaces declared their intention to work like well-oiled machines but which often failed to take advantage of the opportunity offered by mechanization to make buildings really comfortable for human occupants, psychologically and even physically. He criticized an architecture which capitalized on certain signs of modernism, using them to accomplish a visual illusion of functionalism without really achieving a truly functional architecture.[32]

Among those who in the forties joined the call for buildings designed with the occupant in mind was Alvar Aalto. In 1940 he wrote an article called "The Humanizing of Architecture," in which he pointed out that an object may function successfully from one point of view and unsuccessfully from another, and that the first period of modern architecture had considered function chiefly from the technical point of view.

> But, since architecture covers the entire field of human life, real functional architecture must be functional mainly from the human point of view. If we look deeper into the processes of human life, we shall discover that technic is only an aid, not a definite and independent phenomenon therein. Technical functionalism cannot create definite architecture.[33]

He described the newer trend in modern architecture as being motivated by a human and psychological examination of function. He describes as typical of its methods his own consideration of various functional aspects of his Paimio Tuberculosis Sanatorium in Finland: that is, the planning of a room around the central fact that its inhabitant would be horizontal, not vertical. This fact, Aalto says, necessitated a reexamination of all the characteristics of the room, including the colors used on walls and ceiling, the source of artificial lighting, the direction of warm air flow, the location of doors and windows. Consideration of the patient's feelings and realization of the pressures of collectivity in institutions led to some ingenius and very thoughtful decisions in the design.

In his *Space, Time, and Architecture* of 1941, Sigfried Giedion wrote of a schism between thinking and feeling during the nineteenth century which had not yet been healed. Throughout the early twentieth century, too, technology and science had developed far beyond man's ability to feel, to express feelings, and to communicate.

> At the moment when there is a schism, the inner kernel of personality is split by a difference of level between the methods of thinking and those of feeling. The result is the symbol of our period: the maladjusted man.
>
> It is possible that it may not be long before this situation will be recognized everywhere, and the schism may then disappear. But just now it is much easier to forward the most difficult scientific theory than the simplest of new artistic means.[34]

In a later edition of *Space, Time and Architecture,* Giedion was beginning
to see some hopeful signs of improvement, including a group of architects
who aim at "reestablish[ing] a union between life and architecture."[35]
Among these architects Giedion places Alvar Aalto, saying, "People are at
least as important to him as architecture."[36]

Before Giedion was able to make any such optimistic statement, however, there were other attempts to produce a "warmer" architecture, some
of which were misled and short-lived. In England in the forties, a large fac-
tion of the Architect's Department of the London City Council advocated
rejecting the modern style in favor of returning to the more romantic nineteenth-century brick-building in the style of William Morris's *Red House.*
This movement came to be called the "New Humanism." A related movement, supported by the editors of the *Architectural Review,* advocated a
return to the "picturesque" planning of the eighteenth and early nineteenth
centuries. The proponents of this position enjoyed not only the backing of
the *Architectural Review* but also that of the man who, probably more
than any other, had been responsible for introducing the new architecture
to England — J. M. Richards.[37] Richards's book *The Castles on the
Ground,*[38] which Banham calls "a specimen example of wartime 'home
thoughts from abroad,' "[39] was looked upon by the younger architects of
England as clear apostasy.

Yet the defense of the movement sounds very much like a direct
response to Giedion's call for a healing of the split between thinking and
feeling. In discussing the New Picturesque, Nicolaus Pevsner refers to
"feeling disciplined by judgment" and says, "Is it not highly desirable that
decisions on architecture and planning should be taken by men of sensitivity who take trouble to sharpen their visual understanding?"[40] J. M.
Richards refers to the movement as an effort to "humanize the modern
idiom by laying still more stress on the need for particularization."[41] He
describes it thus:

> ...there is a logical next step, the functionalism of the particular. There is therefore no
> call to abandon functionalism in the search for an architectural idiom capable of the
> full range of expression its human purposes require; only to understand that functiona-
> lism itself, by its very nature, implies the reverse of what it is often allowed to imply:
> not reducing everything to broad generalizations — quality in architecture belongs to the
> exact not the approximate — but relating it ever more closely to the essential particulars
> of time and place and purpose. That is the level on which humanity and science meet.[42]

In words this sounds like a perfect marriage of rational functionalism and
sensitivity to human feeling. Unfortunately, what it produced was a style
of building which was quite evidently a sentimental retreat into a more
romantic past.

In direct opposition to this reactionary trend the younger architects of England, led by Alison and Peter Smithson, formed a group which came to be called the New Brutalists. Although the New Brutalism was a reaction to supposedly humanizing development, it too was motivated by a desire to make architecture more human. The Brutalists felt that the intentions of the original masters of the modern movement had been distorted and lost. Among the important elements which they believed the more recent architects had lost sight of was the social conscience of the founders—their desire to establish an "affinity...between buildings and man" through reverence for materials and through the reform of urbanism.[43]

This overview of the "humanizing" trends in architectural theory of the forties and fifties has been cursory. It has not included the details of the developments mentioned, nor has it included all the related ideas which have appeared in architectural writing.[44] My purpose here again has been only to point to a tendency in the more theoretical writings on architecture which helps to shed light on the changing nature of the applied criticism in general, and on the increased concern for the psychological effects of buildings in particular. In summary, there has been, in the applied criticism, as in the developments in theory and in building itself, an observable trend beginning around the start of the forties away from emphasis on the machine toward emphasis on the human being, away from preoccupation with the exterior of buildings toward attention to the interior, away from an exclusive attention to visual effect and style toward a concern for total effect and function. The accompanying increase in attention to the social ramifications of architecture, to be discussed next, shows that concern for the occupant was not always encountered on an individual basis but was also manifested in attention to problems of urban planning and embodiment of common values.

6

Social Function

One of the higher levels on which buildings function is in their capacity to provide a meaningful milieu for society, for man as a social animal. This means that architecture, more than just providing an adequate sheltered space to house a certain group activity, provides forms which serve to symbolize the nature of that activity. On this level, architecture contributes to the institutionalization of man by giving visible, physical form to a social institution. To the extent that creating a durable shelter and symbol for an activity tends to preserve the activity from disintegration, architecture contributes to the progressive civilization of man. On the other hand, architecture is a conservative element to the extent that creating a durable shelter and symbol for an activity tends to preserve the nature of the social institution as it was when the building was designed.

This chapter deals with what architectural critics have said concerning the social function of architecture. Some of their discussion is related to building types: that is, what a building "says" about its role in society and about the activity or institution which it houses. In the past, for example, the forms of certain building types have been quite clearly understood and accepted. A Renaissance town hall has a shape which distinguishes it clearly from a church or private dwelling and which identifies it for the people of the town whether or not they ever step inside it. Part of the critics' discussion of building types has to do with those types which have originated in the twentieth century.[1] The critics also have been concerned with the ways in which modern architects have reinterpreted traditional building types. In addition, in discussions which may or may not make mention of specific building types, critics have investigated the characteristics of modern architecture in terms of what it "says" about the nature of our society. Critics frequently have seen in new buildings a sort of commentary on contemporary life. The critical statements dealing with architecture as revealing "signs of our times" are among the most interesting because of the verbal link they provide between the worlds of architect and inhabitant. The investigation into the ways in which architecture and society influence each other's shapes and symbols is among the more important developments in architectural thought of this century.

One of the new building types whose architectural value was established during the early modern movement is the business building, later exemplified by the skyscraper. In a caption for a photograph of Sullivan's Carson, Pirie, Scott building, for example, appears the statement, "thus the [business] building takes its place with all the other architectural types...the Greek temple, the Gothic cathedral, the medieval fortress."[2] Another of the new building types of this century is realized in Kahn's medical laboratories. One critic points out a peculiarly *architectural* problem related to this type:

> ...architecture, for Louis Kahn, is always marked by two overreaching qualities—"a harmony of systems" and a "hierarchy of ennobling spaces." The first of these will be found even in good building but the latter is the *sine qua non* of true architecture. As a type, the laboratory not only does not call for this type of exalted spatial experience, it does not by its very nature permit it. This fact conditions Kahn's judgment of his University of Pennsylvania building. But it need not limit the judgment of others.[3]

Thus the very principles of architecture are having to be reexamined in light of some of the new "functions" of the technological age.

Among the statements of architectural critics of this century are remarks concerning the reinterpretation of traditional building types by the architects of the modern movement. For instance, in Aalto's building at M.I.T., "the sober program of a dormitory is given a new interpretation. All means are employed in the attempt to avoid the ant-hill atmosphere often emanated by such buildings. Aalto gives the individual his personal rights through a great variety of means...."[4] In the area of domestic architecture, Wright's Robie house is seen to have "completely reorganized and reformulated the theory of the individual house of moderate size and cost":

> In part this reorganization was motivated by aesthetic experimentation—"the sense of the within as reality." Yet more important was the new analysis of the house, not perhaps as a *machine à habiter,* but as an instrument for the new possibilities of expansive modern life.[5]

Mies's Farnsworth house also has been seen as a reinterpretation of what "house" means:

> The house for Dr. Farnsworth is for America the house of the century.... [It] is austere and it is beautiful. If as a house it disdains the paraphernalia of comfort and convenience, it does this so compellingly that any house less disdainful is tawdry by comparison.

The structure...transform[s] a rural house into a pavilion—into a temple [Pl. 39].[6]

Whether or not a temple is habitable by ordinary mortals this critic does not venture to say, but he implies approval of the design and its translation of the traditional idea of "houseness."

The psychological effects of the spiral ramp in the Guggenheim Museum were discussed in Chapter 5. Here it is interesting to notice the remarks made in reference to the function of the building as a representative of the building type, "museum:"

> In 1943 Solomon Guggenheim gave his architect the unprecedented task of building directly for modern art. Hitherto, nineteenth-century ideas of organization and construction had dominated new museums. What could a living art gallery be, a natural environment for the art of today comparable to the temples, the cathedrals, the palaces of the past? The first need: to grasp what modern art was. No longer in the service of gods and rulers, art was free; not without bewilderments but, essentially, free to be itself. The forms of art that unfolded in the new freedom were—a painting as a thing in itself; a sculpture as an independent focus of forces; symbols of realities experienced far within and beyond the shell of conventional expressions. These could not imaginably be served by assimilation into overriding programmes, didactic or decorative.[7]

The effectiveness of Wright's solution has been much disputed, particularly its functional value. In fact, Wright has been accused of exploiting the opportunity given him by Guggenheim in order to create a spirally rising room, a design idea which had intrigued him for years. One critic defends him thus:

> The Guggenheim Museum, however, is not a prototype for a museum as such and certainly not for a gallery-type museum of Renaissance painting, but it poses the question, whether a space of this kind where movement and therefore time play such a decisive role, may not be a suitable frame for pictures in which, as in Cubism, movement and time are determining elements of form. There is also hardly another design in which Wright's conceptions of continuity and plasticity are so uncompromisingly realized.[8]

Perhaps even more than the Guggenheim, Le Corbusier's chapel at Ronchamp has caused much dispute concerning whether or not its design is an appropriate one for a place of worship. The issue is compounded by the complexity, intangibility, and variety of religious and artistic experience which its viewers bring to it. One critic points to "the basically primitive, pre-Christian, pagan quality of Ronchamp Chapel" and says:

> In this sense it is perhaps a very inappropriate design for a Christian sanctuary—unless one is to think of a catacomb—especially since the interior, with its sloping floor echoing the curve of wall and vault, is suggestive of a stone age cavern. The space created under this concrete canopy at Ronchamp is lacking in orientation, unstable, unanchored: "ineffable" to use the word of its creator.[9]

One critic expresses amazement at the chapel's acceptance by the French villagers:

> [They] proceed quite happily to service in the bowels of Le Corbusier's plastic expression of a stranded whale [Pl. 46].
>
> Could one say then that the design of worship houses has become so fragmented, that almost any kind of worship could go on in almost any kind of building? Provided the architect has talent and understanding of building techniques, the symbol building may be beautiful and appreciated by many people, but it will be a symbol only of himself.[10]

This writer expresses a fairly common nonacceptance of buildings which do not conform to the traditional characteristics of the building types they represent, as well as, I believe, the assumption that the more an architectural object is a personal expression of its designer the less it can be of value to others.

Yet many who have appraised Le Corbusier's chapel have found themselves forced to admit that it is a very successful building. In spite of the uniqueness of its personal expression, they find it having just the effect on its users that its programme demands. One critic, for example, feels that although Le Corbusier's design did not grow out of a religious programme, he was very successful at achieving the proper atmosphere for prayer because the emotional expression captured by the design corresponds to the emotional fervor of prayer (Pls. 48 and 49).[11]

One writer has pointed out that the chapel does not adequately "focus the attention of the worshippers on the shrine" and that "there is even competition between the pulpit and the statue of the Virgin"; "but the east wall," he continues rather lamely, as if in spite of himself, "remains impressive and eye-arresting [and since] what happens before this wall serves the main purpose of the shrine, we might ask no more."[12] In the following extended example one can sense how rather ill-at-ease the critic is in encountering such an unorthodox chapel design. In an attempt to deal with its power, he attempts to "translate" it into verbal theological concepts:

> In the great south wall of the Chapel of Notre Dame du Haut, religious feeling is expressed in a way entirely new to the world, yet conveying a timeless sense of its ancient sources. Here, the underlying theme of the chapel, only subtly visible in plan and structure, is crystallized, intensified, and revealed for all to see. One can only assume that, consciously or subconsciously, Corbusier meant this theme to symbolize the opening out of the human soul toward the passion and mystery of the Christian faith.... In opposition to the gradual opening out of nave and wall and windows stand the three chapel towers. Here, like a symbol of solitary religious experience, space shoots upward, heavenward, within slender columns. Here, the opening is not out, but up, the church's final declaration of human destiny. And here, windows set high in the tower walls cast light down their shafts, making each tiny chapel glow with a soft radiance, the source of which is not immediately discernible.[13]

In spite of such literal translation of symbols by these writers, one senses that most critics feel that such an iconographic "reading" of this chapel is not possible as it was with medieval, Renaissance, and Baroque churches. Most are content to accept its success at "expressing something of the symbolic, cosmological function which...belongs to the House of God,"[14] without attempting to be more specific about the respective origins of religious and artistic feeling.

One further aspect of the design of building types that has figured in the criticism of this century is the relationship between the building and its environment. Critics of architecture have pointed out that certain functions are expressed by certain attitudes of buildings as sculptural objects. For example, Ronchamp's location on top of a hill that can be seen for miles is appropriate to its function as a pilgrimage chapel: "Ronchamp is designed to be seen from a considerable distance, to be a visual magnet inexorably leading the pilgrim on to his goal [Pl. 44]."[15] The critic contrasts Ronchamp's visibility to the "hiddenness" of Le Corbusier's monastery of La Tourette at Eveux-sur-l'Arbresle, which "nestles into the wooded slope of a hill instead of occupying the summit."[16]

Related to this idea of correspondence between building type and attitude in environment is the idea that a building located in a city has a social responsibility to the urban environment. In a city it becomes quite evident that the exteriors of buildings—that is, architecture as mass, rather than interior space—shape the public space used by people who may never be concerned with the interior functions of them; thus the effect of a building on its environment is a subject which has been treated by architectural critics. The "empathic" relationship between Rudolph's Art and Architecture building and Kahn's Yale Art Gallery across the street has been mentioned in connection with the Art and Architecture building's "psychological effect."[17] That critic proceeds to relate his comment to the urban scene when he says that in their exact complementing of each other, the two buildings, in his opinion, "constitute a triumph of urbanistic design."[18]

One of the characteristics of the "prima donna role" that Katherine Bauer Wurster accused some architects of playing in the thirties[19] is the disregard for urban planning, the attitude that the building being designed should be a striking statement in itself, neighbors be damned. Increasingly since that time, there has been more emphasis on "environmental planning," in the hope that architects, highway engineers, park commissioners, and city-planners will all work together to coordinate their efforts. Rudolph's Art and Architecture building has been praised repeatedly for its visual "cooperation" with the neighboring buildings. One critic says:

> Not only is Rudolph's building stylistically unified, but the relationships between site and shell, shell and interior, and type and scale are all fully integrated. The building

even takes up, amplifies, or comments upon the series of earlier buildings along Chapel Street. It turns what had been a collection of good but heterogeneous buildings into a procession. It not only fits its environment, but gives a direction and force to that environment.[20]

The architect himself has explained his choice of the pinwheel scheme in his design partly on the basis of the building's location: "Since the building is on a corner its role in the cityscape is to turn the corner. A pinwheel scheme has been adopted because...it turns the corner [Pl. 58]..."[21]

Every building on the list of key architectural monuments forming the basis for this study has been discussed by critics as in some way symbolic of its time. For example, the importance of the machine in the early architecture of the century led to the following discussion of Gropius's Bauhaus:

> The new buildings there had a machine-shop as well as studios, and the architecture school—as befitted the eagles' nest of a new age that Gropius savoured as sharply as the Futurists did—was on a bridge spanning a road between two blocks. This was not an ingenious necessity inspired by a difficult site, for the ground had been wide-open and suburban when Gropius began to design; the relationship of building to road was of Gropius's own making, the road was there because he put it there. A manifesto building, then, for a motorised age.... It is a shrine to the belief that the Machine Age is good [Pls. 13 and 14].[22]

The Villa Savoye, because of its driveway, also has been seen as expressing the arrival of the machine age: "the house began by acknowledging that access by car was the foundation of its existence [Pls. 21 and 22]."[23] And Wright's architecture was described thus: "The forms of the Robie house, the long horizontal bands, the series of windows, the garden walls, are sharply cut as if by a machine."[24]

All of the private dwellings under discussion here, except the Farnsworth house, have been seen as in some way expressive of a new, more informal and leisurely lifestyle.

> ...Rietveld, with his glass walls and sliding screens, created in the Schröder house in Utrecht the best example of the "liberated dwelling." Here the emotional life of our era is convincingly expressed for the first time. The landscape is drawn into the house, so to speak, through the glass walls [Pls. 7 and 10]; and the interior, community space can be organized into four separate spaces [Pl. 8].[25]

Likewise, Wright's Kaufman house:

> But "Falling Water" is something more than a perfect answer to a romantic question, its irregular, assymmetrical plan is contrived with amazing cunning to reflect the informal existence of a Pittsburgh executive on his weekends in the country, and is as admirable an expression of the casual manners of our day as the Bruce house by McKim, Mead and White of the formality of 1906 [Pls. 24-28].[26]

Le Corbusier's Villa Savoye, a house which "revealed Corbu...as a rational analyst of modern urban life,"[27] is described as "reflecting, no doubt, the indoor/outdoor ambiguity of the daily routine of a fashionably sun-loving family of the period."[28] According to one critic, it also, because of its being raised off the ground and its "self-contained and self-conscious" geometry, "shows a city-dweller in the country [Pl. 20]."[29]

Related to this view of domestic life is the drawing of a parallel between homes and steamships. During the early part of this century, when some of these examples of domestic architecture were being constructed, the steamship cruise was the ultimate in informal, leisurely life. Sometimes the analogy was drawn quite literally comparing specific features of a house with those of the ship, with its long horizontal outlook between decks and above deck, its open promenade, its gangway and cantilevered bridge:

> The ship's deck, however, is not that of the sailor but of the passenger, free to sun himself, or to play deck-tennis, or to swim in the ship's pool, or to dance and to flirt. It is a symbol of the paradise of the cruising tourist who is involved in no responsibility, but can flex or relax his muscles for no other reason than the pleasure of flexing or relaxing them. This is a very characteristic holiday compensation for the dweller in the mechanical hive [Pls. 22 and 23].[30]

The Robie house also has been compared to a cruising ship—unjustly so, according to this statement:

> Chicagoans who did not like the Robie house, who were offended by the novelty of its appearance and its long stretched-out horizontal lines, sought to deride it by comparing it to a steamship, just as later Le Corbusier's critics were to refer similarly to his buildings. Without knowing it, they were implying that the house was built in the spirit of the age out of which it came, that, like the steamship, it had been born naturally out of its period [Pl. 5]. What is decisive in it is not a superficial and misunderstood similarity to a steamship but its inner relationship with the aims of its time.[31]

In this statement Giedion is arguing that the parallel with the cruise ship is a legitimate one as long as it is understood that it is the spirit which is analogous, but hardly the specific structures.

Norris Kelly Smith, an important biographer of Wright and analyst of his work, speaks of Wright's profound concern with the nature of family life and of the manner in which this concern shows up in his domestic architecture. Smith explains that the period which gave rise to the Robie house was one during which Wright fluctuated between two conceptions of the family:

> We find Wright oscillating in this early period between two conceptions of the family as the nuclear social group: on the one hand he wanted to establish its integrity and to

insist upon the inter-dependence of its members—a concern that leads him to stress the oneness of the sheltering roof, the centrality of the family hearth, and the simple regularity of the whole; while on the other, he sought, both in architectural imagery and in the conduct of his own life, to assert the independence of the individual—a desire that is expressed in broken roofs, irregular silhouettes, and highly variable groupings of architectural components.[32]

Later in his career, "Falling Water" also made a statement in plastic form about the nature of the family.

The house celebrates a mode of familial relatedness that is based upon a lively process of interaction rather than upon an architectonic pattern of orderly submission. We have here Wright's best expression of the ideal that first became fully clear to him when he and Mamah Borthwick established their unconventional household at Taliesin in 1911—a household away from the city, sustained entirely by natural endeavor and without benefit of law or custom or ceremony.[33]

As mentioned above, Mies's Farnsworth house is the one private dwelling of those on which this study is based that has not been described as the expression of the modern, more leisurely lifestyle. It was once described as "the apotheosis of the compulsive, bureaucratic spirit" because of its disregard for "the necessary intimacies and informalities" of life;[34] nevertheless, it has been seen more often as a house which refused to express any particular lifestyle but rather provided "a timeless background against which men can develop freely through generations, a background that is quiet and simple, objective and impersonal."[35] A more complete explanation for the creation of such a structure is given in another critical article:

Mies is convinced that architecture should be no more than the shell within which each occupant produces his or her own dwelling. . . . It may be that the people who live in Mies' architecture will change, that new generations with new customs and traditions will occupy the "shell." But this subtle influence is likely to remain—the influence of a great artist, of a great work of art, of a great discipline, of a great belief that man in architecture should be free.[36]

Thus, whereas critics have seen in some of the homes under examination for this study a reflection of the changed societal conditions, particularly in relation to family lifestyle, the work of Mies has been interpreted as standing aloof from the changes and providing a space frame which supposedly could accommodate any lifestyle.

In several of the architectural monuments of this century, critics have seen commentaries on the growing lack of provision for individuality in modern society. In the forms of the Bauhaus, for example, one critic sees reflected "the aims then limited to the teaching program of the Bauhaus,

[that] are identical with those slowly becoming accepted as the aims of our whole way of life, the reconciliation and interpenetration of the individual and communal spheres."[37] In a discussion of the stress on the unity of interior spaces by the International Stylists and particularly by Mies van der Rohe in the twenties and thirties—something which is characteristic of his Tugendhat house but also of the Farnsworth house twenty years later—a parallel has been seen with modern life in general:

> [The mergence of the interior spaces] is, of course, a practical necessity in an industrial complex, in which there must be a maximum freedom of transportation, locomotion and transmission of power. The application of the same principles to domestic interiors is something of the nature of a cultural curiosity.... You will notice a reduction of provision for personal privacy, almost to the minimum consistent with ordinary standards of physiological decency.... What is important here is the mergence of the individual into his society, such as is demanded by technological and industrial developments to which modern architecture is related.[38]

A discussion of Sullivan's Carson, Pirie, Scott building written in 1959 describes it as an early expression of the will to combat the infringement of the collectivized, technological age on the human sphere:

> ...one can feel, in Sullivan's buildings, a curious power of potential action, since they are not so rooted [in the earth, as are Wright's]. Turn your back and Carson-Pirie-Scott may cast off and float silently down the street behind you.... For Sullivan,...buildings were not so much ambients within which human beings might move—which has always been the Wrightian position—as sculptural presences which might compliment and challenge human beings and, through physical association, awaken in the new mass age a renewed sense of the possible dignity of an active human presence in the world.[39]

Although the following statement about Ronchamp deals with the relation between form and technics, it seems to me by analogy also to speak about the plight of modern man. In any case it does deal with the situation of the modern architect:

> The more that an irregular non-rectilinear building approaches the condition of being "a whole thing," the less it can take one of the main advantages of being made in the middle of the twentieth century and dip into the larder of mass-produced equipment. Le Corbusier was able to keep his chapel at Ronchamp almost a whole thing because it had no equipment and only one straight wooden staircase at the back to shatter the fluid harmony [Pl. 45]. The exciting buildings are in fact most significant because they are not expressions of mass-production techniques. They are anti-universal. They remind architecture that all the technical potentialities of the twentieth century are not bound to mass-production. The structure is still free, more free than ever before (though how long this may last is another question) and the architect still has every justification—indeed, a duty—to exploit this freedom whenever the opportunity arises by creating forms and spaces precisely appropriate to the occasion.[40]

Critics have seen various other aspects of modern society "symbolized" or "expressed" in architectural works of this century. Mies's Barcelona Pavilion, for example, has been called an expression of "the highest aspirations of a Europe wracked by war and inflation":

> Here was that clarity, order, and peace that Europe longed for. Here were noble spaces, unpolluted by any connotation to a discredited, futile past. Here were fine materials, freed of decadent motifs and moldy symbolism, glowing with their own intrinsic beauties.[41]

In 1929, it was called the symbol of the new Germany:

> Violà l'esprit de l'Allemagne nouvelle: simplicité et clarté de moyens et d'intentions — tout ouvert au vent, comme à la franchise — rien ne ferme l'accès à nos coeurs. Un travail honnêtement fait, sans orgueil. Voilà la maison tranquille de l'Allemagne apaisée![42]

Wright's Guggenheim Museum has been called "an external symbol for contemporary abstract art.... [a building which] has a genuine fitness in its severe rationality of form."[43] Similarly, Kahn's medical research building has been called "an unbending monument to the human confrontation with death."[44]

The critics' use of the word "expression" in discussions of the social function of architecture is worth noticing. Most of the examples quoted above contain the word "expression" or a roughly synonymous term, such as "reflection" or "symbol." This concept of architecture's ability to "express" something has not figured in the discussions of physical or psychological function, levels on which architecture is thought of as "doing" something rather than "saying" something. The term did appear, however, in the discussion of structural articulation. Yet there is a basic difference between what architecture "says" in terms of structural articulation and what it "says" in terms of social function. Generalizing from the critics' use of the concept, I believe the difference can be stated this way: in terms of structural articulation, architecture says, "*I* am..." ("I am a steel cage wrapped in a curtain wall," for example), whereas on the level of social function, architecture says, "*You* are..." ("You are a mechanized society," or "You are no longer individuals but masses," for example).

Quite obviously architecture does not have a subject matter, as literature and painting and sculpture do, or can. Yet in this area of social function, architecture perhaps comes as close as any nonliterary or nonpictorial medium can come to having something like subject matter. At least, one can see that the critics have "read" statements about modern society in, or from, the buildings they examine.

Recognizing this underlying assumption of the critics' statements — that is, that architecture "says" something to man *about himself* — one is not surprised that the level of social function has been an important one in the overall picture of architectural criticism in this century. Statements about the social function of specific buildings appeared as early as any of the other types of statements; that is to say, after the almost complete absence of applied criticism during the first three decades of this century, critiques of modern buildings were about as likely to discuss their social significance as their articulation of structure. And this level of function has continued to be of interest to critics throughout the century, particularly from about 1950 on, at which time there was a noticeable rise in the attention given to the social "meanings" of architecture.

The increased interest in architecture as a social statement undoubtedly is related to the call for a more humanizing architecture which appeared in the forties. Soon after Sigfried Giedion's exposition of his theory of the split between thinking and feeling in his *Space, Time and Architecture* of 1941, he began to talk about a specific aspect of that split — what he called "the need for a new monumentality."[45] In 1944 Giedion described this need with these words:

> People desire buildings that represent their social, ceremonial, and community life. They want these buildings to be more than a functional fulfillment. They seek the expression of their aspirations in monumentality, for joy and for excitement.[46]

Giedion declared that monumental architecture had become empty, that it was no longer representative of the spirit of the people.

Soon after Giedion put forth this concept, a great deal of published discussion took up the argument of what a meaningful "monumentality" really is. In September of 1948, the *Architectural Review* published statements on this subject submitted by some of the leading architects and critics of the day. In April of the same year, Lewis Mumford published his article "Monumentalism, Symbolism and Style," in which he said:

> Now we live in an age which has not merely abandoned a great many historic symbols, but has likewise made an effort to deflate the symbol itself by denying the values which it represents. . . . Because we have dethroned symbolism, we are now left, momentarily, with but a single symbol of almost universal validity: that of the machine. . . . What we are beginning to witness today is a reaction against this distorted picture of modern civilization.[47]

I believe that the rise in critical attention to social symbolism in architecture around 1950 can be seen as a part of that reaction.

Later analyses of this problem point out the privatization of architecture that had taken place especially in the United States: modern architecture had done its best work with the individual house, usually a country house for someone who could afford to put a great deal of money into such a project.[48] Lewis Mumford, as early as 1925, deplored the fact that such country homes were designed as escapes from the world of business in the city,[49] while the cities became more and more the product of the engineer rather than the artist. In the control of the engineer, the cities ceased to be made up of real communities and so no longer represented the social and ceremonial life of the people. In addition, as Giedion pointed out, governmental leaders and administrators, being just as much victims as the common man of the split between thinking and feeling, were insensitive to the creative power of the artist and failed to commission successfully monumental buildings.[50] Thus, the split which grew between business and humane home life paralleled the split between thinking and feeling, between "person" and "society."

In his essay of 1948, Mumford spoke of the need for a trend away from an ideology of the machine to an ideology of the organism and the person, and he related this trend to functionalism:

> We must erect a new hierarchy of function in which the mechanical will give place to the biological, the biological to the social, the social to the personal. For this new order the machine can no longer serve as symbol: indeed, the emphasis on the impersonal, the anti-organic, the non-humanistic, the "objective" must now be counteracted by a temporary over-preoccupation, perhaps, with the organic, the subjective, the personal. On these terms Frank Lloyd Wright in 1900 was far in advance of Le Corbusier in 1920; indeed in a sense L'Art Nouveau was, despite its ill-conceived ornament, often closer to the human and the organic than the architects of cubism were. To say this is not to desert functionalism in architecture, but to relate it once more to every human function.[51]

In using the word organic to describe this trend, Mumford anticipates other architectural writers who began to report the beginning development of a less cerebral, more *feeling,* expression in architecture.

One of these was Bruno Zevi, who, in his book *Towards an Organic Architecture,* published in 1950, defines organic as a "product of intuitive sensations" (as opposed to "product of thought"), "in close contact with nature" (as against "contemptuous of nature"), "the search for the particular" (as opposed to "the search for the universal"), "realism" (instead of "idealism"), "Naturalism" (not "stylism"), "the structure like an organism that grows in accord with the law of its own individual existence" (as opposed to "the structure like a mechanism in which all the elements are disposed in accord...with the immutable law of an *a priori* system"), "product of contact with reality" (as opposed to "product of education").[52]

Zevi saw the organic movement as having been foreshadowed by Sullivan and Wright; and now in the middle of the century, citing the "latest work" of Le Corbusier and Gropius, he felt that finally other architects were showing signs of going in that direction.[53] Relating organic architecture to functionalism, Zevi says,

> Organic architecture...satisfies more complex needs and functions; it is functional not only in technics and utility, but also in terms of human psychology. It bears a post-functionalist message which speaks of the humanization of architecture.[54]

In 1954, Giedion wrote two essays entitled "Social Imagination" and "Spatial Imagination" in which he talked about recent developments which seemed to him possibly to promise a healing of the split between thinking and feeling.[55] What he saw was a number of instances in which society's leaders were coming around to an understanding of the human need for monumentality. An example of the "social imagination" of an architect which had been allowed to take actual physical form was Le Corbusier's Unité d'Habitation. An example of "spatial imagination" which had taken form and was accepted by the "establishment" and common people alike was Le Corbusier's Pilgrimage Chapel at Ronchamp. Giedion, who attended the dedication ceremonies of Notre Dame du Haut, quotes a segment of the Archbishop's address, and then continues hopefully:

> It was one of the first recognitions from such a quarter than contemporary architecture is a symbol of the inner strivings of our period—a courageous recognition of the present.... Does this signify a radical change on the part of those authorities who hold power in their hand?.... It is an event that cannot be brushed aside: that such a work, which brings to expression the secret boldness that dwells within our times, has not had to wait to achieve recognition.... Have we reached a moment of change? Is the ruling taste, that has befuddled the innate strength of the general public for a century and a half, disappearing at last, and, with it, the tragic conflict between feeling and thinking? From now on will those few great spirits who have the gift of spatial imagination be able to concentrate upon real achievements rather than upon clever imitations? It almost seems so.[56]

With these optimistic words, Giedion heralded a movement in architecture which, though not yet arrived at its goal, is continuing to progress in its effort to fulfill man's need for a "monumentality," a social/communal significance in buildings. The material of the next chapter, that concerned with the cultural/existential function of architecture, in my opinion shows the image of that continuing progress as it is reflected in criticism.

7

Cultural-Existential Function

Writing about Mies van der Rohe's Farnsworth house, one critic said, "It is intended to challenge not only the standards of architecture; it challenges, also, the standards by which most men work and live — for it restates certain simple and lasting values that have sometimes been lost in the shuffle."[1] This statement points to a level of architectural function which can perhaps best be called "cultural/existential."

A clear explanation of this title is very difficult — even impossible — to give at the present time because the function of architecture on this level is so little understood. The effort to discuss it at all grows out of the conviction — which itself is by no means new — that architecture has an even more profound task than any of those discussed in the previous chapters, a task which somehow intimately involves both the more permanent and widespread beliefs and values of an entire cultural tradition and the most basic orientation of each individual in time and space. In phrasing the conviction in these terms, I have moved from the previous discussion of social function in two seemingly opposite directions: toward the more general "culture" and toward the more particular individual "existence." Yet as the discussion proceeds, this dichotomy should dissolve as the fundamental unity of the two poles becomes evident.

The discussion cannot proceed, however, before tackling certain problems of logistics which arise out of the nature of the material at hand. Because of the complexity of these problems, it may be helpful first to look back at the procedure used in preceding chapters as a point of comparison.

In the case of each level of function so far discussed, the procedure has consisted of the following steps: first, to introduce the level of function in terms of the general nature of the "task" or "effect" of architecture referred to on that level;[2] second, to illustrate the nature of the category, as well as its subdivisions, by reference to the examples of applied criticism which appraise buildings on their "performance" in that category (during this step, analysis of the content of the examples both contributes to the "definition" of the level of function itself and reveals the particular issues with which critics have been concerned during the course of this century); third, to observe the history of the critics' concern with that level of function in relation to the larger body of functional criticism in quantitative terms; and fourth, to analyze that history in light of information derived both from the content of the examples themselves and from the larger events of architectural history and theory.

In the case of "cultural/existential" function, however, problems are encountered at each step. At the outset, introducing this level of function in terms of the general nature of the "task" or "effect" of architecture referred to here is difficult because, as mentioned above, the "task" is so little understood. We of the twentieth century are now realizing that, historically, cultural symbolization has generally formed an important part of the building task, but the study of how architecture functions in this way is so recent that understanding of the phenomenon is far from complete and vocabulary for dealing with it is crude.[3] Thus in terms of the level of function itself, a concept is in the process of forming but is not yet clearly formed.

With regard to the second step of the previous procedure, problems arise out of those encountered in the first step. First, since attempts at a "definition" of this level of function still yield such unclear boundaries, determining just which critical statements help to illustrate the category and deal with issues properly belonging to it is a difficult task. Second, since the category itself, as a subject of investigation, is so new, and since statements of applied criticism by nature are not revelatory of full-fledged theoretical concepts, most examples of applied criticism referring to the cultural/existential function of architecture are recognized as such only in juxtaposition with more complete statements of a theoretical nature. In terms of the past procedure in this study, this is to say that step two can hardly be accomplished without at the same time partially performing step four.

A further complication encountered in the second procedural step arises out of the very *content* of the critical examples themselves. Since the cultural/existential level of architectural function has to do with the world view of a culture, the content of the critical statements pertinent to this chapter refers to aspects of our own world view. But our world view is presently in the midst of a change which has been compared, in its nature and magnitude, with that which accompanied the waning of the Middle Ages.[4] In architectural criticism, as in other areas of twentieth-century thought, there is an underlying recognition that new understanding of all aspects of existence is gradually generating drastic change in some of our most basic assumptions about ourselves and the world. Since understanding of our own orientation in space and time lies at the core of the evolving world view, and since more and more of our environment is man-made, creative architects are at the vanguard of change and architectural theorists are among those whose enormous task it is to analyze that change verbally. As a result, the material under examination in this chapter is doubly slippery: not only is the concept of the level of architectural function itself in flux, but so is the world view which architecture on the cultural/existential level of function has the task of symbolizing. And so intimate is the relation between our understanding of how architecture works and our view of the world and self that change in one both influences and is influenced by change in the other.

The third procedural step is complicated by the incomplete boundaries of the category itself, since "measuring" the "amount" of critical concern with the particular level of function depends on how one defines the level. And the fourth step is quite obviously rendered incomplete by the rapidity of change and growth in the material one would attempt to summarize.

In the face of such obstacles, one might wonder whether the whole effort should not simply be abandoned. But it cannot be abandoned, for a discussion of architectural function which ignores cultural/existential function communicates a misconception very like that of early "narrow functionalism." It leaves out the level of the *artistic* function of architecture. It leaves out the very factor of our survival as a humane culture, the factor which can have a healing effect on our existential neurosis, which Giedion referred to as a split between thinking and feeling.

Thus, discussion of cultural/existential function must proceed in spite of the difficulties. Recognition of those difficulties, however, does give rise to several important differences between the discussion in the chapter at hand and that in previous chapters. First of all, the nature of the level of function itself cannot be satisfyingly defined at the outset but must evolve through the suggestions contained in the examples themselves. Second, the examples of applied criticism will be presented in conjunction with frequent reference to more theoretical writings, for it is in association with the theoretical writing that the relevant meaning of the applied criticism becomes clear. And third, the final analysis will take the shape of "directional signals" rather than description of an historical *fait accompli*. With these procedural changes, I believe a worthwhile attempt can be made to deal with this difficult subject.

One final preliminary point must be made. In discussing cultural/existential function, one frequently needs to refer to what architecture *does* with regard to cultural beliefs or values: a verb is needed which will designate this function. The word "symbolize" is adequate if it is understood to mean more than simply "reflect" or "express." Paul Tillich has said that a symbol, in addition to pointing to something beyond itself, *participates in* that to which it points.[5] The discussion below will, I believe, contribute to an understanding of how architecture, as a symbol, "participates in" cultural values. A second term which I shall use synonymously with "symbolize" is "concretize." That is, architecture gives form to cultural values. The important thing to keep in mind here is that "without form" equals "void." Thus there is a real sense in which the value does not exist until it is concretized.

In the critical statement quoted at the beginning of this chapter, the Farnsworth house is seen as having aspects which "restate certain simple and lasting values," values which (1) are independent of the current social situation, and (2) thereby present a challenge to the consciousness of man. Independence from the social situation and ability to challenge accepted ways of thinking and acting are two important characteristics of the cultural/existential level of architectural function with which this discussion must deal; the former should be understood first of all.

Critics indicate their perception of a level of function which is independent of the more superficial and transitory effects of architecture by the use of such phrases as "simple and lasting values," as in the example above. The following example, concerning Le Corbusier's Villa Savoye, also indicates these qualities:

> . . .Le Corbusier. . .seems to be giving a perenially valid formula for the construction of the house of Man, but it is the house of Everyman and is outside the parameters of time and space and, therefore, outside the individual character of the individual man. . . .[6]

Although there are what I believe to be basic misconceptions revealed in this statement,[7] it shows an attempt to communicate the fundamentality and permanence of cultural values. This statement represents very well the tendency of applied criticism in general to point in the direction of a truth about cultural/existential function without being based upon a coherent theory of how architecture operates on this level. Such statements typically communicate an "aura" of cultural/existential function just as this example does. I believe that this phenomenon is symptomatic of the unfinished state of a comprehensive theory and that eventually even applied criticism may manifest a much more coherent understanding.

Exemplifying the discussion of architectural issues which are independent of social causes is that of the concretization of two opposed responses to nature. The critics of this century have been inspired to tackle this issue by their inevitable comparison of the work of Wright to that of Le Corbusier. In 1941, Giedion contrasted the two men, saying,

> This is another instance of two eternally opposed responses to nature: a contemporary reflection of the differences between the Greek temple, sharply outlined against its

background [Pl. 20], and the medieval town, attached like a plant to the site on which it stands [Pl. 4].[8]

Carl B. Troedsson bases a discussion of the two responses to nature on Kant's dichotomy of "earth-son" and "world-citizen" (i.e., empirical man and speculative man) and upon Spengler's idea of Totem and Taboo as an underlying polarization in cultural history.[9] Critics have referred to Le Corbusier's use of pilotis and picture windows as means of emancipating man from the earth and controlling his contact with it,[10] while Wright's low-slung roof planes and use of "the smallest crevices in the rocks to help bind his houses still more closely to the earth" also have elicited frequent comment.[11] Clearly this dichotomy parallels those of Classical/Romantic and abstract/organic as well as calling to mind Giedion's "split between thinking and feeling." These two opposite poles of man's response to nature thus exist independently of the tendencies of societies and of individuals towards one or the other.

The second major quality already mentioned as characteristic of cultural/existential function is the capacity to challenge man's currently accepted patterns of thinking and acting. By concretizing values which remain independent of social developments, an alternate standard is given form, offering man a larger vision and a degree of freedom from prejudice and "group-think." The following example refers to such a quality in Kahn's Richards building:

> It is as clear and astringent as a sermon by Martin Luther [Pls. 53 and 57]. It says that architecture is a serious affair, in need, just now, of an original bedrock reexamination of its fundamentals. It ridicules, by its very presence, the lace-edged mush that surrounds modern man, the kindergarten result of his acting like a four-year-old and then hoping to escape the consequences of his own foolishness with a singing commercial or a couple of multicolored curtain walls.[12]

Another critic sees nature as the source of a larger vision in the case of Wright's Guggenheim Museum:

> Wright always felt that an architectural form that grew out of some truth in nature would, more often than not, challenge preconceived notions of function, and force men to reexamine such notions in the light of a new architectural truth. That certainly became necessary in the Guggenheim Museum.[13]

This example calls to mind the earlier presentation (in Chapter 4) of critical acceptance, even praise, of Wright's Guggenheim design for its artistic value in spite of rather obvious practical failings. At that time, the term "artistic value" was not defined. Now, however, we have reached the part of this study which provides a vocabulary for dealing with artistic value. It is my opinion that in most cases in which a critic praises a building for its artistic value in spite of practical failings, what he senses about the building—though he often does not verbalize it—is that it "functions" well on the cultural/existential level. Some specific ways in which critics have interpreted the artistic value of the Guggenheim design will be discussed presently.

Implied in the notion that architecture challenges and can bring about change in man's patterns of thought and action is the suggestion of an *interaction* between the architectural object and the viewer. The building is seen not as a passive object to be merely observed but as an active force capable of taking part in a "dialogue." This implication finds more explicit discussion in some theories of perception recently being posited by philosophers and psychologists. For example, the phenomenologist Merleau-Ponty expresses his belief with these words:

> [B]etween my body as the potentiality for certain movements, as the demand for certain preferential planes, and the spectacle perceived as an invitation to the same movements and the scene of the same actions, a pact is concluded which gives me the enjoyment of space and gives to things their direct power over my body.[14]

The relation between observer and object, or between subject and object, has received concentrated attention from existentalist thinkers. Indeed, Rollo May describes existentialism as "the endeavor to understand man by cutting below the cleavage between subject and object which has bedeviled Western thought and science since shortly after the Renaissance."[15]

The initial attack against this disastrous separation of subject and object was made by Søren Kierkegaard in his formulation of truth-as-relationship. In 1846, he wrote:

> When the question of truth is raised in an objective manner, reflection is directed objectively to the truth, as an object to which the knower is related. Reflection is not focused upon the relationship, however, but upon the question of whether it is the truth to which the knower is related. If only the object to which he is related is the truth, the subject is accounted to be in the truth. When the question of the truth is raised subjectively, reflection is directed subjectively to the nature of the individual's relationship; if only the mode of this relationship is in the truth, the individual is in the truth, even if he should happen to be thus related to what is not true.[16]

With this statement, he anticipated by eighty-one years Heisenberg's "uncertainty principle," which reversed the Copernican view of the separation of man and nature,[17] turning physical *laws* into statements of probability, and initiated a movement whose impact is still reverberating and increasing in amplitude. Gestalt psychologist Frederick Perls, for example, refers to the interacting of organism and environment as the "organism/environment field" and says that all theories of perception, motivation, and behavior must be related to such an interacting field, never to an isolated organism.[18] More recently, in the approach to meaning in architecture known as semiology, or the science of signs, Charles Jencks constructs a "semiological triangle" whose "main point...is that there are simply *relations* between language, thought and reality." Jencks shows his alignment with the existentialist view when he says:

> One area does not determine the other, except in rare cases, and all one can really claim with conviction is that there are simply connections, or correlations. Unfortunately more is claimed, much more. In fact the behaviourists hold that reality determines both thought and language and the Whorfians that language determines the other two, whereas the Renaissance Platonists claimed that thought is determinant. Each semiologist points the arrows in the direction he believes in, but...[the semiological triangle shows that] the relations are always two-way and never absolute.[19]

Thus the viewpoint expressed in architectural criticism that architecture and man interact — that even as man makes art, so art makes man — reflects the present day increase in emphasis on relational rather than objective truth.

A further manifestation of this idea found in the criticism under examination here is the suggestion of a dialogue between building and environment. The responsibility of urban buildings to participate with their neighbors in a meaningful larger form rests upon a visible interaction. One critic discussed Le Corbusier's chapel at Ronchamp in such a way as to draw attention to the building as an active force in its environment. He first quotes a statement by the architect and then interprets it:

> "...It is toward the four horizons that the Chapel speaks through 'an acoustical phenomenon introduced into the realm of forms.' It is an intimacy which ought to penetrate every object, capable of provoking the radiation of ineffable space." In other words, Le Corbusier envisions his Chapel as more than an object. To him it is a sort of animate creature placed on a raised and open stage, capable of conversing with the surrounding landscape [Pls. 43 and 44]. It might be said that this is a kind of penetration of inner and outer space (one of the original ideals of the International Style) here raised from the inert material level to one that is philosophic and contemplative.[20]

Such a relationship of building and environment cannot, of course, be interpreted as existing independently of the observer. It is probably through the observer's identification with the prime figure in the perceptual field — the building — that the dialogue can be experienced by him. Thus, this building/environment relationship may be seen as a specific manifestation of the building/observer relationship.

A more common interpretation of the architectural object as an active force is found in statements concerning the relationship between the artist and his evolving work. The notion of the art object as a pseudo-independent entity is not new in this century, but it tends to accompany a more romantic and organic view of art than was dominant during the early "functionalist" era. The work of Louis Kahn has been spoken of in terms of an entity emerging out of itself.

> In his work, space is neither archaized by classical rules nor pressed into the rhythmic repetitive forms of frame structure, as in early modern; rather space is "phenomenologically" determined and evaluated. A new typology is allowed to emerge out of "servant space" and "served space," the former housing together the new elements in building equipment.... They are allowed to develop their own significant expression, as seen in Kahn's design for a science building [Pl. 57].[21]

In this case, the critic may have taken his cue from Kahn's own reference to "what the thing wants to be."[22] Architects, like other artists, frequently describe their experience of the creative process as one in which certain aspects of the design simply "appear" to them as if of their own accord, without the conscious will or effort of the artist. Since the design thus seems to "grow" by itself out of the soil of the problem which the artist's mind has been presented with, the result has often been referred to as an "organic" design.

As is stated in the above example, the approach to design under consideration here is not one of imposing a formula onto a design but rather of "allowing" the elements of design to "develop their own significant expression." Although the main point of the present discussion is to *describe* a characteristic metaphor, not to explain it, subsequent consideration of the critics' view of the subconscious mind as a source of form will contribute to an explanation of the impression of the separateness of the art object. Our society, being characterized by "thinking" rather than "feeling," has tended to regard the functions of "feeling" as split off from the more "real," *thinking* functions. Thus, during an era in which objective knowledge is thought of as true knowledge, while subjective knowledge is considered false or distorted, an object which is intellectually and technically the product of conscious thought processes, where *conscious* decisions control each aspect of it — such an object is one which the maker can look upon as her own creation; while one which is to some extent the offspring of her unconscious mind, her subjective processes of knowing, she feels less control over: it even seems to have an *animus* of its own. The critical statements referred to here reveal a recognition of the validity of unconscious processes in creation, but they still reflect the split between objective and subjective knowing that existentialism attempts to undercut.[23]

Also related in the criticism of this century to the suggestion of buildings as active forces in a dialogue with man and to the creation of an "organic" architecture is a respect, even reverence, for the natural qualities of physical objects. Such an attitude was so important to the New Brutalists that some observers of their work remain unaware that they were motivated by any other desire than to glorify the nature of raw, functional materials. Recent critical statements indicate that, with regard to his attitude toward materials, Frank Lloyd Wright seems, as in so many other respects, to have been about fifty years ahead of his time. It is interesting to see in juxtaposition first a passage from an article on structural analysis written in 1966 and then a paragraph from an interpretation of one of Wright's early works. First, from "Structural analysis in art and anthropology":

> Natural space, and more especially its solid-object constituents, are not however merely passive and static. In addition to mere extension, they have the property of embodying or being permeated by *forces*. In the natural world the more obvious of these forces are of two kinds: one, omnipresent in all solids, is that of gravity; the other is the vital, animal energy resident in living creatures. One is mechanical, predictable and rational; the other organic, spontaneous and irrational. These energies, singly or in interaction, contain within themselves a repertory of imagery and a structural logic which permeate the work, and radically affect the manner in which it charges and transforms the space of the beholder, making it a space in which certain interactions of force prevail, and certain kinds of action are possible.[24]

The following critical statement seems almost a paraphrase of the theoretical one. The critic is speaking of the "pure and unbroken horizontals" of the Robie house:

> The meaning embodied by them would seem again to be double: it is first of the earth, with its clefts, hollows and climatic masses, felt as full of life, always moving and lifting itself like some great beast, as Cézanne saw it. The second meaning grows out of the first. As the earth and objects upon the earth are pulled into the rhythm of flux and change, it and they fragment into their components, which then oscillate around each other in an "eternal becoming." This is the world as the cubists saw it. The Robie House thus combines Cézanne's reverence for the majesty of solid things and his recognition of the forces that pull at them with Picasso's and Braque's fragmentation of solids into planes which move continuously through space [Pl. 5]. Lacking contact with these contemporary European expressions in painting, Wright was still creating many of the same meanings with his forms.[25]

Although critics generally tended not to emphasize this attitude of Wright's until more recent years, Lewis Mumford in 1929 spoke of Wright's "great sense of tact—the tact of the artist with his materials, of the lover of nature with the earth, and of a man with other men."[26] Wright himself, as a critic later pointed out, "encourages man to be 'natural by living in accord with what he judges the phenomenal world of nature to be.'"[27] This philosophy is much more compatible with the present-day consciousness of ecology than with the early twentieth-century fascination with the machine and its potential for replacing many elements of nature, which is perhaps the reason that critics are *now* discussing this aspect of Wright's philosophy.

One of the principal characteristics which distinguish critical discussions of architecture's cultural/existential function from those of the "lower" levels of function is the tendency to point to the unconscious mind of the architect as the source of form. For example, a discussion of Kahn's work refers to the unconscious in connection with a term Kahn himself has used:

> His design has a monolithic singleness of vision for which he himself has claimed the term "archaic," not in the conventional meaning of superannuated but in the psychoanalytic sense of a return to subconscious or intuitive fundamentals.[28]

This statement and the next one illustrate not only a typical allusion to the unconscious mind but also the idea, mentioned earlier, of the quality of fundamentality of architecture which is effective on the cultural/existential level.

> There is throughout this design [of the Dominican convent of La Tourette], just as there is at Ronchamp, a suggestion of the fundamental and the primordial; the feeling that these forms spring from the depths of the unconscious, from some compulsive and automatic provocation [Pls. 47 and 48].[29]

The use of the terms "compulsive and automatic" in association with the origins of the design suggests something of that separateness of artist and art object already discussed above: it seems to imply that the forms materialized, as it were, *in spite of* the artist's conscious "will."

Characteristic of the critical statements which attempt to deal with the cultural/existential function of architecture is a recognition of the difficulty of verbalizing about the unconscious meanings sensed in the works. Their terminology is noticeably different from that which is suitable even for the social level of function. A clear statement of the difficulty is made by a critic writing in 1964 about the ornament on Sullivan's buildings:

> [It] is...difficult to interpret in symbolic terms. It is radically subjective, and it evokes from the observer so many different responses and associations that it is scarcely possible to find objective experiences that might have led to the feelings out of which it grew [Pl. 3].[30]

Thus, whereas on the level of social function the critic frequently says that a building *expresses* such-and-such a recognized social phenomenon, on the level of cultural/existential function he says that (nonverbal) associations, images, or feelings are *evoked* in the observer by the work.[31] In the previous chapter, the primary syntactical relation was between the building —an object of the viewer's perception—and a characteristic trait of society—also an object of the viewer's perception; now the primary relation is between the building and the viewer himself—or, more precisely, the viewer's *self*, since the associations "evoked" in him stem from experiences which have been so assimilated by him that it is now difficult for him to perceive them as objects separate from himself.

Two critical responses to Rudolph's Art and Architecture building at Yale University further demonstrate the manner in which critics describe their perception of a significance they cannot verbalize:

> ...his building has not only a Larkin aspect and a Richards Medical aspect but a Kenzo Tange aspect, a George Vantangerloo aspect, and even a Sir John Soane aspect [Pl. 58]..... And yet all these reminiscences are mere marginal reflections, a dim halo of associations.[32]

> ...few who visit this building can resist the mnemonic quality of its spaces, its light, its inventive furnishings, its use of art works. Like a museum, it displays the essences of design and architecture. Like a shell from the sea, it will sound the source of its being to those who will hear.[33]

These statements describe an experience which has received direct attention in at least two recent philosophical publications.

One of these, *The Tacit Dimension* by Michael Polanyi, posits the function of a basic process of thinking which enables us to "know more than we can tell."[34] The unverbalizable knowledge consists of the particulars *from* which we attend *to* the specifiable knowledge. The particulars are the elements of the bodily processes of knowing—we rely on our bodies for our knowledge—and we know the particulars only tacitly, only as we attend from them to the specifiable whole. Polanyi illustrates his theory with a description of an experiment performed by Lazarus and McCleary in 1949:

> These authors presented a person with a large number of nonsense syllables, and after showing certain of the syllables, they administered an electric shock. Presently the person showed symptoms of anticipating the shock at the sight of "shock syllables"; yet, on questioning, he could not identify them. He had come to know when to expect a shock, but he could not tell what made him expect it. He had acquired a knowledge similar to that which we have when we know a person by signs which we cannot tell.... Here we see the basic structure of tacit knowing. It always involves two things, or two kinds of things. We may call them the two terms of tacit knowing. In the experiments the shock syllables and shock associations formed the first term, and the electric shock which followed them was the second term. After the subject had learned to connect these two terms, the sight of the shock syllables evoked the expectation of a shock and the utterance of the shock associations was suppressed in order to avoid shock. Why did this

connection remain tacit? It would seem that this was due to the fact that the subject was riveting his attention on the electric shock. He was relying on his awareness of the shock-producing particulars only in their bearing on the electric shock. We may say that he learned to rely on his awareness of these particulars for the purpose of attending to the electric shock.

Here we have the basic definition of the logical relation between the first and second term of a tacit knowledge. It combines two kinds of knowing. We know the electric shock, forming the second term, by attending to it, and hence the subject is *specifiably* known. But we know the shock-producing particulars only by relying on our own awareness of them for attending to something else, namely the electric shock, and hence our knowledge of them remains *tacit*. This is how we come to know these particulars, without becoming able to identify them. Such is the *functional relation* between the two terms of tacit knowing: *we know the first term only by relying on our awareness of it for attending to the second.*[35]

His theory constitutes, then, grounds for accepting the critics' description of their unspecifiable experience of architecture and counters the possible assumption that their inability to verbalize is merely a result of lazy thinking.

Another philosophical approach to such unspecified experience of art objects is that of Gaston Bachelard to the function of a poetic image, a function which he calls "reverberation."

[W]hen I shall have occasion to mention the relation of a new poetic image to an archetype lying dormant in the depths of the unconscious, I shall have to make it understood that this relation is not, properly speaking, a *causal* one. The poetic image is not subject to an inner thrust. It is not an echo of the past. On the contrary: through the brilliance of an image, the distant past resounds with echoes, and it is hard to know at what depth these echoes will reverberate and die away. Because of its novelty and its action, the poetic image has an entity and dynamism of its own; it is referable to a direct ontology.... To say that the poetic image is independent of causality is to make a rather serious statement. But the causes cited by psychologists and psychoanalysts can never really explain the wholly unexpected nature of the new image, any more than they can explain the attraction it holds for a mind that is foreign to the process of its creation. The poet does not confer the past of his image upon me, and yet his image immediately takes root in me. The communicability of an unusual image is a fact of great ontological significance.[36]

Thus when a critic writes that associations and analogies with aspects of Classic and pre-Classic Mediterranean tradition are "poetically evoked" by Le Corbusier's Villa Savoye,[37] he may be describing his own experience of "reverberation" or "tacit knowing."

While some critical statements elicited by twentieth-century architecture have stopped with a still vague reference to such "reverberations," other have attempted to attend *to* those particulars in the hope of gaining a better understanding of the power and meaning of an architect's design.

That is, critics have sometimes attempted to make contact with and name "an archetype lying dormant in the depths of the unconscious," as Bachelard phrased it, which they believe to be the underlying source of meaning in a design. Often the critic refers to forms of the remote past or of primitive cults as the source of such an archetype or as being analogous to the modern building which embodies that archetype. Several discussions by Vincent Scully of Wright's Guggenheim Museum provide excellent examples of this tendency:

> These two compelling movements — the first, toward immurement in the ideal hollow, and the second (deeply traditional also but now Nietzschean-heroic in its force) toward the conquest of time itself through the use of the continuous spiral, "beyond time and infinity," which returns cyclically and never seems to end — are climaxed in the Guggenheim Museum of 1946-59. Here is was purely these mystical drives which formed the design.... The domed and spiralling space is the whole, causing the building to hollow outward among its starched neighbors, like the pulsing sanctuary of a primitive cult drumming on Fifth Avenue [Pl. 31].[38]

> In the end, therefore, Wright seems, like many modern men, to have rejected all immediate heritages in favor of remote ones, assumed by himself out of the deep past. Here, too, was another specific rejection of Europe — a rejection explicit in much of America's most patent mythology — and a concentration once more upon the archetypal character of those instincts which I mentioned earlier: upon mobility and security, the road in the spiral, the perfect peace of engulfment in the circle's continuous shell [Pls. 34 and 37].[39]

Gaston Bachelard, whose writings have explored the phenomenological impact of architecture on the inhabitant, has discussed the inherent images of shells in *Poetics of Space.*[40] The recurrent appearance of such "archetypes" in various writings, both theoretical and practical, not only lends credence to the critic's own description but also increases the "reverberations" in the reader. A recently published article on the symbolic content of Paul Rudolph's design for the State Service Center of Boston, for example, dwells on the mythological significance of the conch, the spiral, the labyrinth, the cave.[41]

Although the tendency to discuss architectural significance in terms of archetypes is primarily a recent phenomenon — most common since about 1960 — there are two particular archetypes of a spatial nature which seem to underlie some of the earliest responses to the space of twentieth-century buildings. In reading the statements concerning architectural space in chronological order, one has the impression of viewing the evolution of two complimentary archetypal concepts — "place" and "path." The structure of "place" develops out of the early preoccupation with free plan, space-in-motion, and interpenetration of inner and outer space, while an early appearance of the notion of "path" can be seen in Le Corbusier's concern with "route" in architectural design. As architecture (along with city planning) is uniquely a space-molding art, and its cultural/existential significance resides primarily in the handling of space, the manner in which critics have dealt with space in this century is a subject pertinent to the present study. A brief look at the history of space as an architectural concern will help to place the discussion of its treatment by critics in perspective.

The handling of space generally is recognized by contemporary critics and theorists of architecture as one of the architect's primary concerns, but Peter Collins has pointed out that the emphasis on space is a relatively recent development.

> The notion of space as an essential element of architecture must have existed in some rudimentary form from the time man first built enclosures or made structural improvements to his caves; but it is a curious fact that until the eighteenth century no architectural treatise ever used the word, whilst the idea of space as a primary quality of architectural composition was not fully developed until the last few years.[42]

Prior to the eighteenth century the primary concern of architectural theorists was not space but structure, and the word space was used only in discussions of decoration to refer to such things as the blank areas of a painted ceiling: as yet it "had no three-dimensional significance whatsoever."[43]

Collins suggests that, like so many modern architectural ideals, the new attitude toward space probably had its beginnings in the middle of the eighteenth century. Whereas for the Classical theorist architecture was primarily a matter of structure and the word space was used only to designate "amorphous unproportionable surfaces,"[44] the introduction of Romantic gardens in the mid-eighteenth century brought an emphasis on the positive qualities of spaces themselves. Yet it was not until about a century later that the term "space" began to be widely understood in its modern three-dimensional sense, and this development Collins attributes almost exclusively to the writings of German theorists of the first half of the nineteenth century. He traces the lineage from Hegel's use of the term in his *Philosophy of Art* to its development by Heinrich Wolfflin's English-speaking followers.

The real key, however, to the new architectural significance of space was not theoretical work but, in the words of Collins, "the intuitive creative endeavours of Frank Lloyd Wright."[45]

> It was he who, at the beginning of the century, by the judicious application of new structural materials, first exploited the spatial possibilities which had lain dormant since the end of the Baroque, and applied them to buildings appropriate to the new age.... Whereas the Rationalists, such as Viollet-le-Duc, could conceive only the *structure* of churches as providing the archetype for a new way of building, Wright took the *space;*

and it is this which distinguishes Wright from the other great architects of his generation (such as Perret) as the first great architect of the twentieth century.[46]

Wright's Larkin building marks the beginning of the new era: "henceforth, space was regarded as a twin partner with structure in the creation of architectural compositions, and the sensation of spatial relationships resulting from successive viewpoints (which had been such an important feature of the *jardin anglais*) became the principal aesthetic experience sought.[47] The extent to which this new emphasis upon the experience of spatial relationship began to dominate architectural thought is reflected in the quantity of critical statements dealing with movement in or of space.

Of the two primary approaches to the relationship between architectural space and the observer — space-in-motion and observer-in-motion — the former is largely metaphorical — but still very important to an understanding of twentieth-century architecture.[48] And, as mentioned above, it seems to have evolved toward the "archetype" of human spatial orientation, "place."

The notion of space-in-motion refers to the feeling of an observer that space "flows" through the building: around partitions, up steps, through glass walls. Although Reyner Banham, in describing the phenomenon, says that it is "axiomatic" that space flows *away* from the observer since he is the "source of spatial experience,"[49] I find that in the critical statements I have been concerned with which speak of space as flowing, an observer is not mentioned. A description of the Barcelona Pavilion, for example, says:

> The building was embellished not only by the richness of the colorful marbles used but also through the succession of different compartments [Pl. 19]. None was closed. All led from one to the other. The space seemed to be in motion, flowing from one part to another, merging with the enclosed water court and finally with the outside space.[50]

One might ask, "What moves when space moves? If space is nothingness, how can it 'move'?" Quite clearly the critics are not referring to moving *air* since they have referred to "flowing space" even in the Farnsworth house where, according to the owner, the air was suffocatingly still. Thus, we must conclude that space-in-motion is a fallacious and seductive idea which is perhaps best viewed as a metaphor for observer-in-motion, since what *can* move through the building is the observer or, at least, the observer's line of vision. Nevertheless, critics *have* spoken in terms of flowing space, particularly in discussing buildings which provide a relatively unobstructed line of vision. In fact, the much admired "free plan," made possible by the new structural methods, is a nearly universal characteristic of those buildings in which space is said to be "in motion."

Bruno Zevi finds the origins of free plan in Frank Lloyd Wright's new concept of continuous space. The free plan as used by Wright, says Zevi, "is not an initial formula but results from the concept of continuous space."[51] Zevi refers to the early works of Wright and says:

> Everywhere the same tendency is apparent: to amalgamate the rooms, to animate the building as if it were a continuous spatial discourse rather than a series of separate words, to break with geometry—often even with the right angle—for the sake of forms more adequate for human use and movement. Above all, to feel interior space as a reality, as the substantive, pulsating reality of architecture—that reality which, through the artist's intuition, expresses and transforms all practical requirements...this is the true meaning of Wright's work.[52]

Zevi feels that after the free plan had been used so successfully and so famously by Le Corbusier, it became, in the hands of less gifted architects, a cliché of the modern movement, divorced from its original meaning; rather than the meaningful channeling of space, it came to mean simply the absence of walls.

The flow of space and the extensive glass walls made possible by new structural techniques brought about an impression, mentioned particularly by critics in the fifties, of an "interpenetration of inner and outer space." Although works by other architects have been praised for the experience they provide of inward and outward movement of space, Mies van der Rohe is the architect whose works best exemplify this principle. A description of the Barcelona Pavilion, for example, says:

> There the unit of design is not the enclosed volume anymore but the free standing wall extending into space, the wall which does not enclose space but channels it, producing a continuous movement. Here the interior and exterior spaces are not defined, and the whole emphasis is placed on the flow of horizontal space [Pls. 18 and 19].[53]

Another writer speaks of the way in which the Pavilion unites inner and outer space and, at the same time, combines the extremely "rational" grid structure with the "irrational" space concept.[54] Here in the use of the word irrational is perhaps recognition of the metaphorical character of the "flow of space" idea, yet the value of the image is by no means diminished by such a recognition.

An extension of the idea of interpenetration of inner and outer space which appears in the criticism of the sixties is the notion of limitation or intensification of infinite space. For example, a discussion of Rietveld's Schröder house deals with space as follows:

> Dans l'évolution de l'homme, l'habitat a perdu peu à peu sa fonction d'abri contre le danger pour se transformer en un espace construit qui est comme une intensification de l'espace universel. Dans cette évolution l'habitation construit par Rietveld à Utrecht en 1928 [sic] a marqué une phase décisive [Pls. 8 and 10].[55]

In a similar vein, a description of Mies's Farnsworth house says that "the dominant visual function of those verticals [of the structure] is to establish the regular rhythm that measures, controls, the piece of infinite space that has been marked off to form the house."[56]

The idea expressed in these statements closely parallels or is identical to one found in a number of theoretical sources. Very early in the century, Gerrit Rietveld himself stated that only the limitation of space—by "clouds, trees or something else that gave it a size and that reflected light and sound"—could bring segments of it to life, make them real.[57] In 1965, Herbert Read wrote:

> The specifically aesthetic act is to take possession of a revealed segment of the real, to establish its dimensions, and to define its form. Reality is what we thus articulate, and what we articulate is communicable only in virtue of its aesthetic form.[58]

It almost seems as if, in this instance, the applied criticism was catching up to concurrent events in the realm of theory, and that a necessary step for applied criticism had been the direct encounter with infinite space in "wall-less" architecture, particularly that of Mies. I am reminded of methods of contemporary Gestalt therapy in which one seeks to regain contact with a repressed emotion by exaggerating in "psycho-drama" the bodily experience of that emotion. Perhaps the exaggeration of interpenetration of inner and outer space brought critics into direct awareness of infinite space and the psychological/aesthetic significance of walls, so that the experiencing of architecture as limitation or intensification or concretization of space could become conscious. (It is interesting in this context that the urge to build wall-less houses seems to have run its course; architects now are exploring other aspects of "house-ness," in ways which tend to make the limitation of space more easily felt.)

Critical statements which speak of architectural space as limitation or intensification of infinite space have much in common with recent publications by philosophers and psychologists in which they attempt to analyze the functioning of man's orientation in space. Many writers have contributed to this endeavor, but one who has a particular interest in the ramifications of such research for architecture—he is himself an architect—is Christian Norberg-Schulz, whose *Intentions in Architecture* represents an effort to provide a much needed, comprehensive theory of architecture for twentieth-century architects, critics, and laymen, and whose *Existence, Space, and Architecture* summarizes the present state of research into spatial orientation.

Limitation and intensification of infinite space are the two most important characteristics of one of the primary elements of existential space discussed by Norberg-Schulz—the element of "center," or "place."

Norberg-Schulz asserts that existential, or life-, space is composed of a number of interpersonal, universally common elements, which he refers to as topological schemata. These schemata, or structures, develop as the individual develops, following a universal sequence of steps.

> The topological schemata are in the beginning tied to the things themselves. The most elementary order obtained is based on the proximity relation, but the "collection" thus established, soon develops into more structured wholes, characterized by continuity and enclosure. . . . The elementary organizational schemata consist in the establishment of *centres* or places (proximity), *directions* or paths (continuity) and *areas* or domains (enclosure). To orient himself, man above all needs to grasp such relations, whereas the geometrical schemata develop much later, to serve more particular purposes. In fact, primitive man mostly manages very well without any geometric notions.[59]

The element of "path" will be discussed subsequently, in connection with the concept of observer-in-motion. The element of "domain" does not figure in this discussion of architectural criticism of function, because it is not one that seems to be indicated by the critics's statements and because it can be seen both as another level in a hierarchy of "places" and as the "ground" on which place and path are the two kinds of meaningful figures.

The element of "place" is the earliest to develop and is therefore the most basic. Norberg-Schulz has said, "Only when space becomes a system of meaningful places, does it become alive to us."[60] In the defining of space, he says that a "place," such as a home, must be small and that it needs a pronounced limit or border.[61] Thus he presents the concept of the *limitation* of infinite space which has appeared in critical statements. Norberg-Schulz also says that areas which take on a high level of meaningfulness by virtue of the activities which have gone on within them tend to become "places," that "human identification with the environment presupposes *varying* densities, and above all, dense foci which serve as basic points of reference.[62] The dense foci or "places" thus are characterized by their having become *intensified* areas within unlimited space.

The second important approach to the relationship between architectural space and the observer is the idea that architecture is to be experienced by an observer-in-motion, that architecture is a series of segments of infinite space through which the architect, by arrangement of steps, hallways, even floor patterns, provides a prescribed route. Early in this century Le Corbusier spoke of the idea of *route* as one of the important experiences in architecture,[63] and critics frequently point to this aspect of his buildings, such as the ramps in the Villa Savoye. A recent critical discussion of Le Corbusier's work pointed out that his use of ramps and slightly inclined passageways was an effective means of increasing the muscular experience of procession through a building.[64] This recognition of other than visual means of sensing architecture is significant in view of the increasing awareness among philosophers and psychologists of the proprioceptive and subceptive powers of man.[65]

An architect in addition to Le Corbusier in whose work critics frequently see the concept of observer-in-motion is Frank Lloyd Wright. A discussion of one of his earlier designs reads:

> [In] the Robie plan by Wright...you have once again the very strong idea of the barely defined continuity of space which comes alive only in the movement of the inhabitant. It is no longer an aesthetic succession of room unity, but it is the dynamic movement of the occupant that actually creates the space experience [Pl. 5].[66]

The following description of Wright's Guggenheim Museum emphasizes the "route" which is its primary design feature:

> It does not exalt man standing fixed and upright within it. The meaning is in the journey, since from above, upon leaving the elevator, the visitor finds the space dizzying and vast, while the great downward coil of the ramp insistently invites him to movement [Pl. 37]. Upon arriving at the ground floor once more [Pl. 33], he will find that the building seems much longer than before because the long journey through it is remembered. But as that memory fades, the heavy vertical piers (not, as in the Larkin Building, intrinsic to the spatial experience but counter to it), the dome struts, and the bright side-lights catch the eye and reduce the space in size once more [Pl. 35], so that he must move again soon if the sensation of freedom and vastness is to be regained. Thus he is kept, in all truth, "on the road."[67]

The idea of architecture as an experience of "movement *through*" has figured large in the statements written by the architect/critic Philip Johnson. He has declared his conviction that architecture is a temporal art and that it finds its significance not in the organization of volumes nor even in the arranging of spaces, but rather in the "organization of procession."[68] In this regard, Johnson finds the Guggenheim to be a highly successful building:

> The experiences are not static but temporal. The beauty consists in how you move into the space. There are as many ways of introducing space as there are architects, but it strikes me that clarity is one of the prerequisites. At least in the Guggenheim...the processional is as clean as the Acropolis or St. Peter's. The walker-through-the-space is never lost, never in the slightest doubt as to his orientation, whence he has come or whither he aims. *Whence* and *whither* are positive, not negative, architectural virtues which are basic to the entire discipline of the art.[69]

A subsidiary emphasis, related to the idea of architecture as a processional experience, is that placed by critics of this century upon the quality of the entrances of the buildings they appraise. They express their concern in terms of the quality of experience afforded the moving observer as he walks toward and through the entrance and then into the building itself, judging, for example, the logic of the placement of the entrance, the appropriateness of scale, and the clarity of direction once inside. Philip Johnson has included, in his discussion of procession in the Guggenheim, praise for the "breathtaking effect" of being "sprayed" into the domed space from a relatively small entryway.

The recent attention given in applied criticism to procession and entrance experience in architecture parallels an interest, manifest in theoretical writings, in the archetypal "path" and its role in the meaningful design of architectural space. Norberg-Schulz introduces the element of "path" in this way:

> Man's taking possession of the environment always means a departure from the place where he dwells, and a journey along a path which leads him in a direction determined by his purpose and his image of the environment.... The *path,* therefore, represents a basic property of human existence, and it is one of the great original symbols.[70]

As an element in man's structuring of space, paths are the connecting links between "meaningful places" in a system the basic elements of which underlie all human experience of space. Two critical statements elicited by the most recent of the thirteen buildings on which this study is based show that critics are finding Paul Rudolph's Yale Art and Architecture building to be a successful design incorporating aspects of both of these primary archetypes. Both of these examples speak of the separate space units, each of which has its unique character. The second one particularly emphasizes the importance of the users' path through the building:

> It is nominally a six-story structure, but actually has 36 different levels [Pl. 61]. Floors step up and down; ceilings soar or suddenly descend near head level, each room is as if invented as a new kind of space, and these volumes are ingeniously assembled in a great, burly, rough-textured concrete and glass frame.[71]

> Light influx from four sides, broken by varying textures on columns and parapets, creates space units interlocked by the movement of the users. Within each level, shallow steps change the eye-focus, as on a Piranesi engraving making vertical and horizontal dynamics a self-sufficient perceptive experience. Applied to teaching spaces, this learning-in-motion is as old as Aristotle's peripatetic method.[72]

Thus the research of "archetypes" — of universal symbolic structures of spatial organization — and the growing understanding of man's faculties of perception shed light on the possible significance of the applied criticism of twentieth-century architecture. A look at the "profile" of the cultural/ existential category of function suggests a trend in the direction of increasing concern with this aspect of architecture. Before 1950, concern for the cultural/existential aspect of architecture was far outweighed, along with that for physical, psychological, and social function, by the overriding preoccupation with structural articulation, a primarily stylistic, external "effect" of architecture. During the fifties, however, increasing signs of interest in cultural/existential function began to appear and, during the decades of the sixties and seventies, statements dealing with the existential meaning of architecture seem to be about as frequent as those reflecting attention to the purely stylistic aspects of structural articulation. Thus, of the categories of architectural function, it is the cultural/existential category which is definitely "on the upswing," the one in which "progress" is most noticeable. One can speak of progress here in both a quantitative and qualitative sense: quantitative in that the "profile" reveals an increasing number of references to cultural/existential meaning, and qualitative in that criticism of function may thus be seen to be moving closer to the firm theoretical base which is growing out of the insights of scientists, philosophers, psychologists, and artists.

This chapter opened with an explanation of why certain procedures of discussion used in earlier chapters must be altered in dealing with the cultural/existential level of function. One of those differences is that this chapter could not *begin* with a clear definition of the cultural/existential level of function, since the category itself is still in a nascent stage in architectural criticism. Now that the critical examples have been viewed and related to the various theoretical ideas toward which they seem to be pointing, it is possible to indicate one defining characteristic of this level of function. Indeed, it is not only possible but necessary, since to leave this point unmade would be to permit a false understanding of the breakdown of function into the categories which have formed the backbone of this study.

It should be noted that the division of the concept of function into categories according to various "levels" of human experience perpetuates the very same alienation that has been exposed by such writers as Kierkegaard, Tillich, and others as the prevalent pathology of our culture. The separation of experience into physical, psychological, social, and cultural or symbolic levels denies the essential unity of human experience. And yet most of the functional criticism produced in this century rests upon these divisions: they reflect the prevalent attitude of architectural critics throughout most of the seventy-five-year period under examination in this study.

What is crucial to a proper understanding of these categories, however, and particularly to the understanding of cultural/existential function, is that the latter category encompasses all of the others, thereby healing the schizophrenia of categorization. Although the fundamental unity of human experience is most clearly expressed in the theoretical sources cited in this chapter — particularly in Michael Polanyi's explication of "tacit knowing," a pattern of sensory-motor functioning which permeates all levels of human knowing and acting — the signs of growing insight on the part of architectural critics can be seen in their statements, especially in those pertaining to their experiences of space. The union, in their statements, of symbolic meaning with the necessity of bodily movement through space encompasses the "highest" and the "lowest" levels of architectural function, and demonstrates that their experience is unitary. The advent of such insight in the functional criticism of the last three decades is of profound importance and demands further historical interpretation as well as some discussion of its implications for the task facing the practicing architectural critic.

8

Conclusion

This examination of the concept of function in twentieth-century architectural criticism covers an eighty-year period beginning in 1900. During this period, critics responding to specific contemporary buildings have dealt with several different aspects of architectural function ranging from the pragmatic to the symbolic. Investigating the critics' remarks in terms of several differentiated categories of function has made possible the observation of a profoundly significant development in the recent history of the concept of function. This development can be seen in the growing attention paid by critics to the cultural/existential meaning of architecture and indicates nothing less than the emergence of a new world view or philosophical position in architectural criticism paralleling that enunciated primarily by existentialist thinkers but also by many others including psychologists, physicists, and poets.

When Sigfried Giedion attributed the sterility of much modern architecture to a "split between thinking and feeling," he was lamenting the rationalist approach to building which dominated the production of the first three or four decades of this century. He recognized that until that split was healed, there could be no "living" architecture, no architecture which could answer the needs of the whole man. In the world of architectural criticism, Giedion was a pioneer in the struggle against the crippling effect of rationalism on art and society, but in the larger context, the struggle began long before the turn of the century when Søren Kierkegaard protested against the ruling political and philosophical rationalism of his day, "Hegel's 'totalitarianism of reason.'"[1] The identification of abstract truth with reality was, according to Kierkegaard and those who followed him, a falsehood which had been growing since the Renaissance. By the nineteenth century it had become a "cancer," a sickness which Kierkegaard called the "sickness unto death," in which man was alienated from nature, from his fellows, from his experience, from *himself*. The healing of this sickness could result not from an anti-rational, merely activist approach, however, but, as Kierkegaard, Nietzsche and their followers realized, from the experience of a reality underlying both abstract thinking and concrete action. People needed to experience themselves as neither objects nor subjects, but on a level which undercuts the object-subject cleavage.

It is my conviction that the criticism of architectural function in this century reflects the beginning of a reorientation in the critical approach to architecture which is founded upon a *healing* of the split between thinking and feeling, upon a recognition of the relatedness of man and his experience of architecture, a reorientation which permits the creation and the perception of artistic value in architecture. The change that has taken place since the beginning of the modern movement can best be seen in a comparison of the criticism of function which appeared early in the century with that of the late fifities, sixties and seventies.[2]

The criticism of architectural function throughout this century has been characterized by a preoccupation with structure, particularly with the idea that structure should be made evident to the observer of a building. At the beginning of the century, partly in reaction to the nineteenth-century interest in applied "style" and partly in response to the novelty, beauty, and logic of the new materials and techniques, architects produced and critics admired designs which "honestly" revealed or expressed their steel skeleton construction and which made clearly visible their division into areas according to the activities housed. Such designs were called "functional" because they articulated the function of the structural elements or the differentiated functions of the programme. The attitude toward structure later in the century often retains the preference for such "honest" structural articulation but in addition it places strong emphasis upon the symbolic meaning of a building's structure. This changing attitude toward structure gives rise to shifts in emphasis in several related areas, shifts which provide clues to the new concept of architectural function.

The shift of emphasis from the exterior of a building to its interior is one such change which might easily be overlooked because of its apparent simplicity. The large number of critical statements in the early decades dealing with structural articulation discussed a design primarily from the standpoint of an observer located outside the building studying it as an object of rational investigation, asking himself to what extent it told the "truth" about its technical structure. The presumption of an objective "truth" betrays the rationalist orientation of the critic, and the conviction that the external appearance of the building should be consistent with that truth is characteristic of that orientation. The emphasis is certainly not upon the relationship between the viewer (critic) and the building but rather upon the building as a rationally analyzable *object*. Later criticism, on the other hand, more frequently discusses the interior of a structure: it places the individual in relation to the building by moving her point of orientation inside it. Furthermore, the word "structure" must be understood in a symbolic as well as a "merely physical" sense: the structure of the design *idea* is also placed in relation to the viewer. The critic, as viewer, moves inside the "ideal" structure and at the same time, if he is truly in relation to it, finds that structure within himself: it has meaning for him because it already existed within him, as an element of his perceptual functioning. Thus, the early emphasis on exterior style made man into an *observer,* while later critical writing views him rather as a *participant* in the architectural experience.

Related to the earlier attitude of the critic toward herself as an observer of an object is the almost exclusive emphasis upon *visual* perception. Even when she advised readers that proper understanding of the design could not be appreciated from one angle alone but necessitated movement around the building, the experience was spoken of in terms of a series of views of the building which became superimposed in the mind, giving somewhat the effect of a cubist painting. Vision is the one of our senses which comes into use most often as we observe objects at a distance.[3] Thus, exclusive emphasis on visual perception communicates the unrelatedness of observer and building. In contrast to this visual emphasis, later criticism began to evidence an appreciation of the nonvisual senses that should be particularly called into play by architecture—that is, the proprioceptive, kinesthetic sensors which give the "walker-through" his bodily perception of the spaces which surround him.

The visual and exterior emphasis during the first few decades of the modern movement in architecture contributed to the development of a modern style, sometimes called "functionalist style," and, after 1932, the "International Style," of which the functionalist treatment of structure (i.e., structural articulation) was an important characteristic. Later criticism reflects the acceptance of a diversity of styles: different architects are appreciated for their widely divergent styles, and individual buildings are not expected to conform to a preestablished set of criteria, such as that described by Hitchcock and Johnson.[4] Recent criticism often expresses an appreciation of the uniqueness of each individual's experience of interior organized space and of the meaning contained in various symbolic structures. Similarly, the early critic's dwelling upon certain characteristics of a good modern style is being replaced by an appreciation of the unique vision of the individual artist.

The theoretical undergirding of this particular quality in recent criticism can be found, I believe, in two main ideas: first, the existentialist concept of *Dasein,* the appreciation of the existence of the particular being who *is there,* who has a "there" and a "then" which are unique;[5] and, second, the recognition of the common archetypes of human experience, which give underlying meaning *in* plurality—when underlying meaning is absent (or unrecognized), then the illusion of meaning, of technical meaning at least, can be achieved by consistency and clear organization.

Another shift in emphasis can be seen in relation to this same change in the "location" of meaning. Characteristic of earlier criticism was the association of the modern style with certain non-architectural factors of modern society particularly exemplified in the criticism directed to the social level of function. Buildings were seen to express such concepts as the mechanization of modern life, the depersonalization of mass society, the leisure of cruise life. These are all referential meanings of architecture— they are non-architectural factors to which a building points. Later criticism, with its heightened sensitivity to spatial experience, began to respond to the more intrinsic meanings of architecture, meanings derived from the syntax of structure and known not cognitively but experientially, meanings participated in by the architectural structure rather than merely referred to by it. This is the unconscious or tacit dimension of architectural meaning discussed in the previous chapter.[6]

Faced with these comparisons, one may ask why the architecture of the early part of the century was responded to so differently by critics writing then and more recently. If recent critical statements reveal cultural/existential significance in some of those primary monuments of the early modern movement, why did critics who dealt with those buildings at their completion not speak of them in those terms? I believe that the answer lies in the rationalist orientation of the early twentieth century that I have been describing here. Not only were the critics under the normal pressure of the rationalist orientation of the time, but they were also undoubtedly influenced by the rationalist polemic of some of the major spokesmen of the new movement, such as Le Corbusier—men who themselves were responding to the need to make the new style acceptable on economic and intellectual grounds, since world events were not auspicious toward an undertaking which had as its primary motivation anything so "frivolous" as enriching the "feeling" part of human life. Once the battle for acceptance had been won, however, the damages of war could be computed; the reappraisal of functionalism that occupied critics at the mid-century mark revealed the cost in terms of the impoverishment of our environment and the denial of our human sensibilities.

To summarize these various signs of a shift in orientation in architectural criticism of function—from emphasis on exterior appearance to that on interior structure, from man as observer to man as participant, from visual to proprioceptive perception, from one style to a plurality of styles, from referential to syntactical meaning—one can speak of them as revealing a trend away from the rationalistic world view of the early twentieth century to one in the last three decades which, instead of denying the nonrational side of existence, incorporates it into the total experience. It is important to note that the trend is not from one extreme to the other—that is, not from rationalism to anti-rationalism—but from one extreme to a synthesis. That is, early rationalism was based upon a "split between thinking and feeling"; it was based upon a false dichotomy between what was considered "objective" and "subjective" knowing, in which the former was considered to correspond to reality while the latter could not be trusted. The later criticism shows signs of a *healing* of the dichotomy, so that the essential relatedness of the "objective" and "subjective" is recognized. The implication in criticism that man can know more than he can tell or prove reflects an awareness of those powers of tacit knowing, described by Polanyi, which are neither objective nor subjective but which give thinking-and-feeling individuals their *experience* of and contact with the world—a world which takes on reality for them *as* they experience it.

There are some signs that architecture has, since the early part of the century, passed through a period in which, in reaction to rationalism, an emotionalism or sentimentalism was in vogue. The picturesque architecture of the late forties and early fifties was one such response to the call for a New Humanism, but "humanism" in this case meant cozy warmth and nostalgic anti-rationalism. Even New Brutalism, which arose partly in reaction to picturesque, contained strong elements of anti-rationalism. It seemed to attempt to slap man's physical senses awake again by its bluntness.[7] Perhaps if this study had been made in the late fifties, the conclusion would have to have been that "thinking" had been *replaced* by "feeling," rather than having become one with it.

I have spoken of the present situation in architectural criticism as the beginning of a reorientation, but I recognize that enthusiasm for the hope held forth by such a development does not guarantee its continuation nor even substantiate the claim that it is happening. And, admittedly, the concern for cultural/existential significance in architecture is reflected in only a small portion of the total critical writing that appeared in the sixties and seventies; in addition to that criticism described in the previous chapter, there is that which deals exclusively with the other levels of function as if they were separate phenomena, plus all of that criticism which falls into the category of form analysis. This study is, therefore, a limited one and needs to be supplemented by further endeavors to interpret the events in twentieth-century architectural criticism. In addition, the lack of a firm theoretical base for the criticism of cultural/existential function makes proper interpretation of present events in criticism difficult, as explained above. But even without the handicap of such problems as these, no study could interpret future events. Whether the new orientation of some critics in recent years will continue to pervade the wider circle of architectural criticism, only time can tell.

There are, however, several good reasons why the hope for such a growth may not be unfounded. In the first place, there is the respectability and strength of those theoretical sources in philosophy and psychology referred to in the previous chapter and the diminishing gap between them and the orientation implied in architectural criticism. The insights of men like Kierkegaard, Nietzsche, Tillich, Polanyi, and the psychologists who study perception and human knowing are not likely to be quickly forgotten; their influence, already great, will continue to grow in effect.

Second—and of great importance—the critics of tomorrow will be responding to the architecture of today; and if the bias of rationalism is now finally ceasing to distort the critics' vision, they will see in these works qualities that will encourage a fuller understanding of man's architectural experience on the cultural/existential level. Since present-day events in architecture are among the more substantial supports for the belief that criticism is finding a viable new orientation, some of those events should be explicitly mentioned here.

A small book written in 1966 by the architect Robert Venturi purports only to express the author's preference for a complex and contradictory architecture,[8] but his "gentle manifesto" also seems to describe the character of the present age. If Venturi's book is any indication, the desire for the simplicity and logic of earlier structural articulation seems to be giving way to a recognition that life *is* complex and filled with ambiguity, and that successful architecture cannot be otherwise. In support of his argument, Venturi quotes these words of August Heckscher:

> The movement from a view of life as essentially simple and orderly to a view of life as complex and ironic is what every individual passes through in becoming mature. But certain epochs encourage this development: in them the paradoxical or dramatic outlook colors the whole intellectual scene. . . . Amid simplicity and order rationalism is born, but rationalism proves inadequate in any period of upheaval. Then equilibrium must be created out of opposites. Such inner peace as men gain must represent a tension among contradictions and uncertainties. . . . A feeling for paradox allows seemingly dissimilar things to exist side by side, their very incongruity suggesting a kind of truth.[9]

As our view of man expands to accommodate his nonrational faculties and our view of the world enlarges to see its problems and potentialities, so, too, is architecture changing. And there is reason to believe that criticism is changing with it. Vincent Scully, whose critical statements have appeared frequently in these pages, says this of Venturi's book:

> I believe that the future will value it among the few basic texts of our time—one which, despite its anti-heroic lack of pretension and its shift of perspective from the Champs-

Elysées to Main Street, still picks up a fundamental dialogue begun in the twenties, and so connects us with the heroic generation of modern architecture once more.[10]

At the very least, architecture which is characterized by complexity and contradiction will keep us from lapsing back into the rationalist tendency to exclude that which cannot be neatly integrated into a logical whole.

A description of the architecture of the recent past given by Philip Drew in his book *Third Generation*[11] mentions several characteristics which indicate that buildings now being constructed are embodying an existential position of the unity of subjective and objective knowing. Among these he points to the bringing together of the "rational geometric and intuitive organic ideals in a dynamic synthesis."[12] Jørn Utzon is an architect whose work embodies "the third generation's conversion to an organic conception of environmental order which displaced the first generation's rational bias."[13] Drew describes this new organic as the search for intrinsic systems of order, such as those suggested by nature, to substitute for the superimposition of extrinsic structure. Utzon's search for these intrinsic systems of order led him first to an examination of Mayan and Japanese architectural methodology and then to Taliesin West and an encounter with Frank Lloyd Wright. These influences, combined with his study of unselfconscious architecture,[14] led him to an understanding of architecture which places him, in spirit at least, firmly within the ranks of the "third generation." Whereas the first generation's tightly controlled rationalism had resulted often in outbursts of individual artistic genius under the label of self-expression, Utzon makes use of "the anonymous expression of collective consciousness and symbiosis with landscape."[15] In his handling of the relationship between interior and exterior, Utzon ascribes to the third generation preference for a contrast between the inside and the outside, providing an expression of contradiction, as opposed to the earlier rationalist insistence upon the logical articulation of interior arrangement on the exterior of the building.

The third generation's union of rational-geometric with freer systems of order in a new organic is also exemplified in the work of Moshe Safdie, who, through a study of unselfconscious architecture, was led to conclude that the tradition of "fixed architectural composition [must be rejected] in favour of open vernacular building systems responsive to choice, change and growth."[16] Safdie says:

> . . .we must try to find the genetic code of a particular environment. The genetic code produces an infinite number of adaptations, each in itself not finite — not buildings with beginnings and ends, but continuums capable of growth and change. . . . In each case I search for a solution that is organically valid for the particular problem.[17]

Safdie's three-dimensional grid constructions with "plug-in" units to be placed according to the changing needs of the users exemplify his interpretation of an organic "which permits spontaneous random modifications to the architecture without detracting from its wholeness."[18]

This flexible architecture of the third generation may be contrasted to the static relationship between the whole and its parts found in the rationalist interpretration of organic: "If all the distinguishable parts of a whole are essential and in the proper order and if the whole lacks no part necessary for its completeness, then the parts are 'organically related' and the whole has 'organic unity.' "[19] This interpretation of organic reflects the origins of the "biological analogy" in the new science of biology, a science which began in the analyzing and classifying of organisms. It has more to do with the rationalist emphasis on functional differentiation of building parts in a static arrangement than with the living, growing architecture of the third generation.

The basic factor which makes the difference between these two definitions of organic is the element of time. The third-generation architects seem to be attuned to the existentialist understanding of time. Rollo May points out that "the most crucial fact about existence is that it *emerges*—that is, it is always in the process of becoming, always developing in time."[20] Designing an architecture which can change and grow with its inhabitants guarantees an element of vitality never accomplished by the first generation of modern architects. The metabolism group of younger architects bases its work particularly on an interpretation of the biological analogy that allows for organic growth. Kisho Noriaki Kurokawa describes two types of organic metamorphosis: additive growth, as in the addition of new parts, and multiplicative growth, as in urban renewal.[21] In both cases, change is facilitated in a way not permitted by the rationalist definition of an organic whole. The work of all the metabolists is characterized by "the Japanese empathy with nature [which] led to a view of life as a ceaseless flux in which architecture participated."[22]

The interrelationship of the levels of function is also appreciated by the younger generation of architects. Their work reveals a willingness to take advantage of the functional ambiguity of forms denied by orthodox functionalism. In the Hagi Civic Center by Kiyonori Kikutake of the metabolist group, for example, the architect "sought to optimize the opportunities for spontaneous social contact through the ambiguous consideration of the interlocking public areas which connect the specialized auditorium and meeting-rooms."[23] Similarly, Safdie's design for the Student Union at San Francisco State College allows the building's circulatory system to function like a campus green, providing a focus of informal social activity. Drew describes it thus:

...Safdie heaped up the Union building in a manmade hill which extended the grass and plant life over its inclined walls and terraces. Arched over the campus circulation cross-roads, the open hollowed-out hill invited students to wander over it and through it.[24]

Such efforts to create a humanly meaningful environment characterize the work of the third generation. Their goals and philosophy seem to grow out of a sensitivity to the same sorts of human needs and solutions that have motivated the existentialist philosophers and psychologists and which seem now to be appearing as an important thrust in architectural criticism.

I have said that one of the major problems in this analysis of functional criticism is the lack of a complete theoretical base for understanding the cultural/existential level of architecture. That is also the primary obstacle now facing the critic who might wish to pursue such criticism. The critic is faced with the problem of pursuing his task with an incomplete understanding of how architecture operates on the cultural/existential level.

Although I am personally qualified to say very little concerning the actual shape that theoretical base should take, there is one aspect of the problem that I do want to describe: the matter of recognizing and dealing with the interrelatedness of all the "levels" of function. The levels of function discussed in this study may be looked at in terms of the three existential modes of being-in-the-world: *Umwelt, Mitwelt,* and *Eigenwelt.* The *Umwelt* includes the natural world—the environment—but also the human, biological needs, drives, and instincts; thus it corresponds to the physical and psychological levels of function. The *Mitwelt* is the world of relationships with other human beings, and corresponds to the social level of function. The *Eigenwelt,* the mode of relationship to one's self, can be seen to correspond to the cultural/existential level of function in that it is on that level that architecture as art can be regarded as one of the primary instruments in the development of human consciousness.[25] Rollo May says of these modes:

> It should be clear that these three modes of world are always interrelated and always condition each other.... The human being lives in *Umwelt, Mitwelt,* and *Eigenwelt* simultaneously. They are by no means three different worlds but three simultaneous modes of being-in-the-world.[26]

In their buildings, important architects are demonstrating that physical space is never merely physical space, never purely *Umwelt,* but is conditioned by—and conditions—social and personal/existential orientation. Some critics are beginning to realize that treating architectural space in one of these modes by no means completes the task, and that although they may for the purposes of analysis focus on one of the levels of function for a time, a recognition of the fundamental inextricability of the modes of architectural being must underlie their discussion.

In addition to the philosophical argument for the necessity of the critics' recognition of the interrelatedness of the levels of function, there is the imperative placed upon criticism by the younger generation of architects. Forrest Wilson, writing in 1970, had this to say about the current trend in architecture:

> As we begin...a new architecture for the century's end, we find the architect, as never before, undertaking a great variety of activities. He has expanded all of his concerns, including involvement in the economic, political, and social worlds in his search for the parameters of his profession.
>
> Indeed, the search for limits to violate has become as intensive as the search for defintions to reconstruct. The ideas that structure this new order would not have been considered within the domain of the profession fifty years ago.[27]

This expansion of the area of concern in architecture is analogous to the recognition, growing in criticism, of the many-layered significance of architectural function. If the architecture of today is growing out of an involvement in many areas of contemporary life, then critics also will need to be in touch with those areas in order to respond to the architecture.

The critic has always gone about his task through a combination of two basic means of achieving increased understanding of one's environment: the verbal means—the use of one's own and others' verbal explanations and expressions to increase intellectual understanding; the nonverbal means—the tuning in to one's own perceptions, conscious or unconscious, explicit or tacit, visual or nonvisual, in order to get a "feel" for the object or problem. The research described in these pages carries implications for the critic relating to each of these two basic means at his disposal; they are implications concerning the problems connected with the use of those means in view of new insights into architectural and human functioning.

The "verbal" procedure involves the study and assimilation of insights from many different theoretical sources such as those already referred to in these pages. But this way is difficult in the present era for three reasons: first, as stated above, the sources are to be found in such a wide variety of fields, not only fields that are newly related to architecture but also fields that are themselves new—such as information science, linguistics, cybernetics, humanistic psychology; second, the sources are widely scattered geographically and often, because of language or publication problems, they are practically inaccessible;[28] third, much of the theoretical work is still in a nascent stage, lacking in clarity, accuracy, and substantiation.

The second procedure used by the critic in his work is the primarily nonverbal one involving his ability to encounter the architectural object itself—to experience it phenomenologically. Indeed I believe that it is primarily through this channel that most of the insight into cultural/existential function perceivable in recent applied criticism has been achieved. Yet this way also presents a profound difficulty, which needs to be understood. Gaston Bachelard describes the phenomenon of "reverberation," by which a poetic image communicates its meaning to a reader, as a relationship set up between a poem and its reader in which the profound significance of the image echoes back and forth between the being of the reader and that of the poem's creator.[29] For reverberation to take place, the reader must be open to the images of the poem, an openness which, according to Bachelard, necessitates an attitude involving some degree of admiration for the poem. "We can admire more or less, but a sincere impulse, a little impulse toward admiration, is always necessary if we are to receive the phenomenological benefit of a poetic image."[30]

The question is, can a person who approaches a work of art as a critic take up such an open stance *vis-à-vis* the art object? Bachelard apparently believes not:

> Here the phenomenologist has nothing in common with the literary critic who, as has frequently been noted, judges a work that he could not create and, if we are to believe certain facile condemnations, would not want to create. A literary critic is a reader who is necessarily severe.[31]

And thus arises the overarching problem of the critic of the new modern architecture. Indications are strong that this architecture will not be susceptible to an abstract sort of critical perusal, that it holds its most profound mysteries in safe-keeping for him who is willing to approach it with openness and to experience existentially his own "givenness" to the structural images it contains.

Thus a considerable part of the problem for the contemporary critic is to discover how he should approach a building both receptively (or "admiringly," as Bachelard would say) and critically, both intellectually and experientially, both verbally and nonverbally.

It is my belief that the problem is not insoluble, that the two procedures can be used together—and indeed must be. Whereas either one, pursued without the balancing weight of the other, would be fallacious, the proper combining of them avoids that danger. I believe that the "verbal" method, rather than inhibiting the function of the nonverbal one, can, unless it is locked into an abstract rationalism, actually facilitate the experience of phenomenological knowing. Since the phenomenological way of knowing is not a function that can be *made* to happen but one that must be *allowed* to happen, what often is needed to set it into motion is a sense of "permission." In the rationalist era, the prohibition placed on that part of our beings consisted of the belief that information gained "subjectively" was "false." As we learn more of how human perception functions, we come to respect subjective knowing and thus to allow it to inform us. Simultaneously, we come to *experience* those insights which we learned through intellectual means, thus giving *them* a new credence and a *felt* significance. In other words, we come into relation with our environment.

Thus, although a coherent theoretical base for criticism may be lacking, basic critical procedures are not.[32] And while criticism is operating during these years without that secure theoretical base, it may take comfort in the thought that one of the reasons that the theory is so hard to come by is that we are in the midst of a period of great architectural creativity, a period of the breaking of the very boundaries that a theory would attempt to fasten down. And if that is a somewhat frightening thought, we all may look to the hard-won respect for humanity found in the third generation of modern architects:

> The architects of the 1970s know that if their work is to be relevant, it must recognize that things are replaceable. The only unique and irreplaceable element is man. It is here that revolutionary youth, and the architects of today are in agreement. Architecture means whatever it means, but its material is human adaptability and its subject matter is life.[33]

Plates

1. Louis Sullivan. Carson Pirie Scott Store, Chicago, 1899–1904. *Exterior*. (Albert Bush-Brown, *Louis Sullivan*. New York, 1960, Plate 76). This reference will hereafter be listed as *Louis Sullivan*.

2. Louis Sullivan. Carson Pirie Scott Store. *Entrance pavilion.* (*Louis Sullivan,* Plate 76), [Henry Fuermann].

3. Louis Sullivan. Carson Pirie Scott Store. *Detail of ornament,
    entrance pavilion.* (*Louis Sullivan*, Plate 77), [John
    Szarkowski].

4. Frank Lloyd Wright. Robie House, Chicago, 1909–10.
Exterior. (Vincent Scully, Jr., *Frank Lloyd Wright*. New
York, 1960, Plate 39), [Hendrick-Blessing]. This reference will
hereafter be listed as *Frank Lloyd Wright*.

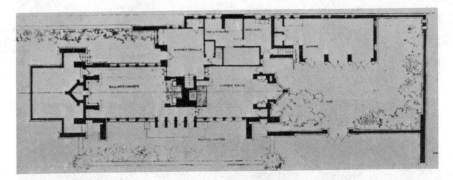

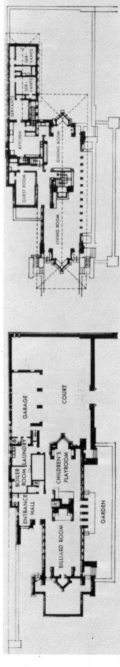

5. Frank Lloyd Wright. Robie House. *View of exterior and plans of ground floor and first floor.* (*Frank Lloyd Wright*, Plates 40 and 41).

6. Frank Lloyd Wright. Robie House. *Living room showing environmental provisions. (The Robie House.* Historic American Building Survey, 1963, Sheet 10). [Drawn by Mary Reyner Banham].

7. Gerrit Rietveld. Schröder House, Utrecht (Holland), 1924. *Exterior from south.* (Theodore M. Brown, *The Work of G. Rietveld.* Utrecht, 1958, Plate 35), [Theodore M. Brown]. This reference will hereafter be listed as *Rietveld.*

8. Gerrit Rietveld. Schröder House. *Exterior view, and plans of three floors.* (Henry A. Millon, *Key Monuments of the History of Architecture.* Englewood Cliffs, New Jersey, p. 507), [Jan Versnel, Amsterdam]. This reference will hereafter be listed as *Key Monuments.*

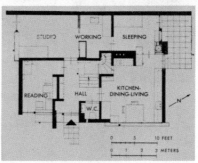

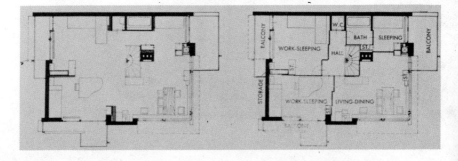

9. Gerrit Rietveld. Schröder House. *Exterior south-west side.* (*Rietveld*, Plate 36), [Jan Versnel, Amsterdam].

10. Gerrit Rietveld. Schröder House. *Detail, corner window, east.* (*Reirveld*, Plate 58), [Theodore M. Brown].

11. Gerrit Rietveld. Schröder House. *Exterior, south-west, showing its visual weightlessness.* (*Rietveld*, Plate 65).

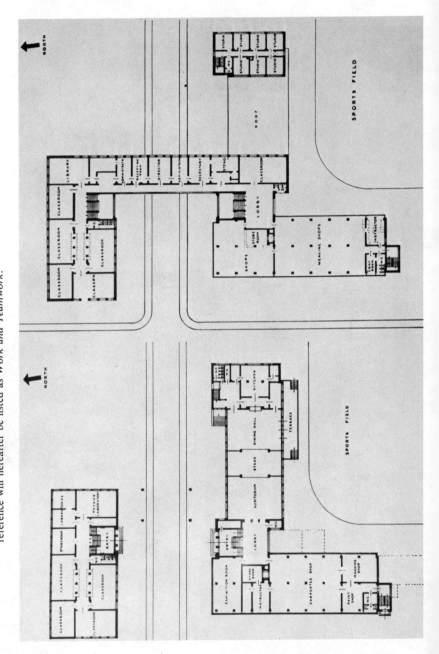

12. Walter Gropius. Bauhaus Buildings, Dessau, 1926. *Ground floor and second floor plans*. (Siegfried Giedion, *Walter Gropius: Work and Teamwork*. New York, 1954, Plates 85 and 86). This reference will hereafter be listed as *Work and Teamwork*.

13. Walter Gropius. Bauhaus Buildings. *View on the left of heavy concrete construction upon which the glass wall (right) was to be hung.* (*Cahiers d'Art,* V (1930), p. 99), [Sigfried Giedion and Lucia Moholy].

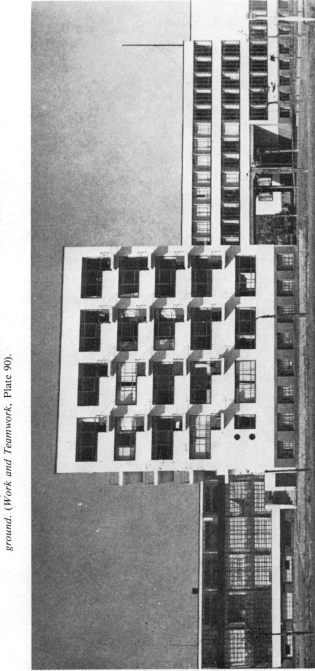

14. Walter Gropius. Bauhaus Buildings. *View from the east with workshop building in the foreground. (Work and Teamwork,* Plate 90).

15. Mies van der Rohe. German Pavilion, International Exposition, Barcelona, Spain, 1929. *Exterior.* (Philip C. Johnson, *Mies van der Rohe.* New York, 1947, p. 67). This reference will hereafter be listed as *Mies van der Rohe.*

16. Mies van der Rohe. Barcelona Pavilion. *Plan and view from end of court. (Key Monuments.* p. 511), [Williams & Meyer].

17. Mies van der Rohe. Barcelona Pavilion. *View across one of the pools.* (Werner Blaser, *Mies van der Rohe: The Art of Structure.* New York, 1965, p. 33). This reference will hereafter be listed as *Art of Structure.*

18. Mies van der Rohe. Barcelona Pavilion. *Interior showing the independence of the walls from the load-bearing columns. (Art of Structure.* p. 29).

19. Mies van der Rohe. Barcelona Pavilion. *Interior with famous
     "Barcelona" chairs. (Mies van der Rohe.* p. 73).

20. Le Corbusier. Villa Savoye at Poissy (France), 1929–31. *North corner.* (Maurice Besset, *Who Was Le Corbusier?* Cleveland, 1968, p. 101). This reference will hereafter be listed as *Who Was.*

21. Le Corbusier. Villa Savoye. *Plan*. (Le Corbusier, *Complete
Works, 1929-1934*. Zurich, 1935, p. 24). This reference will
hereafter be listed as *Complete Works*.

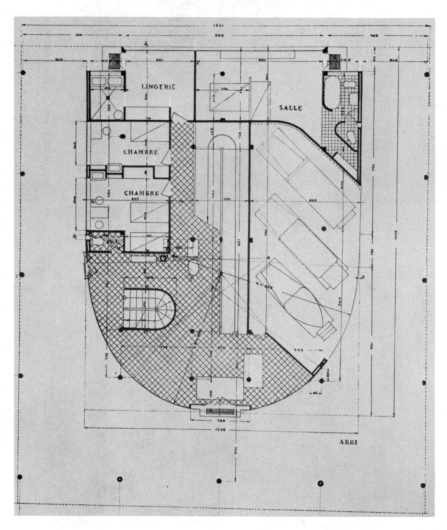

22. Le Corbusier. Villa Savoye. *Entrance vestibule and curved wall with driveway returning toward Paris. (Complete Works.* p. 26).

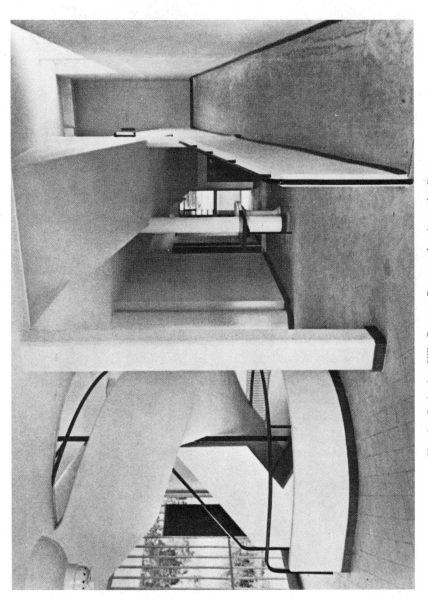

23. Le Corbusier. Villa Savoye. *Ramp and staircase leading to the first floor living quarters.* (*Who Was.* p. 103).

24. Frank Lloyd Wright. Kaufmann House, "Falling Water," Connellsville, Pennsylvania, 1936–37. *From below. (Key Monuments.* p. 515), [Hedrich-Blessing].

25. Frank Lloyd Wright. Kaufmann House. *South elevation.* (*Architectural Forum*, LXVIII (January 1938), p. 41), [Hedrich-Blessing]. This reference will hereafter be listed as *Forum*.

26. Frank Lloyd Wright. Kaufmann House. *Lower terrace and arbor, hanging steps from living room into pool in the stream. (Forum.* p. 40), [Hedrich-Blessing].

27. Frank Lloyd Wright. Kaufmann House. *Exterior corner of living room and guest room with stair well leading to pool.* (*Forum.* p. 43), [Hedrich-Blessing].

28. Frank Lloyd Wright. Kaufmann House. *View from senior Kaufmann's bedroom. (Forum.* p. 39), [Hedrich-Blessing].

29. Alvar Aalto. Baker House Dormitory, Cambridge, Massachusetts, 1947–48. *Exterior, rear, and plans of main floor
(above) and typical floor (below).* (Frederick Guthem, *Alvar
Aalto.* New York, 1960, Plates 46 and 47). This reference will
hereafter be listed as *Alvar Aalto.*

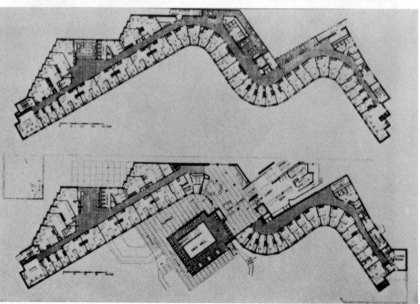

30. Alvar Aalto. Baker House Dormitory. *Exterior, street front. (Alvar Aalto, Plate 48).*

31. Frank Lloyd Wright. Solomon R. Guggenheim Museum, New York, 1946–59. *Exterior, looking southeast across Fifth Avenue. (The Solomon R. Guggenheim Museum, New York, 1960, p. 31). This reference will hereafter be listed as Guggenheim Museum.*

32. Frank Lloyd Wright. Guggenheim Museum. *Entrance*. (*Guggenheim Museum*. p. 34).

33. Frank Lloyd Wright. Guggenheim Museum. *Interior, a few steps inside the entrance.* (*Guggenheim Museum.* p. 38).

34. Frank Lloyd Wright. Guggenheim Museum. *Interior, showing the ramp leading up to the dome. (Guggenheim Museum. p. 39).*

35. Frank Lloyd Wright. Guggenheim Museum. *View of dome.* (*Guggenheim Museum.* p. 41).

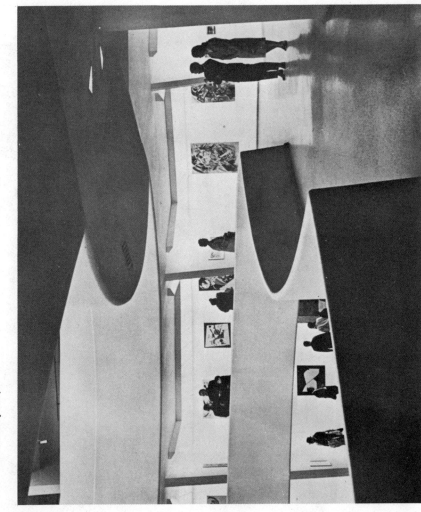

36. Frank Lloyd Wright. Guggenheim Museum. *View of exhibition on upper ramps.* (*Guggenheim Museum.* p. 67).

37. Frank Lloyd Wright. Guggenheim Museum. *View of ramps and main floor from above.* (*Guggenheim Museum.* p. 69).

38.   Mies van der Rohe. Farnsworth House, Plano, Illinois, 1945–50. *View from across Fox River.*   . .
(*Art of Structure.* p. 107).

39. Mies van der Rohe. Farnsworth House. *Terrace, stairs and plan.* (*Architectural Forum,* XCV (October 1951), p. 156), [George H. Steuer].

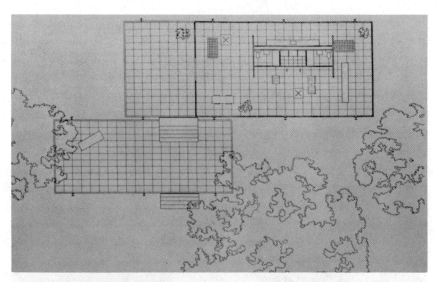

40. Mies van der Rohe. Farnsworth House. *View showing
entrance terrace.* (*Art of Structure.* p. 111).

41. Mies van der Rohe. Farnsworth House. *View from interior looking across Fox River.* (*Art of Structure.* p. 115).

42. Mies van der Rohe. Farnsworth House. *Detail of standard H-Beam column and cornice.* (*Art of Structure.* p. 119).

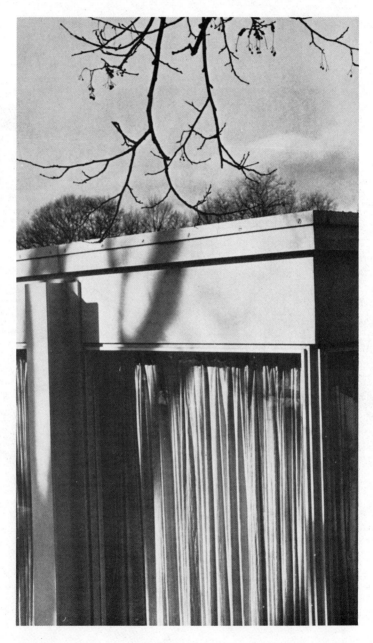

43. Le Corbusier. Chapel of Ronchamp, Notre Dame du Haut, near Belfort (France) 1950-53. *View of east facade and choir.* (*Who Was.* p. 140).

44. Le Corbusier. Chapel of Ronchamp. *View from south east.* (Le Corbusier, *The Chapel at Ron-champ.* New York, 1957, p. 79). This reference will hereafter be listed as *Chapel at Ronchamp.*

45. Le Corbusier. Chapel of Ronchamp. *View from northwest. (Chapel at Ronchamp.* p. 62).

46. Le Corbusier. Chapel of Ronchamp. *View of east facade with pilgrims. (Chapel at Ronchamp.* p. 22).

47. Le Corbusier. Chapel of Ronchamp. *West wall with white plastering and tank of rough concrete under the roof spout.* (*Who Was.* p. 112).

48. Le Corbusier. Chapel of Ronchamp. *The south wall ("light-wall") seen from interior.* (*Who Was.* p. 137).

49. Le Corbusier. Chapel of Ronchamp. *The south wall with worshipers.* (*Chapel at Ronchamp.* p. 16).

50. Le Corbusier. Chapel of Ronchamp. *The south wall showing the gap between wall and roof.* (*Chapel at Ronchamp.* p. 30).

51. Le Corbusier. Chapel of Ronchamp. *The south wall showing the triangular frames of reinforced concrete which support the roof and divide the embrasures and splays of the windows.* (*Chapel at Ronchamp.* p. 97).

52. Le Corbusier. Chapel of Ronchamp. *Isometric diagram.*
    (*Chapel at Ronchamp.* p. 106).

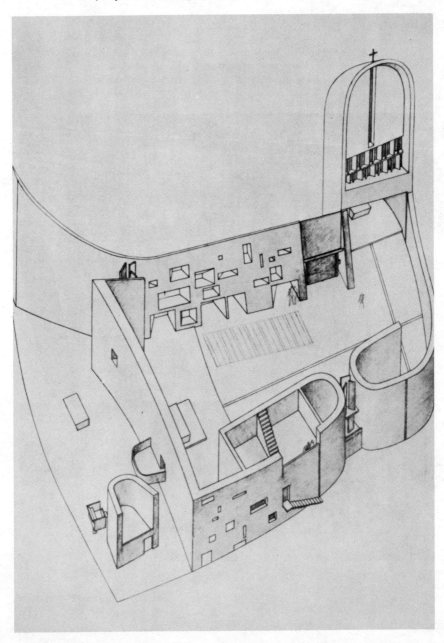

53. Louis Kahn. Richards Medical Research Building, Philadelphia, Pennsylvania, 1960. *Exterior stair towers (right and left) and four air-intake stacks from the south.* (Vincent Scully, Jr., *Louis I. Kahn.* New York, 1960, Plate 71), [John Ebstel]. This reference will hereafter be listed as *Louis I. Kahn.*

54. Louis Kahn. Richards Medical Research Building. *Laboratory towers and service stacks from the north.* (*Louis I. Kahn,* Plate 70), [Malcolm Smith].

55. Louis Kahn. Richards Medical Research Building. *A. North elevation. B. First-floor plan. C. Fifth-floor plan. (Louis I. Kahn,* Plate 66).

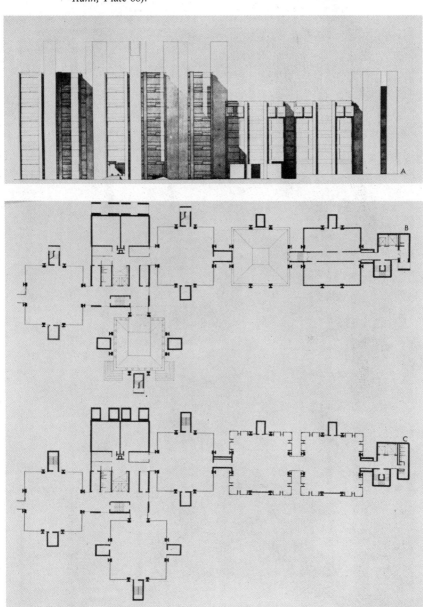

56. Louis Kahn. Richards Medical Research Building. *Entrance.*
(*Louis I. Kahn,* Plate 68), [Crevin Robinson].

57. Louis Kahn. Richards Medical Research Building. *Main
laboratory tower, showing precast concrete structure, vertical
exhaust stacks, stair tower and entrance steps (model).*
(Museum of Modern Art *Bulletin,* XXVIII (1961), p. 12),
[Malcolm Smith].

58. Paul Rudolph. Yale School of Art and Architecture, New Haven, Connecticut, 1964. *Exterior.* (Nikolaus Pevsner, *Studies in Art, Architecture and Design, II.* London, 1968, p. 260).

59. Paul Rudolph. Yale School of Art and Architecture. *Exterior from east, showing the York Street elevation and the main entrance.* (*Architectural Review*, CXXXV (May 1964), p. 324), [Cervin Robinson].

60. Paul Rudolph. Yale School of Art and Architecture. *Main Entrance.* (*Architectural Review*, CXXXV (May 1964), p. 329), [Cervin Robinson].

61. Paul Rudolph. Yale School of Art and Architecture. *Plan of main floor and cutaway view from Chapel Street.* (*Architectural Forum,* CXX (February 1964), 67).

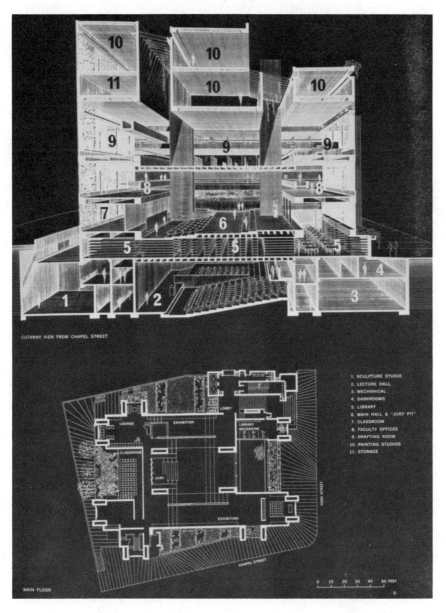

Notes

Chapter 1

1. Although a few architectural theorists in Germany at the turn of the century were pursuing this problem, the effects of their work are only now being felt in this country. See Paul Zucker, "The Paradox of Architectural Theories at the Beginning of the 'Modern Movement,'" *SAHJ,* X (October 1951), pp. 8–14.

2. David R. Weimer, "Lewis Mumford and the Design of Criticism," *Arts and Architecture,* LXXIX (September 1962), p. 14.

3. *The Shape of Time* (New Haven, 1962).

4. There are two reasons for the sparsity of foreign-language examples quoted in the following pages. The first is related to the method of research: the Art Index catalogs considerably fewer foreign-language journals than English-language ones. The second is related to historical events: the two world wars greatly hindered the consistent publication of European architectural journals. My research has indicated, however, that the foreign-language criticism which did appear corroborates consistently that of the English and American critics.

5. *Intentions in Architecture* (Cambridge, Massachusetts, 1965).

Chapter 2

1. *Origins of Functionalist Theory* (New York, 1957).

2. Ibid., p. 232.

3. Peter Collins, *Changing Ideals in Modern Architecture: 1750–1950* (Montreal, 1965), p. 247.

4. Ibid., p. 224.

5. De Zurko, p. 232.

6. Ibid., p. 233.

7. Collins, p. 206.

8. De Zurko, p. 118.

9. Collins, pp. 159–66.

10. For Sullivan's use of the word "function" see his *Kindergarten Chats* (New York, 1947) or Hugh Morrison's *Louis Sullivan, Prophet of Modern Architecture* (New York, 1952), pp. 247–48, 252. For Gropius's use of the word "function" see his "First Proclamation of the Weimar Bauhaus," reprinted in *Bauhaus: 1919–1928*, ed. Herbert Bayer et al. (Boston, 1952), p. 27; *The New Architecture and the Bauhaus* (London, 1955), p. 23; and further references quoted in Marcel Francescano's *Walter Gropius and the Creation of the Bauhaus* (Chicago, 1971), p. 23; and Ludwig Grote's "The Bauhaus and Functionalism," *Bauhaus and Bauhaus People,* ed. Eckhard Neumann (New York, 1970), p. 207.

11. Quoted in Philip Johnson, *Mies van der Rohe* (New York, 1947), p. 192.

12. *Towards a New Architecture* (New York, 1952), p. 7.

13. Morrison, p. 252.

14. Ibid., p 253.

15. Quoted in Collins, p. 152.

16. Quoted in Bruno Zevi's *Towards an Organic Architecture* (London, 1950), p. 99.

17. *The New Architecture*, pp. 23-24.

18. *Towards a New Architecture*, p. 7.

19. Ibid., pp. 12, 89.

20. See particularly "In the Cause of Architecture," *Arch. Record,* XXIII (March 1908), pp. 155–221.

21. Collins, pp. 149–58.

22. *Towards a New Architecture,* pp. 33, 97, 166.

23. "First Proclamation of the Weimar Bauhaus," *Bauhaus: 1919–1928,* p. 27.

24. Quoted in Johnson, p. 184.

25. *An Introduction to Modern Architecture* (Baltimore, 1940), p. 37.

26. Quoted in Morrison, p. 231.

27. Reyner Banham, *Theory and Design in the First Machine Age* (New York, 1960), pp. 220, 223.

28. Henry-Russell Hitchcock and Philip Johnson, *The International Style* (New York, 1932), p. 14.

29. L. Hilberseimer, *Contemporary Architecture: Its Roots and Trends* (Chicago, 1964), pp. 141, 142.

30. Ibid., p. 142. For an English translation of this entire article, see Ulrich Conrad's *Programs and Manifestoes on 20th-Century Architecture* (Cambridge, Massachusetts, 1970), pp. 117–20.

31. Hitchcock and Johnson, p. 36.

32. Zevi, *Organic Architecture,* p. 38.

33. Quoted, idem.

34. He left in 1930 after two years.

35. It is interesting to note that strict functionalism could be used to defend essentially opposite points of view. In the "capitalist" United States the new architecture was heralded as an approach to building which guaranteed "the most advantageous ratio between investment and profit return," while in "communist" Russia it was espoused as an architecture of the people and as such was opposed to a "class-enemy mentality" or a "consumer's psychology."

36. *Theory and Design*, pp. 320–21.

37. Ibid., p. 311.

38. "Machinery and the Modern Style," *New Republic,* XXVII (August 3, 1921), pp. 263–65.

39. "Architecture and the Machine," *American Mercury,* III (September 1924), pp. 77–80.

40. "The Social Background of Frank Lloyd Wright," *Wendingen* (Santpoort, Holland), VII, no. 5 (1925), pp. 65–67. Wright, however, was for Mumford one of the "new poets and artists" who, unlike the group of modernists who "would make the machine and machine-principles dominant," was going to "take possession of the machine, modify it, remold it, humanize it, restoring man to the central position which the 'advance' of the last two hundred years has undermined." (Ibid., pp. 71, 74.)

41. "Machines for Living," *Fortune,* VII (February 11, 1933), p. 78–80.

42. Alberto Sartoris's *Gli Elementi dell'architettura Funzionale* (Milan, 1932) had a similar effect on Italian readers.

43. *Theory and Design*, p. 321.

44. See Barbara Miller Lane's *Architecture and Politics in Germany* (Cambridge, Massachusetts, 1968); Paul Schultze-Naumburg's *A B C des Bauens* (Berlin, 1926) and *Das Gesicht des deutschen Hauses* (Munich, 1929); Bruno Zevi summarizes the situation in France in his *Towards an Organic Architecture,* pp. 39–45.

45. *American Architect*, CXXXVII (May 1930), p. 41.

46. Collins, pp. 243–64.

47. Collins notes that Victor Hugo in the preface to his play *Cromwell* expresses some ideas which relate the idea of ugliness to the concept of the organic in a way similar to a tendency I have noticed in architectural criticism of the 1960s: "Victor Hugo...asserted that beauty was simply that small and almost negligible part of nature which was pleasing to man, whereas everything organic was pleasing to God." (p. 244.)

48. Collins points out that there is a strategic difference between this desire for sincerity, which is subjective, and the desire for truth, such as is demonstrated in the "honest" use of materials and techniques, which is objective. The former, not being susceptible to judgment, is what had an adverse effect on criticism. The latter, being susceptible to judgment, did not have such an effect. It is the importance of the former that Collins stresses. I, however, see great import in the latter because of its influence on the principle of structural articulation found both in early functionalism and later in the Brutalist movement.

49. "...by the end of the nineteenth century,...[architectural periodicals] had virtually

abandoned their original role as diffusers of technical knowledge to become fashion magazines, and this change is well exemplified in the exaggerated publicity given to Art Nouveau, which was certainly never as popular as its publicists contended, or as the numerous magazines devoted to this emphemeral and rootless vogue might lead the uninstructed observer to believe." (Collins, p. 262.)

50. Robin Boyd, "The Functional Neurosis," *Arch. Review,* CXIX (February 1956), p. 87.

Chapter 3

1. Lyndon P. Smith, "An Attempt to give Functional Expression to the Architecture of a Department Store," *Arch. Record,* XVI (July 1904), pp. 53, 59.

2. Richards, *Introduction to Modern Architecture,* pp. 132-33.

3. "Houses USA: A Brief Review of the Development of Domestic Architecture in America," *Arch. Forum,* LXXXVI (May 1947), p. 82.

4. Walter Curt Behrendt, *Modern Building: Its Nature, Problems, and Forms* (New York, 1937), pp. 120, 121.

5. Hilberseimer, *Contemporary Architecture: Its Roots and Trends,* pp. 98-100.

6. *Louis Sullivan: Prophet of Modern Architecture,* p. 199.

7. Henry-Russell Hitchcock, *The Architecture of H. H. Richardson and His Times* (New York, 1936), pp. 293-94.

8. Smith, "An Attempt to give Functional Expression to the Architecture of a Department Store," p. 59.

9. Fiske Kimball, "Louis Sullivan — An Old Master," *Arch. Record,* LVII (April 1925), pp. 302-3.

10. The works of Frank Lloyd Wright have elicited comment on this same basis. Critics frequently have pointed to his honest use of materials in ways which suit their individual natures. See Elizabeth Mock, *Built in USA — Since 1932* (New York, 1943), p. 27; Stow Persons, *Evolutionary Thought in America* (New York, 1956), p. 383; Henry-Russell Hitchcock, *Painting Toward Architecture* (New York, 1948), p. 18.

11. Vincent Scully, *Frank Lloyd Wright* (New York, 1960), p. 16.

12. James Marston Fitch, "Mies van der Rohe and the Platonic Verities," *Four Great Makers of Modern Architecture* (New York, 1963), p. 156.

13. Arthur Drexler, *Ludwig Mies van der Rohe* (New York, 1960), p. 28. See also Howard Dearstyne, "Miesian Space Concept in Domestic Architecture," *Four Great Makers of Modern Architecture* (New York, 1963), pp. 134-35; Jürgen Joedicke, *Architecture Since 1945* (New York, 1969), p. 86; Peter Blake, *Mies van der Rohe: Architecture and Structure* (Baltimore, Maryland, 1960), p. 83.

14. Smith, "An Attempt to give Functional Expression to the Architecture of a Department Store," p. 59.

15. Vincent Scully, "Frank Lloyd Wright and Twentieth-Century Style," *Problems of the 19th and 20th Centuries: Studies in Western Art* (Princeton, 1963), p. 11.

16. Henry-Russell Hitchcock, *Modern Architecture: Romanticism and Reintegration* (New York, 1929), p. 114.

17. Henry-Russell Hitchcock, *Modern Architecture: International Exhibition* (New York, 1932), pp. 58, 60-61. See also Martin van Treeck and François Loyer's "Bauhaus," *L'Oeil,* CLXII-CLXIII (June-July 1968), p. 22.

18. See Museum of Modern Art, *What is Modern Architecture?* (New York, 1942), p. 28; Hilberseimer, *Contemporary Architecture: Its Roots and Trends,* p. 139; Cranston Jones, *Architecture Today and Tomorrow* (New York, 1961), pp. 50-51.

19. Hilberseimer, *Contemporary Architecture: Its Roots and Trends,* p. 139; van Treeck and Loyer, p. 22; James Marston Fitch, *Walter Gropius* (New York, 1960), p. 22.

20. Hitchcock, *Modern Architecture: International Exhibition,* p. 58.

21. Hitchcock, *Modern Architecture: Romanticism and Reintegration,* p. 189.

22. James Marston Fitch, "Utopia Revisited, the Bauhaus at Dessau Forty Years On," *Arch. Review,* CXLI (February 1967), p. 99.

23. Robin Boyd, *The Puzzle of Architecture* (Melbourne, Australia, 1965), pp. 72-73.

24. Joedicke, *Architecture Since 1945,* p. 115; cf. p. 64.

25. Vincent Scully, "Doldrums in the Suburbs," *Perspecta,* IX/X (1965), p. 290.

26. Robert Venturi, *Complexity and Contradiction in Architecture* (New York, 1966), p. 88.

27. Robert Venturi refers to a dual function of Kahn's brick service towers in his discussion of the "double-functioning element" in *Complexity and Contradiction in Architecture,* pp. 41-42.

28. Boyd, *The Puzzle of Architecture,* pp. 132-33. A decidedly negative appraisal of the effects of this dichotomy is offered by Reynor Banham in "On trial: The Buttery Hatch Aesthetic," *Arch. Review,* CXXXI (March 1962), p. 203-6. Banham's primary objection is that the towers housing mechanical services are given an importance out of proportion to their subsidiary relation to the parts of the building which house the human occupants.

29. John Jacobus, *Twentieth Century Architecture: The Middle Years* (New York, 1966), pp. 192-93.

30. Boyd, *The Puzzle of Architecture,* p. 133.

31. Jacobus, *Twentieth Century Architecture: The Middle Years,* p. 193.

32. One critical statement said that Kahn had been dubbed by some a "Neo-Brutalist," but wrongly so. See Henry-Russell Hitchcock, "Notes of a Traveller: Wright and Kahn, *Zodiac,* VI (1960), p. 20.

33. William H. Jordy, "Medical Research Building for Penn. U., Phila," *Arch. Review,* CXXIX (February 1961), p. 100.

34. Boyd, *The Puzzle of Architecture,* pp. 132-33.

35. Jordy, "Medical Research Building for Penn. U., Phila.," p. 100.

36. In addition, I observed the relative importance of the two divisions of structural articulation, and found that during the period before 1950, articulation of structural methods and materials was of primary concern, while after that time the two divisions were of about equal interest to critics. By way of an attempt to offer some explanation of the phenomenon I should say that I see a possible relationship between the increased con-

cern with architecture as a frame for human activity and the call for a new humanism in architecture that arose particularly in the forties and fifties. This trend in criticism will be discussed more fully in Chapters 5 and 6.

37. Peter Collins, as mentioned in Chapter 2, puts the emphasis on sincerity, a subjective aspect of artistic creation. I am here emphasizing truthfulness, a more objective quality (more objective in this case because measurable against the standard of revelation of structure), because it seems to be pertinent to the twentieth-century idea of structural articulation and to have been an outgrowth of nineteenth-century Romanticism via the Realist school. (See above p. 29).

38. *The International Style,* p. 20.

39. Ibid., pp. 56–57.

40. Ibid., p. 70.

41. "Form follows function — or does it?" *Arch. Forum,* CVIII (April 1958), p. 99.

42. Scully, "Doldrums in the Suburbs," pp. 36–47.

Chapter 4

1. Norberg-Schulz, *Intentions in Architecture,* pp. 112ff.

2. Reyner Banham, *The Architecture of the Well-Tempered Environment* (Chicago, 1969).

3. Cranston Jones, *Architecture Today and Tomorrow* (New York, 1961), p. 38.

4. Peter Blake, *The Master Builders* (New York, 1961), p. 61.

5. See "Art Serves Science," *Arch. Record,* CXXVIII (August 1960), p. 152; see also Banham's attack on the effectiveness of the solution in "On Trial: The Buttery Hatch Aesthetic," pp. 203–6.

6. Fitch, "Mies van der Rohe and the Platonic Verities," pp. 161–62.

7. Banham, *The Architecture of the Well-Tempered Environment,* pp. 231–32.

8. Blake, *The Master Builders,* p. 62.

9. Idem.; Fitch, "Utopia Revisited, The Bauhaus at Dessau Forty Years On," *Arch. Review,* CLXI (February 1967), p. 98.

10. *The Architecture of the Well-Tempered Environment,* pp. 232–33.

11. Ibid., p. 121.

12. Idem.

13. Ibid., pp. 151–52.

14. Morrison, *Louis Sullivan: Prophet of Modern Architecture,* pp. 198–99.

15. Grant C. Manson, *Frank Lloyd Wright to 1910* (New York, 1958), p. 199.

16. Jones, *Architecture Today and Tomorrow,* p. 38.

17. Sigfried Giedion, *Space, Time and Architecture* (Cambridge, Massachusetts, 1941), p. 413.

18. Jones, *Architecture Today and Tomorrow,* p. 66.

19. Idem.

20. Colin St. John Wilson, "Gerrit Rietveld: 1888–1964," *Arch. Review,* CXXXVI (December 1964), p. 399.

21. Robert A. M. Stern, *New Directions in American Architecture* (New York, 1969), p. 11.

22. Philip Johnson, quoted in Susan Braudy's "The Architectural Metaphysic of Louis Kahn," *The New York Times Magazine,* Nov. 15, 1970, p. 92.

23. Lewis Mumford, "Skyline: What Wright Hath Wrought," *The New Yorker*, December 5, 1959, p. 112.

24. Peter Blake, "The Guggenheim: Museum or Monument?," *Arch. Forum,* CXI (December 1959), pp. 89–90.

25. See above p. 8ff. and p. 17ff.

26. The call for a "New Humanism" in architecture will receive further discussion in the next chapter as will the criticism by Lewis Mumford dealing with the psychological results of mechanized environmental control. Mumford is perhaps the one critic who before 1940 was consistently and urgently concerned about environmental control and with the attitude toward the machine manifested by early modern architecture in this country. Since his primary concern, however, had to do with the psychological effects of the common practice, further detail on this subject belongs in Chapter 5.

27. My interpretation of this tendency in criticism is corroborated by Reyner Banham's findings as reported in *The Architecture of the Well-Tempered Environment* (pp. 12–13): "...the art of writing and expounding the history of architecture has been allowed—by default and academic inertia—to become narrowed to the point where almost its only interest outside the derivation of styles is haggling over the primacy of inventions in the field of structures. Of these two alternatives, the study of stylistic derivations now predominates to such an extent that the great bulk of so-called historical research is little more than medieval disputation on the number of influences that can balance upon the point of a pinnacle." Banham states that the topic of environmental control has become of interest to critics only as it has begun to shape the visible external form of buildings, and he points to Kahn's Richards building of 1961 as a case in point. The noticeable rise in the 1960s of criticism dealing with environmental control and of negative appraisal in criticism coincides, thus, with the appearance of that building. Banham points out that Wright's Larkin building of 1906 might justifiably have had the same effect if it were not for the strength of the visual bias in architectural writing. Interestingly, a good proportion of the criticism of the sixties characterized by negative appraisal and/or concern with environmental control, as I stated above, pertains to buildings completed earlier in the century.

28. "Mies van der Rohe and the Platonic Verities," p. 162.

29. Ibid., p. 163.

30. *Mies van der Rohe: Architectur and Structure,* p. 56.

31. Ibid., pp. 56–57.

32. *Frank Lloyd Wright: Architecture and Space* (Baltimore, 1960), p. 118.

33. "The Guggenheim: Museum or Monument?," p. 87.

34. Ibid., p. 91.

35. Stern, *New Directions in American Architecture,* p. 34.

36. Jan C. Rowan, "Editorial: The New School of Art and Architecture," *Progressive Arch.,* XLV (February 1964), p. 107.

37. "The Functional Neurosis," pp. 85–88.

38. *The Puzzle of Architecture,* p. 151.

Chapter 5

1. Jones, *Architecture Today and Tomorrow,* p. 78.

2. "The Modern Gallery," *Arch. Forum,* LXXXIV (January 1946), p. 82.

3. "Solomon R. Guggenheim Memorial Museum," *Arch. Forum,* LXXXVIII (January 1948), p. 137.

4. Alexander Elliot, "Notes Toward an Ideal Museum," *Art in America,* No. 1 (1960), p. 66.

5. Norris Kelly Smith, *Frank Lloyd Wright* (Englewood Cliffs, New Jersey, 1966), pp. 75–76.

6. Carl Binger Troedsson, *Two Standpoints Towards Modern Architecture* (Goteborg, 1951), p. 9.

7. *Complexity and Contradiction in Architecture,* p. 25.

8. Jones, *Architecture Today and Tomorrow,* p. 67.

9. Blake, *The Master Builders,* p. 66.

10. Manson, *Frank Lloyd Wright to 1910,* p. 200.

11. Giedion, *Space, Time and Architecture,* p. 545.

12. Paul Rudolph, "Regionalism in Architecture," *Perspecta,* IV (1957), p. 16.

13. Jordy, "Medical Research Building for Penn. U., Phila.," p. 105.

14. Thomas H. Creighton, "Seagram House Re-Reassessed," *Progressive Arch.,* XL (June 1959), p. 143.

15. Reyner Banham, *Guide to Modern Architecture* (London, 1962), pp. 49–50.

16. Alvar Aalto and K. Fleig, eds., *Alvar Aalto: Verlag für Architektur* (Zurich, 1963), p. 135.

17. Anonymous, "M.I.T. Senior Dormitory," *Arch. Forum,* XCI (August 1949), p. 63.

18. If the critic permits his feelings to distort his perception of the forms which have evoked them, however, he risks committing what Monroe C. Beardsley and W. C. Wimsatt, Jr., have called the "Affective Fallacy." *The Verbal Icon* (Lexington, 1954), pp. 21–39. Although Beardsley and Wimsatt discuss poetry, I feel that their conclusions are also quite applicable to a discussion of architecture. In their definition of the Affective Fallacy, the word "building" can be substituted for "poem" (p. 21): "The Affective Fallacy is a confusion between the poem and its results (what it is and what is does).... It begins by trying to derive the standard of criticism from the psychological effects of the poem and ends in impressionism and relativism. The outcome of...[the Affective Fal-

lacy] is that the poem itself, as an object of specifically critical judgment, tends to disappear." See also Mark Spilka, "The Affective Fallacy Revisited," *Southern Review: An Australian Journal of Literary Studies,* I (Adelaide, 1965), pp. 57–72, 77–79, and John V. Hagopian, "In Defence of the Affective Fallacy," Ibid., pp. 72–77.

19. Arthur Drexler, *Built in USA: Post-War Architecture* (New York, 1952), p. 21.

20. "M.I.T. Senior Dormitory," p. 68.

21. Jacobus, *Twentieth-Century Architecture: The Middle Years, 1940–65,* p. 22.

22. Manson, *Frank Lloyd Wright to 1910,* p. 199.

23. "Art and Architecture Building, Yale University, Architect: Paul Rudolph," *Arch. Review,* CXXXV (May 1964), p. 332.

24. Sibyl Moholy-Nagy, "Yale's School of Art and Architecture: The Measure," *Arch. Forum,* CXX (February 1964), p. 79.

25. More about this trend in the sixties will appear in Chapter 7.

26. *The Architecture of Humanism* (London). See also Vincent Scully's discussion of this concept in relation to Scott and the architecture of Sullivan in "Louis Sullivan's Architectural Ornament: a brief note concerning humanist design in the age of force," *Perspecta,* V (1959), pp. 74–75, and Reyner Banham's critique of Scott's theory in his *Theory and Design in the First Machine Age,* p. 67.

27. Vincent Scully, Jr., "Frank Lloyd Wright and Twentieth-Century Style," p. 12.

28. Art and Architecture Building, Yale University, Architect: Paul Rudolph," p. 326. The use of the concept of empathy in criticism lies very close to the idea of the Pathetic Fallacy, first defined by John Ruskin in the third volume of his *Modern Painters.* ("Of the Pathetic Fallacy," Chapter XII, New York, 1882, pp. 152–67.) His discussion refers to the overuse by certain artists and poets of the device of attributing human feelings and powers to natural objects. Ruskin deals with an artist's representation of natural objects. Ruskin deals with an artist's representation of natural objects, but his remarks may also be applied to a critic's representation of an art object. If Ruskin objects to Kingsley's description of the ocean as "the cruel, crawling foam" in *The Sands of Dee* ("The foam is not cruel, neither does it crawl."), he might also object to the statement quoted above: buildings cannot be taciturn nor do they gesticulate. For further discussion of the Pathetic Fallacy, see James K. Robinson, "Pathetic Fallacy," *Encyclopedia of Poetry and Poetics,* edited by Alex Preminger, (Princeton, 1965), pp. 606–7, and Bertram Morris, "Ruskin on the Pathetic Fallacy, or On How a Moral Theory of Art May Fail," *JAAC,* XIV (December 1955), pp. 248–66.

29. "The Social Front of Modern Architecture in the 1930s," *SAHJ,* XXIV (March 1965), p. 52.

30. "Machinery and the Modern Style," p. 265.

31. "Architecture and the Machine," p. 79.

32. "Architecture and the Machine," p. 77–80; "The Architecture of Escape," *The New Republic,* (August 12, 1925), pp. 321–22; "Towards a Rational Modernism," *The New Republic* (April 25, 1928), pp. 297–98.

33. *Arch. Forum,* LXXIII (December 1940), pp. 505–6.

34. *Space, Time and Architecture,* p. 585.

35. *Space, Time and Architecture,* revised edition (1963), p. 565.

36. Ibid., p. 603.

37. *An Introduction to Modern Architecture.*

38. London, 1946.

39. *The New Brutalism* (New York, 1966), p. 13.

40. "Picturesque," *Arch. Review,* CXV (April 1954), p. 229.

41. "The Next Step?," *Arch Review,* CVII (March 1950), p. 180.

42. Ibid., p. 181.

43. Banham, *The New Brutalism,* pp. 46, 47.

44. Discussions of monumentality and the "new organic" are more relevant to the next Chapters, 6 and 7, respectively.

Chapter 6

1. Reyner Banham has said that this century has seen the invention of more new building types than all of the previous history of architecture. *Guide to Modern Architecture* (London, 1962), pp. 21–22.

2. Edgar Kaufmann, Jr., ed., *Louis Sullivan and the Architecture of Free Enterprise* (Chicago, 1956), p. 10.

3. James M. Fitch, "A building of rugged fundamentals," *Arch. Forum,* CXIII (July 1960), p. 185.

4. Giedion, *Space, Time and Architecture,* p. 528.

5. Hitchcock, *Modern Architecture: International Exhibition,* p. 32.

6. Paul Schweirkher, "One Hundred Years of Significant Building," *Arch. Record,* CXX (February 1957), p. 206.

7. Edgar Kaufmann, Jr., "Centrality and Symmetry in Wright's Architecture," *Architects' Yearbook 9,* edited by Trevor Dannatt (London 1960), p. 126.

8. Joedicke, *Architecture Since 1945,* p. 32.

9. John Jacobus, Jr., "Le Corbusier: Fantasy and the International Style," *Arts and Architecture,* LXXV (February 1958), p. 30.

10. "Chapel at Ronchamp," RAIC Journal, XXXV (November 1958), p. 432.

11. N. Salkauskis, "Mies van der Rohe and Le Corbusier," *RAIC Journal,* XXXV (March 1958), p. 83.

12. John Ely Burchard, "A pilgrimage: Ronchamp, Raincy, Vézelay," *Arch. Record,* CXXIII (March 1958), p. 176.

13. Albert Christ-Janer and Mary Mix Foley, "Chapel of Notre Dame du Haut," *Modern Church Architecture* (New York, 1962), pp. 116–17.

14. Peter Hammond, "A Liturgical Brief," *Arch. Review,* CXXIII (April 1958), p. 244.

15. Jacobus, *Twentieth-Century Architecture: The Middle Years,* p. 89.

16. Idem.

17. See above p. 55.

18. "Art and Architecture Building, Yale University, Architect: Paul Rudolph," p. 326.

19. "The Social Front of Modern Architecture in the 1930s," pp. 48–52; see above p. 100.

20. G. L. Hersey, "Replication Replicated, or Notes on American Bastardy," *Perspecta,* IX-X (1965), p. 230.

21. Paul Rudolph, "Yale Art and Architecture Building," *Arts and Architecture,* LXXXI (February 1964), p. 34.

22. Banham, *Guide to Modern Architecture,* pp. 146–50.

23. Ibid., p. 24.

24. Giedion, *Space, Time and Architecture,* p. 332.

25. G. A. Platz, *Wohnräume der Gegenwart* (Berlin, 1933), p. 39, translated in Theodore Brown, *The Work of G. Rietveld Architect* (Utrecht, 1958), p. 58.

26. Wayne Andrews, *Architecture, Ambition and Americans: A Social History of American Architecture* (New York, 1966), p. 243.

27. Blake, *The Master Builders,* p. 53.

28. Banham, *Guide to Modern Architecture,* p. 25.

29. Troedsson, *Two Standpoints Towards Modern Architecture,* pp. 11–12.

30. John Alford, "Modern Architecture and the Symbolism of the Creative Process," *College Art J.,* XIV no. 2 (1955), pp. 104–5.

31. Giedion, *Space, Time and Architecture,* pp. 332–33.

32. *Frank Lloyd Wright,* pp. 60–61.

33. Ibid., p. 135.

34. Lewis Mumford, "The Case Against 'Modern Architecture,'" *Arch. Record,* CXXXI (April 1962), p. 159.

35. "Six Recent Buildings in the U.S.A.: Farnsworth House," *Architects' Year Book 5* (London, 1953), p. 159.

36. No title or author, *Arch. Forum,* XCV (October 1951), p. 160.

37. Sigfried Giedion, *Walter Gropius: Work and Teamwork* (New York, 1954), p. 56.

38. Alford, "Modern Architecture and the Symbolism of Creative Process," pp. 105–6.

39. Scully, "Louis Sullivan's Architectural Ornament," p. 80. This example, in my opinion, makes use of the concept of empathy discussed in the previous chapter; some may see here also an example of the "Pathetic Fallacy"; see above p. 99.

40. Robin Boyd, "The Engineering of Excitement," *Arch. Review,* CXXIV (November 1958), p. 306.

41. Fitch, "Mies van der Rohe and the Platonic Verities," p. 155.

42. English translation: There it is, the spirit of the new Germany: simplicity and clarity of means and intentions—all open to the air, boldly free—nothing blocks access to our hearts. A work honestly made, without arrogance. There it is, the tranquil house of the pacified Germany." Nicolas M. Rubio Tuduri, "Le Pavillon de l'Allemagne à l'Exposition de Barcelone," *Cahiers d'Art,* IV (1929), p. 410.

43. Mumford, "Skyline: What Wright Hath Wrought," p. 110.

44. Vincent Scully, Jr., "Recent Works by Louis Kahn—Laboratory Towers, Philadelphia, Pa.," *Zodiac,* XVII (1967), p. 67.

45. See *Architecture You and Me* (Cambridge, Massachusetts, 1958), p. 22, for details of how Giedion, together with Fernand Léger and José Luis Sert, arrived at this term.

46. *Architecture You and Me,* p. 28.

47. *The Human Prospect, Collected Essays of Lewis Mumford,* edited by Harry T. Moore (Boston, 1955), pp. 212-13.

48. See Scully, "Doldrums in the Suburbs," pp. 36-47, and Kenneth Frampton, "Labour, Work & Architecture," *Meaning in Architecture,* edited by Charles Jencks and George Baird (New York, 1969), pp. 151-70.

49. "The Architecture of Escape," pp. 321-22.

50. "Nine Points on Monumentality," *Architecture You and Me,* p. 50.

51. "Monumentalism, Symbolism and Style," p. 114.

52. The terms are taken from Walter Curt Behrendt, quoted in Zevi, *Towards an Organic Architecture,* pp. 69-70.

53. Ibid., p. 137.

54. *Architecture as Space* (New York, 1957), p. 157.

55. *Architecture You and Me,* pp. 157-99.

56. Ibid., pp. 196, 199.

Chapter 7

1. No title or author, *Arch. Forum,* XCV (October 1951), p. 157.

2. In the case of structural articulation, this has been done in terms of the critics' own use of the word "function," since the category is qualitatively different from the others. (See above p. 37.)

3. Norberg-Schulz, *Intentions in Architecture,* p. 122.

4. Norberg-Schulz, "Meaning in Architecture," *Meaning in Architecture,* edited by Charles Jencks and George Baird (New York, 1969), pp. 216 ff.

5. "The Nature of Religious Language," *Theology of Culture* (New York, 1964), pp. 54ff.

6. Ernesto N. Rogers, "Le Corbusier's Day Dream," *Arts and Architecture,* LXXX (September 1963), p. 17.

7. I find Rogers's use of the preposition "outside" misleading. It would seem that a "perenially valid formula" for the house of Everyman should not be referred to as "out-

side the parameters of time and space" because it is so dependent upon those two elements for its meaning — indeed, the formula derives its meaning from the parameters of time and space. Similarly, it would seem more accurate to refer to this formula as *underlying* "the individual character of the individual man" rather than "outside" it, since a perenially valid formula is one which is basic enough to be commonly meaningful to all individuals — not to none.

8.   *Space, Time and Architecture*, p. 413.

9.   *Two Standpoints Towards Modern Architecture: Wright and Le Corbusier.* The reference to Kant is on page 3. Troedsson summarizes Spengler's ideas thus:

> The Totem world Spengler refers to is the world of Being, in which our human micro-cosmos lives in an intimate association with the cosmos. Totem man is as one with this existence, his feet planted sturdily on this earth from which he draws his inspiration, strength and courage.
>
> Taboo to primitive man is that which is secret, unfathomable and surrounded by fear. Whereas the primitive man avoids that which is taboo, modern man seeks its causes, its laws. This Spengler calls the world of Waking-Being, in which man stands apart from existence, like a stranger watching a gay party through the windows of a brightly lit-up house, like a child, or a man for that matter, taking a toy apart to appraise it and judge it. The Taboo man turns our taboos around to investigate them, to see how they are made, how they ought to be made, what unknown powers lie behind. This is the incessantly awake, who lives not in harmony with and as one with his existence, but in constant tension with it. (pp. 3–4.)

10.   Troedsson, *Two Standpoints,* p. 11; Giedion, *Space, Time and Architecture,* p. 413.

11.   Ibid., pp. 413–14; Blake, *The Master Builders,* p. 61.

12.   Fitch, "A Building of Rugged Fundamentals," p. 83.

13.   Blake, "The Guggenheim: Museum or Monument?", p. 89. See also the statement quoted on page 46 of this study that the Guggenheim "will be a constant admonition to all those who see it. . .that creation is, among other things, a constant process of challenging and questioning accepted notions, everywhere."

14.   *Phenomenology of Perception,* translated by Colin Smith (New York, 1962), p. 250.

15.   *Existence,* (New York, 1967), p. 11.

16.   "Concluding Unscientific Postscript," *A Kierkegaard Anthology,* edited by Robert Bretall (Princeton, 1951), pp. 210–11.

17.   May, *Existence,* p. 26.

18.   *Gestalt Therapy* (New York, 1951), p. 228.

19.   "Semiology and Architecture," *Meaning in Architecture,* p. 16.

20.   Jacobus, "Le Corbusier: Fantasy and the International Style," p. 30.

21.   G. M. Kallmann, "The 'Action' Architecture of a New Generation," *Arch. Forum,* CXI (October 1959), p. 136.

22.   "Form and Design," reproduced in Vincent Scully, *Louis I. Kahn* (New York, 1962), pp. 115ff.

23. See Rollo May's definition of existentialism quoted above, p. 80.

24. Sheldon Nodelman, "Structural analysis in art and anthropology," *Yale French Studies,* XXXVI and XXXVII (October 1966), p. 98.

25. Scully, *Frank Lloyd Wright,* p. 21.

26. "Frank Lloyd Wright and the New Pioneers," *Arch. Record,* LXV (April 1929), p. 416.

27. Stow Persons, ed., *Evolutionary Thought in America* (New York, 1956), pp. 344-45.

28. Sibyl Moholy-Nagy, "The Future of the Past," *Perspecta,* VII (1961), p. 74.

29. Jacobus, "Le Corbusier: Fantasy and the International Style," p. 30.

30. Carl W. Condit, *The Chicago School of Architecture* (Chicago, 1964), p. 172.

31. In the example just quoted, the critic continues, saying, "In its naturalistic character — its iconographic content, so to speak — it clearly represents the organic world of growth and fertility." I believe he is rightly making a distinction here between the verbalizable *iconographic* content and the nonverbal *iconological* content. The latter is Erwin Panofsky's term for the cultural/existential meaning, while he uses "iconography" to refer to the "conventional subject matter." *Meaning in the Visual Arts* (New York, 1955), p. 26.

32. Hersey, "Replication Replicated, or Notes on American Bastardy," pp. 229-30.

33. "A & A: Yale School of Art and Architecture," *Progressive Arch.,* XLV (February 1964), p. 113.

34. *The Tacit Dimension* (Garden City, New York, 1966), p. 4ff.

35. Ibid., pp. 7-10.

36. *The Poetics of Space* (Boston, 1969), pp. xii-xiii.

37. Jacobus, *Twentieth-Century Architecture: The Middle Years,* pp. 22-23.

38. *Frank Lloyd Wright,* p. 30.

39. "The Heritage of Wright," *Zodiac,* VIII (1961), p. 12.

40. pp. 105-35.

41. Carl John Black, "A vision of human space," *Arch. Record,* CLIV (July 1973), p. 105. For discussion of primitive cult structures in Le Corbusier's chapel at Ronchamp, see Sigfried Giedion, *Space, Time and Architecture* (1967), p. 578. For a detailed description of Ronchamp in terms of a prehistoric megalith, see Jacobus, *Twentieth-Century Architecture: The Middle Years,* p. 86. Ancient symbolic meanings of caves are treated in Christian Norberg-Schulz, *Intentions in Architecture,* pp. 125-126, and Sigfried Giedion, *The Eternal Present: The Beginnings of Architecture* (New York, 1964). Phallic and other symbols in Wright's work are discussed by Vincent Scully, *Frank Lloyd Wright,* pp. 16ff. See also Gaston Bachelard's phenomenological analyses in *The Psychoanalysis of Fire, Water and Dreams, Air and Revery, The Earth and the Reveries of the Will,* and *The Earth and the Reveries of Rest.*

42. *Changing Ideals in Modern Architecture: 1750-1950,* p. 285.

43. Idem.

44. Idem.

45. Ibid., p. 286.

46. Ibid., pp. 286–87.

47. Ibid., p. 287.

48. The concept of Space-Time presented by Sigfried Giedion in his book *Space, Time and Architecture*, although the book itself has been widely read and discussed, does not seem to have influenced greatly the discussions of space in criticism dealing with the cultural/existential level of architectural function. The explanation may be the lack of philosophical precision of Giedion's exposition of his concept. For discussion of the flaws in the concept, see Christian Norberg-Schulz, *Intentions in Architecture*, p. 12; and Peter Collins, *Changing Ideals in Modern Architecture*, pp. 287–93.

49. *Guide to Modern Architecture*, p. 49.

50. L. Hilberseimer, *Mies van der Rohe* (Chicago, 1956), p. 42.

51. "Frank Lloyd Wright and the Conquest of Space," *Mag. Art,* XLIII (May 1950), p. 89.

52. Ibid., p. 88.

53. Salkauskis, "Mies van der Rohe and Le Corbusier," p. 82.

54. L. Hilberseimer, *Mies van der Rohe*, p. 42.

55. English translation: "In the evolution of man, little by little his habitat has lost its function of sheltering him against danger and has transformed itself into a constructed space which is an intensification of universal space. In this evolution, the habitation constructed by Rietveld in Utrecht in 1928 [sic] marks a decisive phase." J. B. Bakema, "Le Bâtiment Public ou l'Architecture des Jonctions," *Arch. d'Aujourd'hui,* XXXIX (December 1967), p. 2.

56. Banham, *Guide to Modern Architecture*, p. 50.

57. Quoted in John Milner, "Ideas and Influences of De Stijl," *Studio International,* CLXXV (March 1968), p. 118.

58. *Icon and Idea* (New York, 1965), p. 20.

59. *Existence, Space, and Architecture* (New York, 1971), p 18.

60. "Meaning in Architecture," p. 244.

61. *Existence, Space and Architecture*, p. 20. Since in Mies's Farnsworth house the limit or border is so extremely minimized, it is difficult for most people to think of it as a suitable home. The more successful Philip Johnson house has the benefit of the trees around it which not only are strategic in the control of climatic elements but also serve to represent a "wall."

62. Ibid., p. 27.

63. *Le Corbusier und Pierre Jeanneret: Ihr Gesamtes Werk von 1929–1934* (Zurich, 1935), p. 24.

64. Maurice Besset, *Who was Le Corbusier?* (New York, 1968), p. 130.

65. For the relation between subception and tacit knowing see Michael Polanyi, *The Tacit Dimension,* p. 7.

66. Sibyl Moholy-Nagy. "Sunday Session," *SAHJ,* XXIV (March 1965), p. 81.

67. Scully, *Frank Lloyd Wright*, p. 31.

68. "Whence and Whither: The Processional Element in Architecture," *Perspecta*, IX and X (1965), p. 168.

69. "Whence and Whither," p. 168.

70. *Existence, Space and Architecture*, pp. 21–22. See also Rudolph Schwarz, *The Church Incarnate* (Chicago, 1958), pp. 114–53; and Sigfried Giedion's discussion of "sacred wandering" in the architecture of ancient Egypt, Mesopotamia, and Greece in *The Eternal Present: The Beginnings of Architecture* (New York, 1964), pp. 396–400.

71. "Building years of a Yale Man: A. W. Griswall," *Arch. Forum*, CXVIII (June 1963), p. 92.

72. Moholy-Nagy, "Yale's School of Art and Architecture: The Measure," p. 78.

Chapter 8

1. Maritain's phrase, quoted by May, *Existence*, p. 11.

2. In the following comparative remarks, those pertaining to the recent criticism of function describe characteristics of the cultural/existential emphasis in criticism since about 1955. Thus they describe only one segment (albeit a highly significant one) of the recent criticism. (See description of "profile," pp. 95ff.) When I refer to "recent critics," therefore, the reader should understand that I am referring only to those whose writing evidences the concern with cultural/existential matters.

3. Frederick Perls discusses this characteristic of visual perception in his treatment of the evolution of man's neurotic separation from real experience. *Gestalt Therapy*, p. 311.

4. *The International Style*, p. 20. Although their three-point summary of the International Style was intended as a description and not as a mandate, the rank-and-file architects who read it seem in many cases to have accepted it as the latter. See Sybil Moholy-Nagy, "Diaspora," *SAHJ*, XXIV (March 1965), pp. 24–26.

5. May, *Existence*, p. 41.

6. It should be noticed that many of the "signs of the times" that earlier modern architecture was seen to embody, such as the suburban escape or the mechanized age or the anonymity of mass society, were symptoms of the schizophrenia inherent in the rationalistic orientation. As man's relationship to himself is reestablished (assuming, optimistically, that such might actually happen in our culture), a new repertoire of social meanings in architecture might grow. Perhaps one of these will be the "expression" of a plurality of individual lifestyles seen in the plurality of architectural styles, an idea discussed below.

7. Peter Collins discusses the Romantic origins of Brutalist aesthetics in the nineteenth-century idea of the artistic value of sincerity. *Changing Ideals*, pp. 251–52.

8. *Complexity and Contradiction in Architecture*.

9. *Complexity and Contradiction*, p. 24.

10. Scully makes this statement in the "Introduction" which he wrote for Venturi's *Complexity and Contradiction*, p. 16.

11. *Third Generation: The Changing Meaning of Architecture* (New York, 1972).

12. Ibid., p. 37.

13. Ibid., p. 44.

14. For the kind of architecture referred to here as "unselfconscious" see Bernard Rudofsky, *Architecture Without Architects* (New York, 1965).

15. Drew, *Third Generation,* p. 45.

16. Ibid., p. 58.

17. Moshe Safdie, *Beyond Habitat* (Cambridge, Massachusetts, 1970), p. 243.

18. Drew, *Third Generation,* p. 38.

19. Frank M. Chambers, "Organism," *Encyclopedia of Poetry and Poetics* (Princeton, 1965), p. 594.

20. *Existence,* p. 66.

21. Drew, *Third Generation,* p. 69.

22. Ibid., p. 79.

23. Ibid., p. 80.

24. Ibid., p. 60.

25. Herbert Read, *Icon and Idea,* p. 17.

26. *Existence,* p. 63.

27. "From Product to Process: The Third Generation of Modern Architects," *Progres. Arch.,* LI (June 1970), pp. 156–67.

28. The work of Guido von Kaschnitz-Weinberg in Structural Analysis is an example.

29. *Poetics of Space,* pp. xi–xx. See above p. 86.

30. Ibid., p. xxii.

31. Ibid., p. xxi.

32. Some attempts to build that theoretical base have appeared in recent years. Christian Norberg-Schulz, for example, attempts a comprehensive theory of architecture making use of contributing ideas from information science, phenomenology, and semiology—the science of signs—in *Intentions in Architecture.* He says little about criticism, however, in spite of the fact that his later *Existence, Space, and Architecture* contains insights into the architectural handling of space that could help to provide material for such a critical foundation. The semiologists Charles Jencks, Françoise Choay, Gillo Dorfles, and others pursue the study of architecture and urbanism with a method derived from general linguistics, considering them to be "non-verbal system[s] of meaningful elements, the structure of which in a given society is linked to that of the other cultural systems." *Meaning in Architecture,* p. 27. This idea of structure as meaning provides the foundation for the only attempt at a systematic critical method resting upon the new orientation which I know of at the present time, that called structural analysis, which is based upon the phenomenology of Husserl and whose most systematic practitioner is Guido von Kaschnitz-Weinberg. See his *Mittelmeerische Grundlagen der antiken Kunst* (Frankfurt, 1944), and the first two volumes of his *Ausgewählte Schriften* (Berlin, 1965). See also B. Schweitzer, "Strukturforschung in Archäologie und

Vorgeschichte," *Neue Jahrbücher* (1938), pp. 162ff.; and H. Sedlmayr, "Zu einer strengen Kunstwissenschaft," *Kunstwissenschaftliche Forschungen* 1 (1931), pp. 7ff. The best introductory statements that I know of in English are Sheldon Nodelman, "Structural analysis in art and anthropology," *Yale French Studies: Structuralism,* XXXVI and XXXVII (October 1966), pp. 89–103; and John W. Dixon, Jr., "Outline of a Theory of Structure," *Cross Currents* (Summer-Fall 1972), pp. 258–80.

33. Forrest Wilson, "From Product to Process," p. 167.

Bibliography

Aalto, Alvar and K. Fleig, eds. *Alvar Aalto: Complete Works, 1922-60.* New York, 1963.
Aalto, Alvar. "Humanizing of Architecture." *Arch. Forum,* LXXIII (December 1940), 505-6.
"A & A: Yale School of Art and Architecture." *Progres. Arch.,* XLV (February 1964), 108-27.
Adams, Robert. "In Defence of Historicism." *RIBA Journal,* LXXXVIII (December 1981), 21-25.
Alford, John. "Creativity and Intelligibility in Le Corbusier's Chapel at Ronchamp." *JAAC,* XVI (March 1958), 293-305.
——————. "Modern Architecture and the Symbolism of Creative Process." *Coll. Art J.,* XIV, ii (1955), 102-23.
Allsopp, Bruce. "Inhuman Design, Whose Fault?" *RIBA Journal,* LXXXI (March 1974), 18-26.
"Alvar Aalto Dormitory for M.I.T. is Finished." *Arch. Forum,* XCI (July 1949), 10.
"Alvar Aalto, Finland's modern master." *Arch. Forum,* LXVIII (April 1938), suppl. 8.
Andrews, Wayne. *Architecture, Ambition and Americans: A Social History of American Architecture.* New York, 1966.
" 'Arcaismo' Technologico." *L'Architettura* (Milan), VI (October 1960), 410-11.
"Architectural Criticism." *RIBA Journal,* LXXI (July 1964), 320.
"Architectural Criticism: 'Architectural Aberrations'; or nothing but the awful truth." *Arch. Record,* CXVIII (November 1955), 24ff.; (January 1956), 24ff.
"Architectural Details (Mies)." *Arch. Record,* CXXXIV (October 1963), 149-64.
"Architecture and Technology." *Arts & Arch.,* LXVII (October 1950), 30.
Arnheim, Rudolf. *Art and Visual Perception.* Berkeley, 1954.
——————. "The Dynamics of Shape." *Design Quarterly,* no. LXIV (1966), 3-32.
——————. "From Function to Expression." *Toward a Psychology of Art.* Berkeley, 1967, 192-212.
——————. *Toward a Psychology of Art.* Berkeley, 1966.
"Art and Architecture Building, Yale University, Architect: Paul Rudolph." *Arch. Review,* CXXXV (May 1964), 332.
"Art & Architecture Faculty Building, Yale." *Arch. Design,* XXXIV (April 1964), 178-80.
"Art Serves Science: Alfred Newton Richards Medical Research Building, University of Penna. Phila, Pa.," *Arch. Record,* CXXVIII (August 1960), 149-56.
Ashbee, Charles Robert. *Frank Lloyd Wright: Ausgeführte Bauten.* Berlin, 1911.
Atkinson, F. "Frank Lloyd Wright's Fallingwater: The House and Its History." *Arch. Journal* CLXIX (April 1979), 794.
Bachelard, Gaston. *The Poetics of Space.* Boston, 1969.

Bakema, J. B. "Le Bâtiment Public ou l'Architecture des Jonctions." *Arch. d'Aujourd'hui,* XXXIX (December 1967), 2ff.

Banerji, Anupam. "Ronchamp: The Home of Le Corbusier's Man." *AAQ,* XI (1979), 36–48.

Banham, Reyner. *The Architecture of the Well-Tempered Environment.* Chicago, 1969.

——————. "Convenient Benches and Handy Hooks." *The History, Theory and Criticism of Architecture.* Edited by Marcus Whiffen. Cambridge, Massachusetts, 1970, 91–105.

——————. "Frank Lloyd Wright as Environmentalist." *Arts and Arch.,* LXXXIII (September 1966), 26–30.

——————. *Guide to Modern Architecture.* London, 1962.

——————. "The history of the immediate future." *RIBA Journal,* LXVIII (May 1961), 252–60ff.

——————. "Last Formgiver." *Arch. Review,* CXL (August 1966), 97–108.

——————. "New Brutalism." *Arch. Review,* CXVIII (December 1955), 355–61.

——————. *The New Brutalism.* New York, 1966.

——————. "On trial: The Buttery Hatch Aesthetic." *Arch. Review,* CXXXI (March 1962), 203–6.

——————. "On Trial: Mies van der Rohe." *Arch. Review,* CXXXII (August 1962), 125–28.

——————. *The Age of the Masters: A Personal View of Modern Architecture.* New York, 1975.

——————. *Theory and Design in the First Machine Age.* New York, 1960.

Bardi, P. M. "Critical Review of Le Corbusier." *RIBA Journal,* LIX (February 1952), 143.

Barnett, Jonathan. "New Collegiate Architecture at Yale: Yale's School of Art and Architecture, Paul Rudolph, Architect." *Arch. Record,* CXXXI (April 1962), 125–38.

——————. "A School for the Arts at Yale." *Arch. Record,* CXXXV (February 1964), 111–20.

Baro, Gene. "The Bauhaus Revisited." *Studio,* CLXXVI (September 1968), 69–73.

Baur, Hermann. "Ronchamp und die neuere kirchliche Architectur." *Werk,* XLIV (June 1957), 187–89.

Bayer, Herbert, Walter Gropius and Ise Gropius, eds. *Bauhaus: 1919–1928.* Boston, 1952.

Behrendt, Walter Curt. "Mies van der Rohe." *Mag. Art,* XXXII, x (October 1939), 591.

——————. *Modern Building: its nature, problems, and forms.* New York, 1937.

Benevolo, Leonardo. *History of Modern Architecture, 2 Vols.* Cambridge, Massachusetts, 1971.

Bennett, Richard M. "Critique on Criticism." *AIA Journal,* XXVIX (May 1963), 51–54.

Berkeley, Ellen Perry. "A Building as a Teacher." *Arch. Forum,* CXXVII (July 1967), 47–53.

Berlage, Hendrik P. "Neuere amerikanische Architectur." *Schweizerische Bauzeitung,* (September 1912), 14–28.

Besset, Maurice. "Ludwig Mies van der Rohe." *Encyclopedia of World Art,* X (1965), 80–4.

——————. *Who Was Corbusier?* New York, 1968.

Betjeman, J. and J. Piper. "Seeing eye; or, How to like everything." *Arch. Review,* LXXXVI (November 1939), 201–4.

Black, Carl John. "A vision of human space." *Arch. Forum,* CLIV (July 1973), 105–16.

Blake, Peter. "Beaux-Arts Blues." *Architettura,* XXI (April 1976), 743–45.

——————. *Form Follows Fiasco: Why Modern Architecture Hasn't Worked.* Boston/Toronto, 1977.

——————. "Form follows function — or does it?" *Arch. Forum,* CVIII (April 1958), 99–103.

——————. *Frank Lloyd Wright: Architecture and Space.* Baltimore, 1960.

——————. "Frank Lloyd Wright: Master of Architectural Space." *Arch. Forum,* CIX (September 1958), 120–25ff.

————. "The Guggenheim: Museum or Monument?" *Arch. Forum,* CXI (December 1959), 86–92.

————. *The Master Builders.* New York, 1961.

————. *Mies van der Rohe: Architecture and Structure.* Baltimore, Maryland, 1960.

————. "Modern Architecture: Its Many Faces." *Arch. Forum,* CVIII (March 1958), 76–81.

————. "Modern Architecture: the difficult art of simplicity (Mies)." *Arch. Forum,* CVIII (May 1958), 126–31.

Blanton, John. "Le Corbusier and the Tragic View of Architecture." *AIA Journal,* LXV (April 1976), 74ff.

Blaser, Werner. *Mies van der Rohe: The Art of Structure.* New York, 1965.

Bloc, André. "La critique architecturale." *Arch. d'Aujourd'hui,* XXXIV (November 1964), 2–5, 23–26, 43–45.

————. "Le Corbusier." *Aujourd'hui,* LI (November 1965), 1–118.

————. "Mies van der Rohe." *Arch. d'Aujourd'hui,* XXXIV (April 1964), 78–81.

Bloom, Martin. "Toward a dynamic architecture." *AIA Journal,* XXXVII (January 1962), 50–52.

Boesiger, W. *Le Corbusier 1910-60.* New York, 1960.

————. *Le Corbusier & Pierre Jeanneret: Oeuvre complète.* 7 vols. Zurich, 1937–70.

Boman, Thorlief. *Hebrew Thought Compared with Greek.* London, 1960.

Bonelli, Renato. "Estetica contemporanea e critica dell'architettura," *Zodiac,* IV (1959), 22–29.

Bonnefoi, Christian. "Louis Kahn and Minimalism." *Oppositions,* XXIV (Spring 1981), 3–25.

Bottero, Maria. "Organic and Rational Morphology in Louis Kahn." *Zodiac,* XIII (1967), 240–45.

Boyd, John Taylor. "Prophet of the New Architecture." *Arts and Dec.,* XXXIII (May 1930), 56–59.

Boyd, Robin. "The Engineering of Excitement." *Arch. Review,* CXXIV (November 1958), 295–308.

————. "The Functional Neurosis." *Arch. Review,* CXIX (February 1956), 85–88.

————. "The New Vision in Architecture." *Harper's Magazine,* CCXXIII (July 1961), 72–81.

————. *The Puzzle of Architecture.* Melbourne, 1965.

————. "Search for Pleasingness." *Progress. Arch.,* XXXVIII (April 1957), 195–205.

Boyne, Colin. "All the Modern Movement Needs is a Shot in the Arm." *Arch. Review,* CLXIII (May 1978), 257–60.

Bragdon, Claude. *Architecture and Democracy.* New York, 1926.

————. "Architecture in the United States." *Arch. Record,* XXVI (August 1909), 85–96; XXV (June 1909), 426–33.

————. "Letters from Louis Sullivan." *Arch.* (New York), LXIV (July 1931), 7–10.

Braudy, Susan. "The Architectural Metaphysic of Louis Kahn." *The New York Times Magazine* (November 15, 1970), 73ff.

Broadbent, Geoffrey H. "Learning From New Research." *RIBA Journal,* LXXX (May 1973), 228–30.

Brolin, Brent C. *The Failure of Modern Architecture.* New York, 1976.

Brooks, C. "The Formalist Critics." *The Kenyon Review,* XIII (1951), 72–81.

Brooks, Harold Allen. "Wright and the Destruction of the Box." *SAHJ,* XXXVIII (March 1979), 7–14.

Brown, Keith C. "Hemlock for the critic: a problem in evaluation," *JAAC,* XVIII (March 1960), 316–18.

Brown, Theodore M. "Rietveld's Egocentric Vision." *SAHJ,* XXIV (December 1965), 292–96.
————. *The Work of G. Rietveld Architect.* Utrecht, 1958.
Brownell, Baker. *Architecture and Modern Life.* New York, 1938.
"Building years of a Yale Man: A. W. Griswall." *Arch. Forum,* CXVIII (June 1963), 92.
Bullock, Nicholas. "Modern Movement: Architecture in Context." *RIBA Journal,* LXXXVI (February 1979), 64.
Burchard, John Ely. "Finland and Architect Aalto." *Arch. Record,* CXXV (January 1959), 125–36.
————. "A Pilgrimage: Ronchamp, Raincy, Vézelay." *Arch. Record,* CXXIII (March 1958), 171–78.
————. "Symbolism in Architecture—the Decline of the Monumental." *Symbols and Society.* Edited by Lymon Bryson, et al. New York, 1955.
Burckhardt, Lucius and Werner Blaser. "Haus Schröder in Utrecht." *Werk,* LI (November 1964), 392–93.
————. "Objektive Architektur: Börse und Warenhaus Carson, Pirie, Scott in Chicago." *Werk,* LI (November 1964), 385–7.
Bush-Brown, Albert. "Architectural Polemic." *JAAC,* XVIII (December 1959), 143–58.
————. *Louis Sullivan.* New York, 1960.
————. "Notes toward a basis for criticism." *Arch. Record,* CXXVI (October 1959), 183–94.
Campbell, William. "Frank Furness, American Pioneer." *Arch. Review,* CX (November 1951), 310–15.
Candilis, G. "Le Corbusier et notre Epoque." *Arch. d'Aujourd'hui,* XXXIV (April 1964), 16–31.
Canty, Donald. "Third Force in Architecture." *Architettura,* XXVII (August/September 1981), 450–51.
Carney, Francis. "Summa Popologica of Robert (Call Me Vegas) Venturi." *RIBA Journal,* LXXX (May 1973) 242–44.
Chamberlain, Betty. "Louis Sullivan." *Arts and Arch.,* LXXIII (December 1956), 12–15.
Chambers, Frank M. "Organism." *Encyclopedia of Poetry and Poetics.* Edited by Alex Preminger. Princeton, 1965, 593–94.
"Chapel at Ronchamp." *RAIC Journal,* XXXV (November 1958), 423.
"Chapel in Concrete: Le Corbusier's Notre-Dame-du-Haut." *Time,* LXVI (July 18, 1955), 68ff.
"Chapelle et chaufferie à l'Institut technique de l'Illinois; Maison Farnsworth à Plano; Immeubles d'appartements Lake Shore drive à Chicago." *Arch. d' Aujourd'hui,* XXIV (December 1953), 26–33.
Chermayeff, Serge and Christopher Alexander. *Community and privacy: toward a new architecture of humanism.* Garden City, New York, 1965.
"Chicago: Veto Demolition on Esthetic Grounds: Garrick Theater and Office Building of Louis Sullivan." *Arch. Forum,* CXIII (October 1960), 9ff.
"Chicagoans Rally to Save Wright's Robie House." *Arch. Forum,* CVI (March 1957), 9.
"Chicago's Sullivan in New Photographs." *Arch. Forum,* CI (October 1954), 128–33.
Choay, Françoise. *Le Corbusier.* New York, 1960.
Chotas, Nicholas E. "The Critic's role in esthetic evaluation of architecture." *Progres. Arch.,* XXXVIII (July 1957), 223–28.
Christ-Janer, Albert and Mary Mix Foley. "Chapel of Notre Dame du Haut." *Modern Church Architecture.* New York, 1962, 103–17.
Churchill, H. S. "Notes on Frank Lloyd Wright." *Mag. Art,* XLI (February 1948), 62–66.

Ciucci, Giorgio. "Invention of Modern Movement." *Oppositions,* XXIV (Spring 1981), 68-91.

Clair, Jacques. *Que Propose Le Corbusier?* Paris, 1946.

Collins, Peter. *Changing Ideals in Modern Architecture: 1750-1950.* Montreal, 1965.

—————. "The form-givers." *Perspecta,* VII (1961), 91-96.

—————. "Modular." *Arch. Review,* CXVI (July 1954), 5-8.

—————. "The Philosophy of Architectural Criticism." *AIA Journal,* XLIX (January 1968), 46-49.

—————. "Symbolism and Architectural Theory." *AIA Journal,* XLVII (March 1967), 80-82.

"Committee plans Restoration of Robie House." *Arch. Record,* CXXXIII (April 1963), 29.

Condit, Carl W. *The Chicago School of Architecture.* Chicago, 1964.

—————. "The Humanization of Technics." *Humanist,* VI (Summer-Fall 1946), 82-88.

—————. "Modern Architecture: a new technical-aesthetic synthesis." *JAAC,* VI (September 1947), 45-54.

Connely, Willard. "Last Years of Louis Sullivan." *AIA Journal,* XXIII (January 1955), 32-38.

—————. "Later Years of Louis Sullivan." *AIA Journal,* XXI (May 1954), 223-28.

—————. "Louis Sullivan and his Younger Staff." *AIA Journal,* XXII (December 1954), 266-68.

—————. *Louis Sullivan As He Lived.* New York, 1960.

—————. "Louis Sullivan in 1917-1918." *AIA Journal,* XXII (October 1954), 172-76.

—————. "Mystery of Louis Sullivan and his Brother." *AIA Journal,* XX (November 1953), 226-29; (December 1953), 292-96.

—————. "New Chapters in the Life of Louis Sullivan." *AIA Journal,* XX (September 1953), 107-14.

—————. "New Sullivan Letters." *AIA Journal,* XX (July 1953), 9-13.

Conrad, Ulrich, ed. *Programs and Manifestoes on 20th-Century Architecture.* Cambridge, 1970.

"Continuing tradition in great architecture (Mies)." *Arch. Forum,* CX (May 1962), 89-95.

"Corbu Builds a Church." *Arch. Forum,* CIII (September 1955), 120-25.

"Corbusier designs a hilltop chapel shaped like a fiddle." *Arch. Forum,* XCIX (July 1953), 35.

Cox, Anthony. "The Retreat from Function." *Arch. Forum,* LXX (June 1939), 21.

Craik, Kenneth H. "The Comprehension of the Everyday Physical Environment." *AIP Journal,* XXXIV, i (January 1969), 29-36.

Creighton, Thomas H. "European Diary: Chapel of Notre Dame du Haut at Ronchamp." *Progres. Arch.,* XLI (August 1960), 120-29.

—————. "Seagram House re-reassessed." *Progres. Arch.,* XL (June 1959), 140-45.

"A Critique on Criticism." *AIA Journal,* XLV (January 1966), 70.

Crook, D. H. "Louis Sullivan and the Golden Doorway." *SAHJ,* XXVI (December 1967), 250-58.

Crosby, Theo. "Modern Movement." *RIBA Journal,* LXXXVI (January 1979), 28.

Day, Douglas. "Background of the New Criticism." *JAAC,* XXIV, iii (Spring 1966), 429-40.

Dearstyne, Howard. "Basic teaching of architecture." *Liturgical Arts,* XII (May 1944), 56-60.

—————. "Miesian Space Concept in Domestic Architecture." *Four Great Makers of Modern Architecture.* New York, 1963, 129-40.

De Fries, H. *Frank Lloyd Wright: aus dem Lebenswerke eines Architekten.* Berlin, 1926.

de Moura, Beatriz and Juan Antonio Solans. "La prensa y la critica," *Zodiac,* XV (1965), 139-42.

De Neyi, Don. "Masters of Light: Frank Lloyd Wright." *AIA Journal,* LXVIII (September 1979), 63–65.

Dennis, James M. and Lu B. Wenneker. "Ornamentation and the Organic Architecture of Frank Lloyd Wright." *Coll. Art J.,* XXV, i (Fall 1965), 2–14.

de Reus, J. "What we learned from Frank Lloyd Wright." *House & Home,* XV (February 1959), 126–33.

"Design Direction: Other Voices." *AIA Journal,* LXVII (mid-May 1978), 160–65 ff.

"Design Jelled for Yale Art and Architectural School: Paul Rudolph, Architect." *Progres. Arch.,* XLIII (Janaury 1962), 62.

"Designs glass house for a Chicago builder." *House & Home,* VIII (July 1955), 62.

Desmond, Henry W. "Another View — What Mr. Louis Sullivan Stands For." *Arch. Record,* XVI (July 1904), 61–67.

De Zurko, Edward Robert. *Origins of Functionalist Theory.* New York, 1957.

d'Hornoncourt, R. "International Style." *Arch. Record,* CXIV (September 1953), 12 ff.

Diamond, A. J. "A Plea for performance standards." *AIA Journal,* L (July 1968), 54–55.

Dixon, John Morris and James T. Burns, Jr. "P/A Observer — Kahn's Second Phase at Pennsylvania." *Progres. Arch.,* XLV (September 1964), 208–11.

Dixon, John W., Jr. "The Ambiguities of Natural Phenomena." *The Christian Scholar,* XLVIII, iii (Fall 1965), 183–97.

————. "Fallacies and Heresies in Art Criticism." *Coll. Art J.,* XXIV (Fall 1964), 143–49 ff.

————. "Fresco as theology." *Theology Today,* XXVI, ii (July 1969), 194–203.

————. "The Matter of Theology: The Consequences of Art for Theological Method." *The Journal of Religion,* XLIX, ii (April 1969), 160–79.

————. "Notes Toward a Theory of Style." *SAHJ,* XXVI, iii (October 1967), 172–77.

————. "The Ontological Intransigence of the Aesthetic Fact." *Comparative Literature Studies,* III, ii (1966), 247–57.

————. "Outline of a Theory of Structure." *Cross Currents* (Summer-Fall 1972), 258–80.

Dorflies, G. "Walter Gropius Today." *Zodiac,* VIII (1961), 34–47.

Dorner, Alexander. *The Way Beyond Art.* New York, 1958.

Drew, Philip. *Third Generation: The Changing Meaning of Architecture.* New York, 1972.

Drexler, Arthur. *Built in USA: Post-War Architecture.* New York, 1952.

————. *Ludwig Mies van der Rohe.* New York, 1960.

Duncan, Hugh Dalziel. "Attualita di Louis Sullivan." *Casabella,* CCIV (February-March 1954), 7–30.

————. *Culture and Democracy.* New York, 1965.

Eaton, L. K. "Banham's View; The Age of the Masters: A Personal View of Modern Architecture." *Progres. Arch.,* LVII (September 1976), 92 ff.

————. "Jens Janson & the Chicago School" *Progres. Arch.,* XLI (December 1960), 144–50.

————. "Louis Sullivan & Hendrik Berlage: a Centennial Tribute to Two Pioneers." *Progres. Arch.,* XXXVII (November 1956), 138–41 ff.

————. "Richardson and Sullivan in Scandinavia." *Progres. Arch.,* XLVII (March 1966), 168–71.

"The Edifice Crumbles: A Symposium." *Arch. Review,* CLXIII (February 1978), 64–68.

"Edith Farnsworth Sues Mies." *Arch. Forum,* XCV (November 1951), 61.

Ehrenzweig, Anton. *The Hidden Order of Art.* New York, 1969.

————. *The Psycho-analysis of Artistic Vision and Hearing.* New York, 1965.

————. "Unconscious Form-Creation in Art." *British Journal of Medical Psychology,* XXI (1948), 185–214; XXII-XXIII (1949–50), 88–109.

"Einweihung der Wallfahrtskapelle von Ronchamp, Frankreich." *Werk,* XLII (August 1955), 155.

Elliot, Alexander. "Notes Toward an Ideal Museum." *Art in America,* XLVIII, No. 1 (1960), 76–79.

Elmslie, G. G. "Functionalism and International Style." *Arch. and Eng.,* CXX (February 1935), 69–70.

—————. "Sullivan Ornamentation." *AIA Journal,* VI (October 1946), 155–58.

Elstein, R. S. "Architecture of Dankman Adler." *SAHJ,* XXVI (December 1967), 245 ff.

"Emergence of a master architect (Mies)." *Life,* XLII (March 18, 1957), 60–68.

Erffa, Helmut von. "Bauhaus: first phase." *Arch. Review,* CXXII (August 1957), 103–5.

"An Essay in critical appraisal." *Pencil Points,* XV (March 1934), 106–14.

"Europe's Great New Churches." *Arch. Forum,* CVII (December 1957), 106–11.

"Famous House Rescued: Robie House in Chicago." *Arch. Forum,* CVIII (February 1958), 69.

Fasla, Garrett Eckbo. "Design and Criticism." *AIA Journal,* XLI (June 1964), 23–26.

Fiedler, Conrad. *Essay on Architecture.* Lexington, 1954.

—————. *On Judging Works of Visual Art.* Berkeley, 1957.

"Finland: a portfolio of Finnish architecture." *Arch. Forum,* LXXII (June 1940), 399–412.

Fisker, Kay. "Moral of functionalism." *Mag. Art,* XLIII (February 1950), 62–67.

Fitch, James Marston. "A Building of Rugged Fundamentals." *Arch. Forum,* CXIII (July 1960), 82–87 ff.

—————. "Frank Lloyd Wright: 1869–1959." *Arch. Forum,* CX (May 1959), 108–12.

—————. "Hazards of Western Criticism." *Arts,* XXXVI (March 1962), 62–66.

—————. "Mies van der Rohe and the Platonic Verities." *Four Great Makers of Modern Architecture.* New York, 1963, 154–63.

—————. "The Shifting bases of contemporary criticism." *Progres. Arch.,* XXXVII (June 1956), 143 ff.

—————. "Three levers of Walter Gropius." *Arch. Forum,* CXII (May 1960), 128–33 ff.

—————. "Utopia Revisited, the Bauhaus at Dessau Forty Years On." *Arch. Review,* CLXI (February 1967), 97–99.

—————. *Walter Gropius.* New York, 1960.

Fitz Patrick, Thomas K. "Have we come of age?" *AIA Journal,* XXIX (May 1958), 213–14.

"Five Questions à Le Corbusier." *Zodiac,* VII (1960), 50–55.

Fleming, C. C. "Golden Mean." *Arch. Forum,* LXXXVIII (February 1948), 30 ff.

Ford, James and Katherine Marrow. *The Modern House in America.* New York, 1940.

"Form Evokes Function." *Time,* LXXV (June 6, 1960), 76.

"Fox River, Farnsworth House." *Arch. Forum,* XCV (October 1951), 156–62.

Frampton, Kenneth. "Labour, Work and Architecture." *Meaning in Architecture.* Edited by Charles Jencks and George Baird. New York, 1969, 151–70.

—————, ed. "Modern Architecture and the Critical Present." *Arch. Design,* LII (1982), 1–120.

Franciscono, Marcel. *Walter Gropius and the Creation of the Bauhaus in Weimar: The Ideals and Artistic Theories of its Founding Years,* Chicago, 1971.

"Frank Lloyd Wright's Masterwork: the Solomon Guggenheim Memorial Museum." *Arch. Forum,* XCVI (April 1952), 141 ff.

Frateili, Enzo. "Louis Kahn." *Zodiac,* VIII (1961), 14–17.

"Functionalism is not new." *Int. Des.,* XXXI (May 1960), 158–60.

Gale, A. L. "Architectural criticism; architects and libel." *RAIC Journal,* XXVIII (February 1951), 39–41 ff.

Gardner-Medwin, Robert. "A Flight from Functionalism." *RIBA Journal,* LXV (October 1958), 408–14.

Gaunt, William. "Remarkable story of the Bauhaus." *Connoisseur,* CLXIX (November 1968), 158ff.
Gebhard, D. "Louis Sullivan and George Grant Elmslie." *SAHJ,* XIX (May 1960), 62–68.
——————. "Note on the Chicago Fair of 1893 and Frank Lloyd Wright." *SAHJ,* XVIII (May 1959), 63–65.
"Genetrix: Personal Contributions to American Architecture: Louis Kahn." *Arch. Review,* CXXI (May 1957), 344–45.
"Genetrix: Personal contributions to American architecture: Mies." *Arch. Review,* CXXI (May 1957), 338–39.
"Gerrit Rietveld: Un Prodiglione, Una Scuola, Una Casa." *Domus,* CDIII (September 1965), 1–9.
Ghyka, M. "Le Corbusier's Modular and the Concept of the Golden Mean." *Arch. Review,* CIII (February 1948), 39–42.
Gibson, James J. *The Senses Considered as Perceptual Systems.* Boston, 1966.
Giedion, Sigfried. "Alvar Aalto." *Arch. Review,* CVII (February 1950), 77–84.
——————. *Architecture, You and Me.* Cambridge, Massachusetts, 1958.
——————. "Aspects de l'Architecture aux Etats-Unis en 1953." *Arch. d'Aujourd'hui,* XXIV (December 1953), 7–9.
——————. *A Decade of New Architecture.* Zurich, 1951.
——————. *The Eternal Present: The Beginnings of Architecture.* New York, 1964.
——————. "Le Corbusier et l'architecture contemporaine." *Chaiers d'Art,* V, iv (1930), 204–15.
——————. "Le Corbusier's Church at Ronchamp: a new era?" *Art N.,* LIV (November 1955), 32–33ff.
——————. "Les Problèmes Actuels de l'Architecture." *Cahiers d'Art,* VII, i–ii (1932), 69–73.
——————. *Space, Time and Architecture.* Cambridge, Massachusetts, 1941. (also Second edition, 1949; Third edition, 1954; Fourth edition, 1963; Fifth edition, 1967).
——————. "Walter Gropius et l'architecture en Allemagne." *Cahiers d'Art,* V, ii (1930), 95–103.
——————. *Walter Gropius: Work and Teamwork.* Zurich, 1954.
Gilbert, Katharine. "Clean and organic: a study in architectural semantics." *SAHJ,* X (October 1951), 3–7.
Giurgola, Romaldo. "On Louis Kahn." *Zodiac,* XVII (1967), 119.
"Glass House Stones: The Farnsworth House." *Newsweek,* XLI (June 8, 1953), 90.
Goetz, H. "Modern art in the World Crisis: the Metamorphosis from a European to a Universal Civilization and Art." *Baroda State Mus. B.,* I, i (1943–44), 1–12.
Goldberger, Paul. "Should Anyone Care About the New York Five? ...Or About Their Critics the Five on Five?" *Arch. Record,* CLV (February 1974), 113–16.
Gombrich, E. H. *Art and Illusion.* London, 1960.
Gowan, James. "Notes on American Architecture." *Perspecta,* VII (1961), 91–96.
Grady, J. "Nature and the Art Nouveau." *Art B.,* XXXVII (September 1955), 187–92.
Graham, Dan. "Not Post-Modernism: History as Against Historicism." *Art Forum,* XX (December 1981), 50–58.
Green, A. W. "Architecture, taste and style." *AIA Journal,* (March 1946), 145–48ff.
Green, Wilder. "Alfred Newton Richards Medical Research Building." *Museum of Mod. Art Bulletin,* XXVIII (1961), 3–24.
"Gropius Symposium at the American academy of arts and sciences, Boston." *Arts & Arch.,* LXIX (May 1952), 27–31.
Gropius, Walter. *Apollo in the Democracy.* New York, 1968.

——————. "Architect in Society." *RIBA Journal,* LXVIII (September 1961), 435-38.

——————. "Education toward creative design." *Am. Arch.,* CL (May 1937), 26-30.

——————. "Eight steps toward a solid architecture." *Arts,* C (February 1954), 156-57ff.

——————. "Necessity of the Artist in a Democratic Society." *Arts & Arch.,* LXXII (December 1955), 16-17.

——————. *The New Architecture and the Bauhaus.* London, 1935.

——————. *Scope of Total Architecture.* New York, 1943.

——————. "Teaching the Arts of Design." *Coll. Art J.,* VII (1948), 160-64.

——————. "Toward a living Architecture." *Am. Arch.,* CLII (January 1938), 21-22; (February 1938), 23-24.

——————. "Tradition and Continuity in Architecture." *Arch. Record,* CXXXV May 1964), 131-36.

——————. "True Architectural Goals yet to be realized." *Arch. Record,* CXXIX (June 1961), 147-52.

Gutheim, Frederick. *Alvar Aalto.* New York, 1960.

——————. "Alvar Aalto Today." *Arch. Record,* CXXXIII (April 1963), 135-50.

——————. "New Corbusier." *Arch. Record,* CXVIII (November 1955), 180-87.

——————. "Wright legacy evaluated." *Arch. Record,* CXXVIII (October 1960), 147-86.

Hagopian, John V. "In Defence of the Affective Fallacy." *Southern Review: An Australian Journal of Literary Studies,* I (1965), 72-77.

Hall, Edward T. *The Hidden Dimension.* Garden City, New York, 1969.

——————. "The Language of Space." *AIA Journal,* XXXVI (February 1961), 71-74.

——————. *The Silent Language.* New York, 1959.

Hamlin, Talbot F. *Architecture: An Art for All Men.* New York, 1947.

——————. *Architecture Through the Ages.* New York, 1953.

——————. "Criticism Might Help Architecture. Let's Try It!" *Am. Arch.,* CXXXVII (May 1930), 41ff.

——————. "F. L. W.—An Analysis." *Pencil Points,* XIX (March 1938), 137-44.

——————. "Greek revival in America and some of its critics." *Art B.,* XXIV (September 1942), 244-58.

Hammond, Peter. "A Liturgical Brief." *Arch. Review,* CXXIII (April 1958), 240-55.

Harms, Hans H. "Trends in Architecture: U.S.A.—Louis I. Kahn." *Bauwelt,* XLIII (October 28, 1963), 1252-61.

Haskell, Douglas. "For all concerned; let's have architectural criticism." *Arch. Forum,* CII (March 1955), 178; (June 1955), 160.

——————. "Jazz in Architecture." *Arch. Forum,* CXIII (September 1960), 110-15.

——————. "L'influence de Gropius en Amerique." *Arch. d'Aujourd'hui,* XXVIII (February 1950), 45-47.

——————. "Newspaper Architecture." *Arch. Forum,* CXVII (October 1962), 142.

——————. "Organic Architecture: Frank Lloyd Wright." *Creative Art,* (November 1928), li-lvii.

Hassid, Sami. "Architects as critics." *Progres. Arch.,* XLIII (November 1962), 146-48.

Hellmann, Geoffrey T. "From Within to Without." *New Yorker,* XXIII (April 26, 1947), 31-36ff; (May 3, 1947), 36-40.

Hennessey, William James. "Wright and the Guggenheim Museum: A New Perspective." *Arts,* LII (April 1978), 128-33.

Henze, A. "Ronchamp, Le Corbusier's erster Kirchenbau." *Werk,* XLIII (August 1956), 160.

Herbert, Gilbert. *The Synthetic Vision of Walter Gropius.* Johannesburg, 1959.

Hersey, George L. "Replication Replicated, or Notes on American Bastardy." *Perspecta,* IX-X (1965), 211-48.

Hesselgren, Sven. *The Language of Architecture.* Lund, 1969.

Heywood, Robert B., ed. *The Works of the Mind.* Chicago, 1947.

Hilberseimer, L. *Contemporary Architecture: Its Roots and Trends.* Chicago, 1964.

——. *Mies van der Rohe.* Chicago, 1956.

Hildebrand, Adolf. *The Problem of Form.* New York, 1907.

Hitchcock, Henry-Russell. "The Architectural Future in America." *Arch. Review,* LXXXII (July 1937), 1-2.

——. "Architecture of Bureaucracy and the architecture of Genius." *Arch. Record,* CI (January 1947), 2-6.

——. *The Architecture of H. H. Richardson and His Times.* New York, 1936.

——. "Berlin Architectural Show, 1931." *Hound & Horn,* V, i (October-December 1931), 94-97.

——. "The Evolution of Wright, Mies and Le Corbusier." *Perspecta,* I (1952), 8-15.

——. *Frank Lloyd Wright.* Paris, 1928.

——. "Frank Lloyd Wright and the 'Academic Tradition' of the early eighteen-nineties." *J. Warburg Courtauld Inst.,* VII (1944), 46-63.

——. *In the Nature of Materials.* New York, 1942.

——. *Modern Architecture: International Exhibition.* New York, 1932.

——. *Modern Architecture: Romanticism and Reintegration.* New York, 1929.

——. "Notes of a Traveller: Wright and Kahn." *Zodiac,* VI (1960), 14-21.

——. *Painting Toward Architecture.* New York, 1948.

——. "The Place of Painting and Sculpture in Relation to Modern Architecture." *Architect's Yearbook,* II, London, 1947, 13-24.

——. "Sullivan and the Skyscraper." *RIBA Journal,* LX (July 1953), 353-61.

——. "Wright's Influence Abroad." *Parnassus,* XII (December 1940), 11-15.

Hitchcock, Henry-Russell and Philip Johnson. *The International Style: Architecture since 1922.* New York, 1932.

Hoesli, Bernard. "Die Synthese der Künste bei Le Corbusier." *Werk,* XLVII (August 1960), 286-88.

Holenstein, Elmar. "Excursus: Monofunctionalism in Architecture Between the Wars—Le Corbusier and the Bauhaus." *Oppositions,* XXIV (Spring, 1981), 48-67.

Holland, L. B. "Function of functionalism." *Arch. and Eng.,* CXXVI (August 1936), 25-32.

Holmes, Ann Hitchcock. "Mies' New Pavilion in Houston, Where More is Better." *Art N.,* LXXIII (March 1974), 72-73.

Hope, Henry R. "Louis Sullivan's Architectural Ornament." *Mag. Art,* XL (1947), 111-17.

Hoppenfeld, Mort. "Always a hot subject." *Progres. Arch.,* XXXV (September 1954), 15-16ff.

Horn, Richard. "Humanism of Alvar Aalto." *Res. Int.,* IV (May 1979), 98-101.

Horne, G. "Functional Aesthetics and the Social Ideal." *Pencil Points,* XIII (April 1932), 215-18.

"House of the Century gets a Reprieve from Demolition." *House & Home,* XIII (February 1958), 68.

"Houses USA: A Brief Review of the Development of Domestic Architecture in America." *Arch. Forum,* LXXXVI (May 1947), 81-88.

Howe, George. "Functional Aesthetics and the Social Ideal." *Pencil Points,* XIII (April 1932), 215-18.

Hudnut, Joseph. "The Church in a Modern World." *Arch. Forum,* CIX (December 1958), 89-93ff.

——. "Le Corbusier & American Architecture." *RAIC Journal,* XXVI (April 1949), 95-99.

Hume, Robert D. "Personal heresy in Criticism: a new consideration." *Brit. J. Aesthetics,* IX (October 1969), 387-406.

Hungerland, H. "Suggestions for procedure in art criticism." *JAAC,* V (March 1947), 189–95.
Huxtable, Ada Louise. "Is Modern Architecture Dead?" *Arch. Record,* CLXIX (October 1981), 100–105.
—————. "Troubled State of Modern Architecture." *Arch. Record,* CLXIX (January 1981), 72–79.
"...il laisse son oeuvre." *Zodiac,* V (1960), 28.
"International Effort to Preserve Wright's Robie House in Chicago." *Arts and Arch.,* LXXX (July 1963), 6.
"Interviewing Aalto." *Progres. Arch.,* XLVI (January 1965), 48ff.
Jacobus, John. "Le Corbusier: Fantasy and the International Style." *Arts and Arch.,* LXXV (February 1958), 14–15ff.
—————. "Modern Architecture." *World Architecture.* London, 1966, 297–341.
—————. *Twentieth-Century Architecture: The Middle Years, 1940–65.* New York, 1966.
Jacobus, John M. "Architects Without Architecture: Reflections on the Beaux-Arts 'Revival.'" *Art in Am.,* LXIV (March 1976), 48–52.
Jaffé, H. L. C. *De Stijl: 1917–1931.* Amsterdam, 1956.
Jencks, Charles. *Architecture 2000.* London, 1971.
—————. *The Language of Post-Modern Architecture.* New York, 1981.
—————. *Le Corbusier and the Tragic View of Architecture.* Cambridge, 1974.
—————. *Modern Movements in Architecture.* New York, 1973.
—————, ed. *Post-Modern Classicism: The New Synthesis.* New York, 1980.
—————. "Semiology and Architecture." *Meaning in Architecture.* Edited by Charles Jencks and George Baird. New York, 1969, 10–25.
—————. *Skyscrapers—Skycities.* New York, 1980.
Jencks, Charles and George Baird, eds. *Meaning in Architecture.* New York, 1969.
Joedicke, Jürgen. *Architecture Since 1945.* New York, 1969.
—————. *A History of Modern Architecture.* New York, 1959.
Johnson, Philip C. "Frontiersman." *Arch. Review,* CVI (August 1949), 105–10.
—————. "Great Reputations in the making: Three Architects." *Art in America,* XLVIII (Spring 1960), 70–75.
—————. "House at New Canaan, Connecticut." *Arch. Review,* CVIII (September 1950), 152–60.
—————. "Is Sullivan the Father of Functionalism?" *Art N.,* LV (December 1956), 44–46ff.
—————. "Mies van der Rohe." *Arch. Record,* CII (September 1947), 81–88.
—————. *Mies van der Rohe.* New York, 1947.
—————. "Twelve Twists on Modern Architecture." *AAQ,* XI (1979), 32–35.
—————. "Whence and Whither: The Processional Element in Architecture." *Perspecta,* IX–X (1965), 167–78.
Johnson, S. F. and R. S. Crane. "Critics and Criticism, a discussion; the Chicago manifesto." *JAAC,* XII (December 1953), 248–67.
Jones, Cranston. *Architecture Today and Tomorrow.* New York, 1961.
Jones, J. C. "Functional innovation." *Design,* no. CCLVIII (June 1970), 78–79.
Jordy, William H. "Medical Research Building for Pennsylvania University, Philadelphia." *Arch. Review,* CXXIX (February 1961), 99–106.
—————. "Place of Mies in American Architecture." *Zodiac,* VIII (1961), 28–33.
—————. "Seagram Assessed." *Arch. Review,* CXXIV (December 1958), 374–82.
—————. "Symbolic Essence of Modern European Architecture of the Twenties and its continuing Influence." *SAHJ,* XXII (October 1963), 177–87.
Kaelin, Eugene F. *An Existentialist Aesthetic: The Theories of Sartre and Merleau-Ponty.* Madison, 1962.
Kahn, Louis. "Order and Form" *Perspecta,* III (1955), 47–63.

————. "Order in Architecture." *Perspecta,* IV (1957), 58–65.

————. "The Room, the Street and Human Agreement." *AIA Journal,* LVI (September 1971), 33–34.

————. "A Statement by Louis I. Kahn: A Paper Delivered at The International Design Conference, Aspen, Colorado." *Arts & Arch.,* LXXXI (May 1964), 18–19ff.

Kahn, Shalom J. "Towards an organic criticism." *JAAC,* XV (September 1956), 58–73; XV (March 1957), 376.

"Kahn's Medical Science Building Dedicated at University of Pennsylvania." *Progres. Arch.,* XLI (June 1960), 59, 61.

Kallmann, G. M. "The 'Action' Architecture of a New Generation." *Arch. Forum,* CXI (October 1959), 132–37ff.

Kaufmann, Edgar, Jr. "Centrality and Symmetry in Wright's Architecture." *Architects' Yearbook* 9. Edited by Trevor Dannatt. London, 1960, 120–31.

————. "Crisis and Creativity: Frank Lloyd Wright, 1904–1914." *SAHJ,* XXV (December 1966), 292–96.

————. "Frank Lloyd Wright and the Fine Arts," *Perspecta,* (1963), 37–42.

————. "Frank Lloyd Wright: Plasticity, Continuity and Ornament." *SAHJ,* XXXVII (March 1978), 34–39.

————, ed. *Frank Lloyd Wright: Writings and Buildings.* New York, 1960.

————. "Frank Lloyd Wright's Fallingwater 25 Years after." *Architettura,* VIII (August 1962), 222–80.

————. "Frank Lloyd Wright's Years of Modernism 1925–1935." *SAHJ,* XXIV (March 1965), 32–33.

————, ed. *Louis Sullivan and the Architecture of Free Enterprise.* Chicago, 1956.

————. "The Word on Design." *Interiors,* CXII (December 1952), 117ff.

Kaufmann, Emil. *Von Ledoux bis Le Corbusier.* Vienna, 1933.

Kennedy, Robert Woods. "Form Function and Expression: Variations on a Theme by L. Sullivan." *AIA Journal,* XIV (November 1950), 198–204.

————. *The House and the Art of its Design.* New York, 1953.

Kepes, Gyorgy. *The New Landscape in Art and Science.* Chicago, 1956.

Kidder-Smith, G. E. "Aalto versus Aalto: the other Finland." *Perspecta,* IX–X (1965), 132–66.

————. "Alvar Aalto." *American Scandinavian Review,* XXVIII (December 1940), 313–20.

Kiesler, Frederick. "Pseudo-functionalism in modern arch." *Partisan Review,* XVI (June 1949), 733–42.

Kienitz, J. F. "Romanticism of Frank Lloyd Wright." *Art in America,* XXXII (April 1944), 91–101.

Kierkegaard, Søren. "Concluding Unscientific Postscript." *A Kierkegaard Anthology.* Edited by Robert Bretall. Princeton, 1951.

Kimball, Sidney Fiske. *American Architecture.* New York, 1928.

————. "Louis Sullivan—An Old Master." *Arch. Record,* LVII (April 1925).

Kimmelman, George. "Concept of tragedy in Modern Criticism." *JAAC,* IV (March 1946), 141–60.

Kliment, Robert M. "Alvar Aalto in Context." *Arch. Record,* CLXIX (September 1981), 106–11.

Koehler, Robert E. "Kudos for the critics." *AIA Journal,* L (August 1968), 5–6.

Koestler, Arthur. *The Act of Creation.* New York, 1964.

Kozloff, Max. *Renderings: Critical Essays on a Century of Modern Art.* New York, 1969.

Kubler, George. *The Shape of Time.* New Haven, 1962.

Kuhn, Ferdinand. "Blighted areas of our press." *AIA Journal,* L (October 1968), 54–58.

Kulski, Julian Eugene. "Virile Roots: American Experimentation of the Nineteenth Century in Structure and Space." *AIA Journal,* XLIV (December 1965), 37.

"Laboratoires de recherches médicales Alfred Newton à l'Université de Pennsylvania." *Aujourd'hui,* XXXV (February 1962), 1, 76–81.

"Laboratoires de recherches médicales Alfred Newton Richards." *Arch d'Aujourd'hui,* XCI–XCII (September–November 1960), 66–67.

Labotut, Jean. "Le Corbusier's Notre Dame du Haut at Ronchamp." *Arch. Record,* CVIII (October 1955), 167–72.

"L'Affaire Savoye." *Arch. Forum,* CX (May 1959), 107.

Laisney, François. "Place Nette Pour Une Typologie du Gratte-Ciel." *Arch. d'Aujourd'hui,* CLXXVIII (March 1975), 20.

Lane, Barbara Miller. *Architecture and Politics in Germany, 1918–1945.* Cambridge, Massachusetts, 1968.

Langer, Susanne K., ed. *Reflections on Art.* Baltimore, 1958.

Langsner, Jules. "Pocket guide to architectural criticism." *Arts & Arch.,* LXXIV (July 1957), 30ff.

Lea, David. "Architectural Essence—Modernist or Natural." *Arch. Journal,* CLXXV (June 1982), 56–57.

"Le Corbusier 1933–1960." *Oppositions,* XIX (Winter/Spring 1980), 1–223.

Le Corbusier. "Architecture, the expression of the materials and methods of our times." *Arch. Record,* LXVI (August 1929), 123–28.

—————. *The Chapel at Ronchamp.* New York, 1957.

—————. *Creation is a Patient Search.* New York, 1960.

—————. *Le Corbusier: Textes et Dessins pour Ronchamp.* Paris, 1965.

—————. *New World of Space.* New York, 1948.

—————. *Towards a New Architecture.* London, 1927.

"Le Corbusier—his impact on four generations." *RIBA Journal,* LXXII (October 1965), 497–500.

"Less is More." *Time,* LXIII (June 14, 1954), 88ff.

"Letter from G. G. Elmslie to F. Ll. Wright." *SAHJ,* XX (October 1961), 140–42.

Line, R. M. "Art & Architecture—the Past: Louis H. Sullivan." *Craft Horiz.,* XXII (May 1962), 18–21.

Lobell, John. "Beaux-Arts: A Reconsideration of Meaning in Architecture." *AIA Journal,* LXIII (November 1975), 32–37.

"Logic and Art in Precast Concrete: Medical Research Laboratory, University of Pennsylvania, Philadelphia, Pa." *Arch. Record,* CXXVI (September 1959), 232–38.

"Logic of Contemporary Architecture as Expression of the Age." *Arch. Forum,* CII (May 1930), 637–38.

"Louis I. Kahn, Works 1963–1969." *Arch. d'Aujourd'hui,* CXLI (February-March 1969), 1–100.

"Louis Kahn and the Living City." *Arch. Forum,* CVIII (March 1958), 114–19.

"Louis Sullivan and the Architecture of Free Enterprise." *Chicago Art Inst. Q.,* L (September 1956), 42–43.

McCollum, Jan. *Architecture, U.S.A.* New York, 1959.

MacCormac, Richard C. "Anatomy of Wright's Aesthetics." *Arch. Review,* CXLIII (February 1968), 143–46.

"The McCormick Building and Dry Goods Store (Carson Pirie Scott), Chicago." *Arch. Record,* VIII (April-June 1899), 423–24.

McCullough, Jane Fiske. "The Haus of the Bauhaus reconsidered." *Progres. Arch.,* XLVII (December 1966), 160–66.

————. "Rise and fall of the functionalist style." *Ind. Des.,* VII (March 1960), 36–37.

McGrath, Raymond. "Looking into glass." *Arch. Review,* LXXI (January 1932), 29–30.

————. *Twentieth-Century Houses.* London, 1934.

McQuade, Walter. "Architect Louis Kahn and his Strong-Boned Structures." *Arch. Forum,* CVII (October 1957), 134–43.

————. "Assorted Bruises." *New Statesman,* LXV (January 25, 1963), 125.

————. "A Building That is an Event." *Arch. Forum,* CXX (February 1964), 62–83.

————. "Building Years of a Yale man: A. W. Griswald." *Arch. Forum,* CXVIII (June 1963), 88–93.

————. "The Exploded Landscape." *Perspecta,* VII (1961), 91–96.

————. "Man standing in the center." *Arch. Forum,* CXXVI (January 1967), 112.

MacQuedy, J. "Criticism (functionalism)." *Arch. Review,* LXXXVIII (December 1940), 183.

Malkiel-Jirmounsky, M. *Les Tendances de L'Architecture Contemporaine.* Paris, 1930.

Manasseh, Leonard. "Alvar Aalto and the International Style." *Arch. Journal,* CLXIX (April 1979), 845.

Manson, Grant C. "Frank Lloyd Wright and the Fair of '93." *Art Q.,* XVI, ii (1953), 114–23.

————. *Frank Lloyd Wright to 1910.* New York, 1958.

————. "Sullivan & Wright: an Uneasy Union of Celts." *Arch. Review,* CXVIII (November 1955), 297–300.

————. "Wright in the Nursery: the Influence of Froebel Education on his Work." *Arch. Review,* CXIII (June 1953), 349–51.

Maritain, Jacques. *Creative Intuition in Art and Poetry.* New York, 1953.

Mather, A. "Functionalism and naive materialism in American Architecture." *Arch. Review,* LXXXIX (May 1941), 115–16.

May, Rollo, Ernst Angel, and Henri F. Ellenberger, eds. *Existence.* New York, 1967.

Meiss, M., ed. *Problems of the 19th and 20th Centuries.* Princeton, 1964.

Merleau-Ponty, Maurice. *Phenomenology of Perception.* New York, 1962.

————. *The Primacy of Perception.* Chicago, 1964.

————. *Sense and Non-Sense.* Chicago, 1964.

Meyer, Leonard B. *Music, The Arts and Ideas.* Chicago, 1967.

Middeldorf, Ubich. "Architecture as an Art." *Coll. Art. J.,* VI, i (1946), 37–40.

————. "Mies van der Rohe." *Coll. Art J.,* VII, i (1947), 34–35.

"Mies and Nature: effect of time on architecture." *Arch. Review,* CIX (March 1951), 185.

Mies van der Rohe, Ludwig. "Tribute to Wright." *Coll. Art J.,* VI, i (1946), 41–42.

Miller, Elizabeth G. "Bauhaus: A Prophet Without Honor." *Progres. Arch.,* LV (July 1974), 58–59.

Miller, Nory. "Design Directions: Looking for What is 'Missing.'" *AIA Journal,* LXVII (mid-May 1978), 152–59.

Milner, John. "Ideas and influences of De Stijl." *Studio,* CLXXV (March 1968), 115–19.

"Mr. Robie knew what he wanted." *Arch. Forum,* CIX (October 1958), 126–27ff.

"M.I.T. Senior Dormitory." *Arch. Forum,* XCI (August 1949), 10.

"Modern antiques: 20th Century Landmarks." *Arch. Forum,* CXXVI (May 1967), 82ff.

"Modern Architecture: Mobocrate or Democratic?" *Art Digest,* XXVII (August 1953), 20.

"The Modern Gallery." *Arch. Forum,* LXXXIV (January 1946), 81–88.

Moholy-Nagy, László. *The New Vision.* New York, 1947.

Moholy-Nagy, Sibyl. "Achievement of Le Corbusier." *Arts,* XL (November 1965), 40–45.

————. *The Architecture of Paul Rudolph.* New York, 1970.

————. "Diaspora." *SAHJ,* XXIV (March 1965), 24–26.

————. "F. Ll. W. and the ageing of Modern Architecture." *Progres. Arch.,* XL (May 1959), 136–42.

————. "Frank Lloyd Wright's Testament." *Coll. Art J.,* IV (Summer 1959), 319–29.

————. "The Future of the Past." *Perspecta,* VII (1961), 65–76.

————. "Sunday Session." *SAHJ,* XXIV (March 1965), 81.

————. "Yale's School of Art and Architecture: The Measure." *Arch. Forum,* CXX (February 1964), 76–79.

Molitor, Joseph W. "Art Serves Science: Alfred Newton Richards Medical Research Building, University of Pennsylvania, Philadelphia, Pa." *Arch. Record,* CXXVIII (August 1960), 149–56.

Moore, Charles W. "Scully's Revenge: The Shingle Style Today or the Historian's Revenge." *Progres. Arch.,* LVI (April 1975), 112ff.

Moore, Jill. "The Tragic Hero of Modern Architecture." *Chicago,* I, xi (January 1955), 26–31.

Moos, Stanislaus von. *Le Corbusier.* Stuttgart, 1968.

Morris, Bertram. "Ruskin on the Pathetic Fallacy, or On How a Moral Theory of Art May Fail." *JAAC,* XIV (December 1955), 248–66.

Morrison, Hugh. *Louis Sullivan: Prophet of Modern Architecture.* New York: 1935.

————. "Louis Sullivan Today." *AIA Journal,* XXVI (September 1956), 98–100.

Mumford, Lewis. "Architecture and the Machine." *American Mercury,* III (September 1924), 77–80.

————. "The Architecture of Escape." *The New Republic,* (August 12, 1925), 321–22.

————. "The Case Against Modern Architecture." *Arch. Record,* CXXXI (April 1962), 155–62.

————. "Frank Lloyd Wright and the New Pioneers." *Arch. Record,* LXV (April 1929), 414ff.

————. "Function and Expression in Architecture." *Arch. Record,* CX (November 1951), 106–12.

————. *The Human Prospect.* Edited by Harry T. Moore. Boston, 1955.

————. "The Lesson of the Master: The Seagram Building." *AIA Journal,* XXXI (January 1959), 19–29.

————. "Machinery and the Modern Style." *New Republic,* XXVII (August 3, 1921), 263–65.

————. "Machines for Living." *Fortune,* VII (February 11, 1933), 78–80ff.

————. "Monumentalism, Symbolism and Style." *The Human Prospect.* Collected essays of Lewis Mumford. Edited by Harry T. Moore. Boston, 1955, 202–206.

————. *Roots of Contemporary American Architecture.* New York, 1952.

————. "Skyline: A Phoenix too Infrequent." *New Yorker,* (November 28, 1953), 133–39; (December 12, 1953), 116–27.

————. "Skyline: At Home, indoors and out." *New Yorker* (February 12, 1938), 58–59.

————. "Skyline: What Wright Hath Wrought." *New Yorker* (December 5, 1959), 105–30.

————. "The Social Background of Frank Lloyd Wright." *Wendingen* (Santpoort, Holland), VII, no. 5 (1925), 65–65ff.

————. *Sticks and Stones.* New York, 1924.

————. "Towards a Rational Modernism." *The New Republic* (April 25, 1928), 297–98.

Mundt, Ernst K. "The Wall." *Art Q.,* V (1942), 301–12.

Munro, Eleanor C. "International Style gone Native." *Art N.,* LIV (May 1955), 36–37.

Munro, T. "Form and value in the arts: a functional approach." *JAAC,* XIII (March 1955), 316–41.

"Musée Guggenheim, New York." *Arch. d'Aujourd'hui,* L–LI (December 1953), 13–14.

Museum of Modern Art. *Falling Water: Monograph on a House at Bear Run, Pennsylvania.* New York, 1938.

————. *What is Modern Architecture?* New York, 1942.

Nahm, Milton C. *The Artist as Creator.* Baltimore, 1956.

"Nature as an Ornamentalist." *Arch. Record,* IX (April 1900), insert.

Naylor, Gillian. "History of Taste: Modernism, Threadbare or Heroic?" *Arch. Review,* CLXII (August 1977), 107–11.

Nehls, W. "Das Ende der funktionalistischen Epoche." *Deutsche Bauzeitung,* i (January 1966), 37–40.

Nelson, George. "Architects of Europe today: Gropius." *Pencil Points,* XVII (August 1936), 422–32.

——————. "Architects of Europe today: Mies van der Rohe." *Pencil Points,* XVI (September 1935), 453–60.

——————. "Wright's Houses." *Fortune,* XXXIV (August 1946), 25ff.

Neuenschwander, E., and C. Neuenschwander. *Alvar Aalto and Finnish Architecture.* New York, 1954.

Neumann, Eckhard, ed. *Bauhaus and Bauhaus People.* New York, 1970.

"New Perceptions for the 1980's." *Arch. Record,* CLXVI (December 1979), 85–136.

"New work of Mies van der Rohe." *Arch. Forum,* CXIX (September 1963), 80–91.

No title or author. *Arch. Forum,* XCV (October 1951), 160.

Nodelman, Sheldon. "Structural analysis in art and anthropology." *Yale French Studies,* XXXVI and XXXVII (October 1966), 89–103.

Norberg-Schulz, Christian. *Existence, Space and Architecture.* New York, 1971.

——————. *Intentions in Architecture.* Cambridge, Massachusetts, 1965.

——————. "Meaning in Architecture." *Meaning in Architecture.* Edited by Charles Jencks and George Baird. New York, 1969, 214–29.

North, A. T. "Architectural Critics." *Arch. Forum,* LIII (August 1930), 260.

"Notes Concerning the Phenomenology of the Limit in Architecture." *Oppositions,* XXII (Winter 1981), 43–45.

"Notre Dame du Haut at Ronchamp," *Arch. Review,* CXVIII (December 1955), 354.

Nowicki, Matthew. "Composition in Modern Architecture." *Roots of Contemporary American Architecture.* Edited by Lewis Mumford. New York, 1952, 404–10.

——————. "Function and Form." *Roots of Contemporary American Architecture.* Edited by Lewis Mumford. New York, 1952, 411–18.

——————. "Origins and Trends in Modern Architecture." *Mag. Art,* XLIV (November 1951), 273–79.

Omoto, Sadayoshi. "Queen Anne style and architectural criticism." *SAHJ,* XXIII (March 1964), 29–37.

"One Hundred Years of Significant Building: Office Buildings." *Arch. Record,* CXIX (June 1956), 147–54.

Onobayashi, Hiroki. "Louis Kahn and Alfred Newton Richards Medical Research Building." *Kokusai Kentiku,,* XXVIII (March 1961), 64–69.

——————. "Louis Kahn: Order for Concrete." *Kokusai Kentiku,* XXVII (June 1960), 49–53.

"On Some Modern Architectural Work." *The Builder,* XXVII (February 27, 1869), 157–58.

"Ornament to Spare." *Harper's Magazine,* CCXIV (January 1957), 80–82.

Padovan, Richard. "Dutch Functionalism." *Arch. Journal,* CLXXV (January 1982), 79–81.

Panofsky, Erwin. *Meaning in the Visual Arts.* New York, 1955.

Paul, Sherman. *Louis Sullivan: An Architect in American Thought.* Englewood Cliffs, New Jersey, 1962.

——————. "Sullivan's Treatise on Ornament." *Arts,* XXXVII (December 1962), 62–66.

Peisch, Mark L. "Modern Architecture and Architectural Criticism in the U.S.A., 1929–1939." *SAHJ,* XXIV (March 1965), 78.

Perls, Frederick, Ralph F. Hefferline, and Paul Goodman. *Gestalt Therapy.* New York, 1951.

Persitz, Alexandre. "Contributions Americaines à l'architecture Contemporaine." *Arch. d'Aujourd'hui,* L–LI (December 1953), 5–156.

————. "L'oeuvre de Mies van der Rohe." *Arch. d'Aujourd'hui,* LXXIX (September 1958), 1–103.

Persons, Stow, ed. *Evolutionary Thought in America.* New Haven, 1950.

"Perspectives: Save the Robie House." *Arch. Record,* CXXI (April 1957), 9.

Peter, John. "Heritage of the Bauhaus." *Print,* XVIII (May 1964), 8–15ff.

Pevsner, Nikolaus. "Gropius and Van de Velde." *Arch. Review,* CXXXIII (March 1963), 165–68.

————. *An Outline of European Architecture.* Maryland, 1963.

————. "Picturesque." *Arch. Review,* CXV (April 1954), 227–29.

————. *Pioneers of Modern Design.* Baltimore, 1960.

————. *The Sources of Modern Architecture and Design.* New York, 1968.

————. "Time and Le Corbusier." *Arch. Review,* CXXV (March 1959), 158–65.

Pickens, Buford L. "H. H. Richardson and Basic Form Concepts in Modern Architecture." *Art Q.,* CXI (1940), 273–91.

Pippin, P. W. "Critical Youth Wields the Flail." *Pencil Points,* XXII (September 1941), Suppl. 9–10.

Pippin, P. W. and R. M. Bennett. "What the student expects of his critic; What the critic expects." *Pencil Points,* XXII (January 1941), Suppl. 12ff.

Platz, G. A. *Wohnräume der Gegenwart.* Berlin, 1933.

Polanyi, Michael. *The Tacit Dimension.* New York, 1966.

Pommer, Richard. "Some Architectural Ideologies After the Fall." *Art Journal,* XL (Fall/ Winter 1980), 353–61.

Porphyrios, Demetri, ed. "Classicism is Not a Style." *Arch. Design,* LII (1982), 1–129.

"Post-Modernism Strikes Home." *Arch. Design,* LI (1981), 1–4ff.

Prak, Niels Luning. *The Language of Architecture.* The Netherlands, 1968.

Purcell, W. G. "Louis H. Sullivan, Prophet of Democracy." *AIA Journal,* XVI (December 1951), 265–68ff.

Ragon, Michel. *The Aesthetics of Contemporary Architecture.* Neuchâtel, 1968.

————. "Power of Doubt." *Connaissance Arts,* CCCXLVI (December 1980), 84–91.

Rapoport, Amos. *House Form and Culture.* Englewood Cliffs, New Jersey, 1969.

Rasch, Heinz. *Some Roots of Modern Architecture.* London, 1967.

Rawls, Marion. "An Exhibition of Architecture by Mies van der Rohe." *Art Inst. Chicago Bull.,* XXXII, vii (December 1938), 104.

Read, Herbert. "Against the Betrayal of Architecture." *New Republic* (November 2, 1953), 20–21.

————. *The Forms of Things Unknown.* London, 1960.

————. *Icon and Idea, The Function of Art in the Development of Human Consciousness.* New York, 1965.

Rebori, A. N. "An Architecture of Democracy. *Arch. Record,* XXXIX (May 1916), 437–65.

————. "Frank Lloyd Wright's Textile-Block-Slab Constructions." *Arch. Record,* LXII (December 1927), 449–56.

————. "Louis H. Sullivan." *Arch. Record,* LV (June 1924), 587.

Reese, Ilse M. and James T. Burns, Jr. "The Opposites: Expressionism and Formalism at Yale." *Progres. Arch.,* LXV (February 1964), 128–29.

Richards, J. M. "Against the Steamroller." *Arch. Review,* CXIII (May 1953), 283–85.

————. "Architect, Critic and Public." *RAIC Journal,* XXVII (November 1950), 372–73.

————. *The Castles on the Ground.* London, 1946.

————. *The Functional Tradition in Early Industrial Buildings.* London, 1958.

————. *An Introduction to Modern Architecture.* Baltimore, 1940.

————. "The Next Step." *Arch. Review,* CVII (March 1950), 165–81.

————. "The Professional Magazine as Critic." *AIA Journal,* XLIX (May 1968), 65–68.

————. "Walter Gropius." *Arch. Review,* LXXVIII (August 1935), 44–46.

"Richards Medical Research Building." *Arts,* XXXV (September 1961), 66.

"Richards Medical Research Building." *South African Architectural Record,* (April 1963), 23–26.

Rienaecker, Victor. "The Philosophy of an Architect." *Apollo,* XLIII (1946), 137–39 and XLIV (1946), 7–9.

"Rietveld's Last Works." *Arch. Review,* CXXXVIII (November 1965), 314–15.

Rippeteau, June. "Movement from Modernism: Cause for Concern or Celebration?" *AIA Journal,* LXVII (January 1978), 49–51ff.

"Robie House." *AIA Journal,* XL (August 1963), 114ff.

Robinson, James K. "Pathetic Fallacy." *Encyclopedia of Poetry and Poetics.* Edited by Alex Preminger. Princeton, 1965, 606–7.

Robinson, John Beverley. "Lessons from Architectural Aberrations." *Arch. Record,* XXVII (February 1910), 180–88.

Rogers, Ernesto N. "Il metod di Le Corbusier e la forms della 'Chapelle de Ronchamp.' " *Casabella,* CCXCVI (August 1965), 73.

————. "Le Corbusier's day dream." *Arts & Arch.,* LXXX (September 1963), 16–17ff.

————. "L'esprit nouveau." *Casabella,* CCLXXIV (April 1963), 1–25.

————. "Walter Gropius." *Encyclopedia of World Art,* VII (1963), 175–81.

Roos, F. J., Jr. "Concerning Several American Architectural Leaders." *Design,* XXXVII (December 1935), 2–5ff.

Rosenberg, Harold. *The Tradition of the New.* New York, 1959.

Roth, Alfred. "Die Wallfahrtskapelle in Ronchamp." *Werk,* XLII (December 1955), 375–85.

————. *The New Architecture.* Zurich, 1940.

————. "Worte und Bauten der Pioniere." *Werk,* XXXIX (December 1952), 389–401.

Roth, Ueli. "Louis Kahn und die Medical Towers in Philadelphia." *Werk,* XLIX (January 1962), 22–25.

Rowan, Jan C. "Editorial: The New School of Art and Architecture." *Progres. Arch.,* XLV (February 1964), 106–29.

————. "Wanting to Be... The Philadelphia School." *Progres. Arch.,* XLII (April 1961), 130–64.

Rowe, Colin. "Mannerism in Modern Architecture." *Arch. Review,* CVIII (May 1950), 289–99.

Rubino, Luciano. "Processo ad un grande architetto europeo: la ricerca incompiuta di Alvar Aalto." *Architettura,* VII (April 1962), 804–28.

Rubio Tuduri, Nicolas M. "Le Pavillon de l'Allemagne à l'Exposition de Barcelone par Mies van der Rohe." *Cahiers d'Art,* IV (1929), 408–12.

Rudofsky, Bernard. *Architecture Without Architects.* New York, 1965.

"Rudolph employs special framework to produce rugged textures that add depth and scale to concrete surfaces." *Arch. Forum,* CXVII (September 1962), 89.

"Rudolph in Sospensione." *Architettura,* XIV (August 1968), 320–21.

Rudolph, Paul. "Colgate: Creative Arts Center." *Progres. Arch.,* XLVIII (February 1967), 114–21.

————. "Regionalism in Architecture." *Perspecta,* IV (1957), 12–19.

————. "Yale Art and Architecture Building." *Arts and Architecture,* LXXXI (February 1964), 26–29.

Rugg, Harold. *Imagination.* New York, 1963.

Ruskin, John. *Modern Painters.* New York, 1882.

————. *The Seven Lamps of Architecture.* New York, 1961.

Rykwert, Joseph. "Ornament Is No Crime." *Studio,* CXC (September 1975), 91–97.

Safdie, Moshe. *Beyond Habitat.* Cambridge, Massachusetts, 1970.

Salerno, Joseph. "Louis Sullivan—Return to Principle." *Liturg. Arts,* XVI (February 1948), 4950.

Salkauskis, N. "Mies van der Rohe and Le Corbusier." *RAIC Journal,* XXXV (March 1958), 82–84.

Sargeant, Winthrop. "Titan of Modern Architecture still flings his Houses and his Insults at Backward Colleagues." *Life,* XXI (August 12, 1946), 85–88ff.

Sartoris, Alberto. *Gli Elementi dell'ar_hitettura Funzionale.* Milan, 1932.

Sasaki, H. "Post-Modernism: An Odd and Empty Expression?" *Japan Architect,* LVII (June 1982), 5.

Sawers, R. "Reflections on some new stained glass in Europe." *Craft Horiz.,* XVIII (May 1958), 32–33.

Schild, Gorou. "Alvar Aalto." *Arch. d'Aujourd'hui,* XXXIV (April 1964), 112–17.

Schindler, P. G. "Form, function, and modern architecture." *Arch. and Eng.,* CXXIII (December 1935), 13–15.

Schröder Huis. Hilversum, 1963.

Schultze-Naumburg, Paul. *ABC des Bauens.* Berlin, 1926.

————. *Das Gesicht des deutschen Hauses.* Munich, 1929.

Schuyler, Montgomery. "An Architectural Pioneer." *Arch. Record,* XXXI (April 1912), 427–35.

————. "Architecture in the United States: the Skyscraper." *Arch. Record,* XXVI, ii (1909), 92.

Schwarz, Rudolf. *The Church Incarnate.* Chicago, 1958.

Schweikher, Paul. "One Hundred Years of Significant Building." *Arch. Record,* CXX (February 1957), 199–202ff.

Scott, Geoffrey. *The Architecture of Humanism.* New York, 1969.

Scully, Vincent, Jr. "Art and Architecture Building, Yale University, Architect: Paul Rudolph." *Arch. Review,* CXXXV (May 1964), 324–32.

————. "Doldrums in the Suburbs." *SAHJ,* XXIV (March 1965), 36–47.

————. *Frank Lloyd Wright.* New York, 1960.

————. "Frank Lloyd Wright and the Twentieth-Century Style." *Problems of the 19th & 20th Centuries: Studies in Western Art,* IV, Princeton, 1963, 7–21.

————. "The Heritage of Wright." *Zodiac,* VIII (1961), 9–13.

————. "Light Form and Power: New Work of Louis Kahn." *Arch. Forum,* CXXI-CXXII (August–September 1964), 162–70.

————. *Louis I. Kahn.* New York, 1962.

————. "Louis Sullivan's Architectural Ornament." *Perspecta,* V (1959), 73–80.

————. *Modern Architecture.* New York, 1965.

————. "Recent Works by Louis Kahn." *Zodiac,* XVII (1967), 58–117.

————. *The Shingle Style Today or the Historian's Revenge.* New York, 1974.

————. "Wright, International Style and Kahn." *Arts,* XXXVI (March 1962), 67–71ff.

————. "Wright vs. the International Style." *Art News* (March 1954), 32–35ff.

Seckel, Harry. "Frank Lloyd Wright." *N. American Review,* CCXLVI (Autumn 1938), 48–64.

Segall, Marshall H., et al. *The Influence of Culture on Visual Perception.* New York, 1966.

Serenyi, Peter. "Le Corbusier's Changing Attitude Toward Form." *SAHJ,* XXIV (March 1965), 15–23.

Sert, Jose Luis. "Remembering Le Corbusier: What we have Lost." *AIA Journal,* XLIV (November 1965), 31–33.

Shaffer, Robert B. "Emerson and his Circle: Advocates of Functionalism." *SAHJ,* VII (July 1948), 17–20.

Shand, P. M. "Scenario for a Human Drama: the House of Character." *Arch. Review,* LXXVII (February 1935), 61–64.

—————. "The Work of Alvar Aalto." *Arch. Review,* LXX (September 1931), 72.

"Shapes of Tomorrow, Two Buildings in Diverging Directions." *Interiors* (July 1961), 41.

Shumaker, Wayne. "Condition of critical valuation." *JAAC,* IX (September 1950), 21–30.

Silver, Nathan. "Klingsor's Castle." *Progres. Arch.,* XLVII (August 1966), 206ff.

"Six Recent Buildings in the U.S.A.: Farnsworth House." *Architects' Year Book 5.* London, 1953, 158–61.

"Sixty Years of Living Architecture—the Work of Frank Lloyd Wright." *Arch. Forum,* XCIX (November 1953), 153–55.

"Slum of the Soul." *Arch. Forum,* LXXX (January 1944), 104ff.

Smith, Lyndon P. "An Attempt to give Functional Expression to the Architecture of a Department Store." *Arch. Record,* XVI (July 1904), 53–60.

Smith, Norris Kelly. *Frank Lloyd Wright.* Englewood Cliffs, New Jersey, 1966.

—————. "Frank Lloyd Wright and the Problem of Historical Perspective." *SAHJ,* XXVI (December 1967), 234–37.

Smithson, Alison and Peter Smithson. "The Heroic Period of Modern Architecture." *Design,* XXXV, xii (December 1965), entire issue.

—————. "Louis Kahn." *Architect's Yearbook,* IX (1960), 102–18.

Sobin, Harris. "Masters of Light: Le Corbusier." *AIA Journal,* LXVIII (September 1979), 56–9.

"Solomon R. Guggenheim Memorial Museum." *Arch. Forum,* LXXXVIII (January 1948), 136–38.

"S.O.M. Rudolph, and Johnson at Yale." *Arch. Forum,* CXVIII (November 1963), 30–31.

Sommer, Robert. "Design for Friendship." *AIA Journal,* XXXVIII (December 1962), 84–86.

—————. "Personal Space." *AIA Journal,* XXXVIII (December 1962), 81–83.

—————. "The Significance of Space." *AIA Journal,* XLIII (May 1965), 63–65.

"Span of Kahn." *Arch. Review,* CLV (June 1974), 318–20.

Spence, Basil. "The Modern Church: Le Corbusier's Church at Ronchamp." *RIBA Journal,* LXIII (July 1956), 372–74.

Spilka, Mark. "The Affective Fallacy Revisited." *Southern Review: An Australian Journal of Literary Studies,* I (1965), 57–72, 77–79.

Spring, Bernard P. "Aalto revisited." *Arch. Forum,* CXXIV (April 1966), 70–79.

Staber, Margit. "Funktion, Funktionalismus: Eine Geschichte der Missverständnisse." *Werk,* III (1974), 286–87.

Stahly, F. "Über den plastischen Sinn in der modernen Architektur; die Wollfahrtskapelle in Ronchamp bei Belfort." *Werk,* XLII (January 1955), 1–5.

Stephens, S. "Architectural Journalism Analyzed: Refelctions on a Half Century." *Progres. Arch.,* LI (June 1970), 138–39.

Stephenson, Gordon. "Le Corbusier." *RAIC Journal,* XXXIII (June 1956), 199–203.

Sterling, James. "Functional tradition and expression." *Perspecta,* VI (1960), 88–97.

Stern, Robert. "Modern Architecture After Modernism." *Arch. Design,* L (1980), 59–61.

Stern, Robert A. M. *New Directions in American Architecture.* New York, 1969.

Stillman, S. "Comparing Wright and Le Corbusier." *AIA Journal,* IX (April-May 1948), 171-78, 226-33.

Stirling, James. "Ronchamp: Le Corbusier's Chapel and the crisis of Rationalism." *Arch. Review,* CXIX (March 1956), 155-61.

Sullivan, Louis. "Architecture as Sophism and Architecture as Ethics." *Arch. Review,* LXXIX (March 1936), 147.

—————. "The Chicago Tribune Competition." *Arch. Record,* LIII (February 1923), 151-57.

—————. *Kindergarten Chats.* New York, 1947.

—————. "Reflections on the Tokyo Disaster." *Arch. Record,* LV (February 1924), 113-17.

"Sullivan Mosaics, Stencils found in Garrick Building." *Arch. Record,* CXXX (September 1961), 26.

"Sullivan Seen by his Contemporaries: in his Centennial Year, Another look." *Arch. Record,* CXX (September 1956), 18ff.

Sutton, Walter. *Modern American Criticism.* Englewood Cliffs, New Jersey, 1963.

Szarkowski, John. *The Idea of Louis Sullivan.* Minneapolis, 1956.

Tallmadge, Thomas E. *The Story of Architecture in America.* New York, 1927.

Tami, R. "Le Corbusier, le dernier des baroques." *Werk,* XXXVI (October 1949), 147.

Taut, Bruno. *Modern Architecture.* London, 1929.

Tentori, Francesco. "Ordine e Forma nell'opera de Louis Kahn." *Casabella,* CCXLI (July 1960), 2-17.

"This new Shell Game: Function, Structure, Symbolism – or Art." *Arch. Record,* CXXI (June 1957), 185ff.

Tillich, Paul. "The Nature of Religious Language." *Theology of Culture.* Edited by Robert C. Kimball. New York, 1964, 53-67.

Tomson, B. "Fair Comment on Architecture." *Progres. Arch.,* XL (July-August 1959), 7.

"Towards Another Architecture: What Is Architecture?" *Arch. Review,* CLX (July 1976) 44-45.

"Towards a Unity (Mies)." *Arts & Arch.,* LXXVIII (April 1961), 10-13.

"Tradition to preserve: Wright's Robie House." *Interiors,* CXVI (May 1957), 10ff.

Treeck, Martin von and François Loyer. "Bauhaus." *l'Oeil,* CLXII-CLXIII (June-July 1968), 14-23ff.

Troedsson, Carl B. *Two Standpoints Towards Modern Architecture: Wright and Le Corbusier.* Göteborg, Elander, 1951.

Tselos, Dimitri. "Chicago Fair and the Myth of the 'Lost Cause.'" *SAHJ,* XXVI (December 1967), 262ff.

—————. "Exotic Influences in the Architecture of Frank Lloyd Wright." *Mag. Art,* XLVI (April 1953), 160-69ff.

—————. "Frank Lloyd Wright and World Architecture." *SAHJ,* XXVIII (March 1969), 58-72.

T., W. A. "Sharp Focus." *AIA Journal,* XXX (November 1958), 53-54.

Untermeyer, Louis. *Makers of the Modern World.* New York, 1955.

"Value of used Architecture: Robie House, Chicago." *Arch. Forum,* CVI (April 1957), 107-08.

Venturi, Lionello. *History of Art Criticism.* New York, 1964.

Venturi, Robert. *Complexity and Contradiction in Architecture.* New York, 1966.

—————. "Diversity, Relevance and Representation in Historicism." *Arch. Record,* CLXX (June 1982), 114-19.

Veronesi, Guilia. "Un architecte, une maison, une dame." *Zodiac,* III (1958), 194.

"Village Chapel by Le Corbusier." *Arts & Arch.,* LXXII (September 1955), 16-17.

Vinson, Robert Jean. "50-75: L'Architecture du Troisième Quart du XXe Siècle." *Connaissance Arts,*CCLXXXVII (February 1976), 67.

Völckers, Otto. "Save the Robie House!" *AIA Journal,* XXVIII (August 1957), 247-48.

Wachsmann, K. "Mies van der Rohe, his work." *Arts & Arch.,* LXIX (March 1952), 16-31ff.

Walden, Russell, ed. *Open Hand: Essays on Le Corbusier.* Cambridge, 1977.

Walker, C. Howard. "Functionalism and Architecture, 2." *Pencil Points,* XIII (March 1933), 7-9, 121-22.

"Walter Gropius." *Arch. d'Aujourd'hui,* XX, xxviii (February 1950), 1-116.

"Walter Gropius: seven illustrations from his outstanding work and his own comments on the status of architecture in the U.S." *Arch. Record,* CXIX (March 1956), 190-96.

Ward, Neville. "Play on possum." *Arch. Review,* CXVI (October 1954), 215-18.

Watkin, David. *Morality and Architecture: The Development of a Theme in Architectural History and Theory from the Gothic Revival to the Modern Movement.* Oxford, 1978.

Watterson, Joseph. "Architectural Criticism." *AIA Journal,* XXXIV (August 1960), 62.

Weimer, David R. "Lewis Mumford and the design of criticism." *Arts & Arch.,* LXXIX (September 1962), 14-15ff.

Weisberg, G. "Frank Lloyd Wright and pre-Columbian Art – the Background for his Architecture." *Art Q.,* XXX, i (1967), 40-51.

Weisman, Winston. "Criticism and Commercial Architecture." *Coll. Art J.,* XL, i (1951), 26-29.

————. "Philadelphia Functionalism & Sullivan." *SAHJ,* XX (March 1961), 3-19.

Wellek, René. *Concepts of Criticism.* New Haven, 1963.

"What Does Society Say Through Architecture?" *Arch. Review,* CLXI (May 1977), 258-60.

White, Morton G. *Social Thought in America, the Revolt Against Formalism.* New York, 1949.

Whittick, Arnold. *European Architecture in the Twentieth Century.* Two volumes. London, 1950.

————. *European Architecture in the Twentieth Century,* Two volumes. London, 1953.

Wijdeveld, Hendricus Th., ed. *The Life-Work of the American Architect, Frank Lloyd Wright.* Santpoort, Holland, 1925.

————. *Work of Wright from 1903-1925.* Santpoort, Holland, 1925.

Wilson, Colin St. John. "Gerrit Rietvald: 1888-1964." *Arch. Review,* CXXXVI (December 1964), 399-402.

Wilson, Forrest. "From Product to Process: The Third Generation of Modern Architects." *Progres. Arch.,* LI (June 1970), 156-67.

Wimsatt, W. K. and Monroe C. Beardsley. *The Verbal Icon.* Kentucky, 1954.

Winfield, David. "An Essay in the Criticism of Architecture." *JAAC,* XIII (March 1955), 370-77.

Winter, R. W. "Fergusson and Garbett in American architectural theory." *SAHJ,* XVII iv (Winter 1958), 25-30.

Wittkower, Rudolf. *Architectural Principles in the Age of Humanism.* New York, 1965.

Wolf, Nancy. "Protest Against the Primacy of Technology Over Humanity." *AIA Journal,* LXII (July 1974), 34-37.

"Word on Design." *Interiors,* CXII (December 1952), 116ff.

Wright, Frank Lloyd. *An American Architecture.* Edited by Edgar Kaufmann. New York, 1955.

————. "America Tomorrow." *Am. Arch.,* CXLI (May 1932), 14-17ff.

————. "Architecture as a Profession is all Wrong." *Am. Arch.,* CXXVIII (December 1930), 22-23ff.

————. *Ausgeführte Bauten und Entwürfe.* Berlin, 1910.

————. "Frank Lloyd Wright." *Arch. Forum* (January 1938), entire.

————. "Frank Lloyd Wright." *Arch. Forum,* LXXXVIII (January 1948), entire.

————. *Genius and the Mobocracy.* New York, 1949.

————. "In the Cause of Architecture." *Arch. Record,* XXIII (March 1908), 155–221.

————. "Louis Sullivan, Beloved Master." *Western Architect* (June 1924), 64–66.

————. "Modern Gallery: for the Solomon R. Guggenheim Foundation: New York City." *Mag. of Art,* XXXIX (January 1946), 24–26.

————. *The Natural House.* New York, 1954.

————. (no title.) *Arch. Forum,* XCIV (January 1951), 73–108.

————. *An Organic Architecture.* Cambridge, Massachusetts, 1939.

————. "Organic Architecture looks at Modern Architecture." *Arch. Record,* CXI (May 1952), 148–54.

————. "Sullivan Against the World." *Arch. Review,* CV (June 1949), 295–98.

————. "Surface and Mass, Again!" *Arch. Record,* LXVI (July 1929), 92–94.

————. "Tyranny of the Skyscraper." *Creat. Art,* VIII (May 1931), 324–32.

————. "What the Cause of Architecture needs most." *Arch. Review,* LXXXI (March 1937), 99–100.

Wright, J. L. *My Father who is on Earth.* New York, 1946.

"Wright Masterpiece Preserved: Fallingwater." *Interiors,* CXXIII (October 1963), 12.

"Wright's Newest: E. Kaufmann House." *Art Digest,* XII (February 1938), 13.

Wurman, Richard Saul and Eugene Feldman, eds. *The Notebooks and Drawings of Louis I. Kahn.* New York, 1962.

Wurster, Katherine Bauer. "The Social Front of Modern Architecture in the 1930s." *SAHJ,* XXIV (March 1965), 48–52.

Wynne, Nancy and Beaumont Newhall. "Horatio Greenough: Herald of Functionalism." *Mag. Art,* XXXII (January 1939), 12–15.

"Yale Art and Architecture Building." *Arts & Arch.,* LXXXI (February 1964), 26–29.

"Yale's New Art and Architecture Building, Paul Rudolph, Architect." *Arch. Record,* CXXXI (Jaunary 1962), 16–17.

Zeidler, Eberhard H. "Architecture: The Fine Art of Survival." *Can. Arch.,* XXV (February 1980), 38–41.ff.

Zervos, Christian. "Le 'Bauhaus' de Dessau." *Cahiers d'Art,* I, ix (1926), 259–62.

————. "Mies van der Rohe." *Cahiers d'Art,* III (1928), 35.

Zevi, Bruno. *Architecture as Space.* New York, 1957.

————. "Frank Lloyd Wright and the Conquest of Space." *Mag. Art,* XLIII (May 1950) 86–91.

————. "La Protesta de Gropius." *Architettura,* IX (April 1964), 866–67.

————. *Towards an Organic Architecture.* London, 1950.

Zucker, Paul. "The Paradox of Architectural Theories at the Beginning of the 'Modern Movement.'" *SAHJ,* X (October 1951), 8–14.

Index